Uneasy Military Encounters

Ruth Streicher

Uneasy Military Encounters

The Imperial Politics of Counterinsurgency in Southern Thailand

Southeast Asia Program Publications
an imprint of
Cornell University Press
Ithaca and London

First published 2020 by Cornell University Press

Library of Congress Cataloging-in-Publication Data
Names: Streicher, Ruth, 1982– author.
Title: Uneasy military encounters : the imperial politics of counterinsurgency in Southern Thailand / Ruth Streicher.
Description: Ithaca [New York] : Cornell University Press, 2020. | Includes bibliographical references and index.
Identifiers: LCCN 2020000457 (print) | LCCN 2020000458 (ebook) | ISBN 9781501751325 (cloth) | ISBN 9781501751332 (paperback) | ISBN 9781501751349 (epub) | ISBN 9781501751356 (pdf)
Subjects: LCSH: Ethnic conflict—Thailand, Southern. | Counterinsurgency—Thailand, Southern. | Militarism—Thailand, Southern. | Islam—Thailand, Southern—Relations—Buddhism. | Buddhism—Thailand, Southern—Relations—Islam. | Race discrimination—Thailand, Southern. | Sexism—Thailand, Southern.
Classification: LCC HM1121 .S768 2020 (print) | LCC HM1121 (ebook) | DDC 305.8009593—dc23
LC record available at https://lccn.loc.gov/2020000457
LC ebook record available at https://lccn.loc.gov/2020000458

CONTENTS

ACKNOWLEDGMENTS

In March 2010, when I first arrived in Yala, one of the provincial capitals in Thailand's southernmost provinces, my train was two hours late and I realized that my phone received no signal. Suddenly, a woman came walking toward me: "Are you Ruth?" I had never met Ajan Arin Saidi before. She was the friend of a friend and a lecturer at the Prince of Songkhla University in Pattani. She had not only offered to pick me up, waiting for hours at the train station, but also arranged for accommodations at a university dormitory and provided me with a list of contacts for my stay. My phone, she explained, had been disconnected because emergency regulations in the three southern provinces required that SIM cards be registered under a Thai identification card—a tacit reminder that I had just entered a "special zone."

Ajan Arin's welcome exemplifies the generosity with which I was received by so many people in this conflict region. My thanks go to her and to Amporn Marddent, who put me in touch with a number of people who became key to my research. The team of Deep South Watch at the Prince of Songkhla University, in particular Srisompob Jitpiromsri and Daungyewa Utarasint, supported my research in many different ways, and introduced me to Beding and his family in the village of Tanyong Luloh, who became dear friends. Surainee Waba generously put me up in her apartment during my longest stay in Pattani; her cousin Leena Ngafa became my dear roommate and helped me out whenever I got stuck with translations. The team of the Asian Muslim Action Network, especially Usman Binhasan and Rohanee Daoh, were of great help. At a later stay in Yala, Wannakanok Phitaedaoh kindly let me stay in her house.

Without the openness and curiosity of many soldiers stationed in southern Thailand, this book could not have been written; I have, however, decided to anonymize all military personnel mentioned in this book because of the sensitivity of the conflict context. I owe particular thanks to the team at Yalannanbaru and the soldiers at Wat Lak Mueang, as well as to the task force 11 at Yala and the female rangers unit at the Ingkhayut Camp in Pattani. In Bangkok, Kasian Tejapira and Jularat Damrongviteetham lent their invaluable assistance.

The germ of this book originated as my doctoral dissertation at the Freie Universität Berlin. I am indebted to the Berlin Graduate School Muslim Cultures and Societies for funding through a scholarship by the German Research Foundation. Cilja Harders has supported this project from its inception with enthusiasm. I owe special gratitude to Schirin Amir-Moazami, who was closely involved with the book in its different stages and has greatly supported my research. Paul Amar, Mark Askew, Allaine Cerwonka, Jovan Maud, Jan Bachmann, and Sven Trakulhun read and commented on different chapters of the book; my friends Moritz Konradi, Sonja Neuweiler, and Christine Rollin aided by debating my work in a long series of dinner discussions. Vorawan Wannalak tirelessly assisted in translating documents and tracing the original meaning of certain Thai terms. Daniel Nethery, Mark Rusch, and Usman Shah assisted in editing.

A German Academic Exchange Service fellowship enabled me to spend a year at the University of California, Berkeley, where I had the privilege to study with Saba Mahmood and Penny Edwards and, thanks to Sarah Maxim, greatly benefited from the activities and the discussion of my work at the Center for Southeast Asian Studies. A fellowship funded by the Fritz Thyssen Foundation enabled me to further develop the book. Ruth Mas not only convinced me to pursue this project but also read the whole manuscript and made invaluable suggestions for its improvement. She has been a critical source of brilliant ideas and friendship throughout the process. Ruth also introduced me to Natalie Rose, who, through countless rounds of editing, helped me to clarify my arguments and restructure my writing; she never ceased to ask important questions and make incisive comments even in the final stages of this project. Thank you!

At Cornell University Press, I am grateful to my editor, Sarah Grossman, who supported the project with great commitment; to the two anonymous reviewers, who took great care and time to make important suggestions for the improvement of the manuscript; and to the members of the editorial board, who made additional helpful suggestions.

My daughter was born the day after I had sent off the book proposal. It is to her and to my partner, Nils Riecken, that I owe my greatest gratitude.

ABBREVIATIONS

BRN   Barisan Revolusi Nasional
BRN-C Barisan Revolusi Nasional Coordinate
ISOC   Internal Security Operations Command
NCPO   National Council for Peace and Order
THB   Thai Baht
USD   United States Dollar

NOTE ON TRANSLITERATION AND REFERENCING

I have transcribed all uses of Thai terms in accordance with the Royal Thai General System of Transcription using the transcription tool provided by the online dictionary Thai-language.com. There are notable exceptions: I deploy conventional spellings of well-known people—for instance, King Vajiravudh instead of Wachirawut; moreover, when transcribing personal and family names I have followed, when known, the preferences of those individuals.

Following Thai studies conventions, Thai authors are referred to by their given names, not surnames; in accordance, all citations by Thai authors are alphabetized in the bibliography and elsewhere by given names.

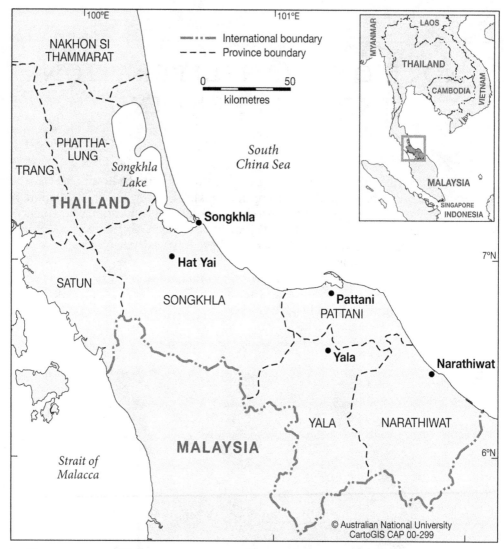

Figure 1. Map of Thailand's southern border provinces. *Source:* The Australian National University, College of Asia and the Pacific, CartoGIS Services.

Uneasy Military Encounters

INTRODUCTION

Policing the Imperial Formation

In August 2016, the conflict in southern Thailand received a sudden and unexpected moment of global media attention. A series of bomb and arson attacks launched across seven central- and upper-southern Thai provinces on August 11 and 12 killed four people and wounded thirty-five, several international tourists among them. In the following days, media reports around the world presented the image of Thailand as a devastated tourist destination; the bombings had shattered the "Thai smile," the tropical travel paradise was in danger, and many foreign offices issued travel warnings.[1] Although Thai officials went out of their way to dismiss any possible connection between the August bombings and the ongoing armed conflict in southern Thailand, forensic evidence confirmed the involvement of southern insurgents: the attackers had used Malaysian mobile phones to detonate the bombs, and their improvised explosive devices resembled those deployed in the southernmost provinces. In September 2016, Thai authorities finally detained a suspect linked to the insurgency.[2]

The Thai military's counterinsurgency strategy in southern Thailand is one of the reasons the August 2016 bombings caught foreign media unawares. As this book will show, the counterinsurgency has included a careful public relations strategy that presents the southern Thai conflict as a "minor unrest."[3] For over a decade, a network of insurgent groups has fought for the independence of an area stretching across three of Thailand's southernmost provinces close to the border with Malaysia (Pattani, Yala, Narathiwat) and four adjacent districts of Songkhla province. This area once belonged to an Islamic sultanate called Patani and is now, in official terminology, considered the home of Thailand's Malay-Muslim minority.[4] During the insurgency, nearly seven thousand people have been killed and many more wounded since 2004, making the conflict one of the most deadly in Southeast Asia. Insurgent attacks targeting both civilians and security forces—most of them small-scale bombings, roadside ambushes, and shootings—have largely been restricted to the southernmost provinces, but there have been several coordinated bombings beyond the main area of conflict. The Thai military's counterinsurgency campaign—the largest in Thai history, deploying over sixty thousand security personnel—has so far not been able to meet its proclaimed goal of stopping the insurgency.

The August 2016 bombings therefore also left in tatters both a counterinsurgency mission that had been celebrated as a success and an official discourse that portrayed the everyday violence in the South as "religious misunderstandings" and "minor cultural conflicts" instigated by misguided individuals.[5] The bombings, which occurred in the very heart of the Thai nation-state and drew international attention to the southern conflict, consequently left officials to assert that "Thailand does not have any conflicts regarding religion, ethnicity, territory or minority groups."[6] In this official framing, the insurgency is made conspicuous by its absence.

This book, by contrast, puts the southern Thai conflict center stage and analyzes such statements as part of a larger counterinsurgency discourse key to understanding the power dynamics of both the present-day Thai state formation and the ongoing insurgency. Counterinsurgency practices, I argue, contribute to producing Thailand as an imperial formation: a modern state formation with roots in the premodern Buddhist empire of Siam that secures its survival by constructing the southern Muslim population as essentially and hierarchically different. Reinforcing notions of the racialized, religious, and gendered Otherness of Patani, counterinsurgency thus fuels the very conflict it has been designed to resolve. From this perspective, it is possible to understand the marginalization of the southern conflict in official discourse, the denials of obvious connections between the insurgency and the August 2016 bombings, and the culturalization of a deeply political conflict as integral parts of imperial policing practices.

THAILAND AS AN IMPERIAL FORMATION

The production and authorization of difference are key principles of rule in imperial formations.[7] The adjective "imperial," in contrast to "colonial," denotes strategies of both formal and informal control that do "not necessarily involve conquest, occupation, and durable rule by outside invaders";[8] the notion of a "social formation," originally a Marxist term, in its poststructuralist rendering presumes the productive vulnerability of structures sedimented through history. Thus, as Ann Laura Stoler highlights, imperial formations are "projects in the making"; by fabricating and managing difference, they produce instability to ensure their own survival.[9] Understanding Thailand as an imperial formation allows us not only to emphasize the continuities between Siam's premodern empire and the structures of the current state formation but also to underscore how Western imperialism has come to shape Thailand in general and, as Tamara Loos shows, its relations with Patani in particular.[10]

PREMODERN ROOTS

One of the key continuities between contemporary Thailand and Siam's premodern empire is the operation of rule through the management of difference generally and the Othering of Islam in particular. The Islamic tradition was widely influential in premodern Siam not only on the Malay Peninsula, where Patani was located, but also in the center of the kingdom, where Muslim traders from India and Persia settled. The Thai term *khaek*, for instance, is today used with derogatory and racialized undertones to refer to southern Thai Muslims, but in the royal chronicles of the Ayutthaya kingdom, which ruled Siam from the fourteenth to the eighteenth centuries, it referred more generally to Muslims of Indian, Persian, Arab, or Malay origin. While *khaek* were allowed to practice Islam and to build mosques in Ayutthaya, a seventeenth-century royal proclamation strictly prohibited the king's subjects from converting to Islam, and the edict became part of Siam's premodern law code, the Three Seals Law.[11] The proclamation also banned Thai, Mon, and Lao women from having "clandestine sexual intercourse with *khaek*, French, English, *khula* [strangers] and Malays who uphold wrong-thinking," thus differentiating subjects adhering to the Theravada Buddhist tradition (Thai, Mon, and Lao) from followers of other traditions such as Islam.[12]

The edict exemplifies how managing the difference of religious traditions hinged on distinctions of gender and ethnicity in premodern Siam. To start with, the Buddhist

Pali terms used to express "wrong-thinking" in the edict underscore the centrality of the Theravada tradition to Siam's premodern system of rule, which consisted of several vassal states structured around a center that represented the power of the universal Buddhist monarch.[13] The decree, moreover, regulated only women's sexual relations and thus mirrors the paternalistic structure of Siam's kingdom, where male sexual prowess symbolized political power and paternal lines of descent determined political loyalties.[14] Last, it demonstrates that ethnic distinctions often correlated with those of religious traditions but did not necessarily match political ties in an empire where the king himself patronized distinct communities and "qualified as . . . emperor by ruling over many peoples," obtaining imperial glory by military conquest.[15]

In this period, Patani was an independent Islamic sultanate that strategically sent tribute to different overlords such as the king of Ayutthaya in order to prevent military aggression. After Ayutthaya fell to the Burmese in 1767, Patani switched allegiance to the Burmese kingdom but suffered a number of severe military defeats when Rama I (r. 1782–1809), the first king of the currently reigning Chakri dynasty, reconstructed the Siamese empire and eventually reestablished rule at a new capital (present-day Bangkok) at the end of the eighteenth century. Notwithstanding its economic and political decline, and the violent dislocation of great parts of its population, Patani had grown into a flourishing regional center of Islamic scholarship by this time, with a mobile Muslim community that linked it to Mecca, Cairo, and other centers of Islamic learning.[16]

SIAM'S MODERN IMPERIAL FORMATION

In the late nineteenth century, the advent of modern Western imperialism had a dual impact on Siam that would, in the end, prove disastrous for Patani. Despite avoiding colonization, Siam became heavily dependent on European powers, while, at the same time, itself deploying modern imperial means to subordinate former tributaries such as Patani in the process of nation-state building.[17] The Franco-Siamese crisis of 1893 exemplifies this dual set of relationships: the Siamese army had aggressively confronted the French military in seeking to expand its control over its former Lao tributaries along the banks of the Mekong River but lost definitively to the French, in the end having to concede vast amounts of territory and allow Asian protégés to remain under French jurisdiction. The defeat, sparked by Siam's own imperial ambitions, demonstrated the helplessness of the "formerly powerful empire" in the face of modern European imperialism.[18]

Only after the 1893 crisis did Siam make efforts to revise the treaties of "friendship and commerce" that it had signed with European powers in the mid-nineteenth century, and not until decades later would scholars call them "unequal treaties"—after the treaties imposed on China by Western powers—to highlight how they had locked Siam into a system of hierarchical relationships with the West.[19] Most crucially, extraterritoriality regulations in the treaties exempted specified foreigners from Siamese jurisdiction and justified the exception on the grounds of the assumed barbarousness of Siam's traditional legal system. In this way, the treaties made the kingdom's sovereignty conditional on a Western "standard of civilization," which "amounted, essentially, to idealized European standards in both external and, more significantly, internal relations," and they were only repealed in 1938 after royal governments had completely reformed Siam's legal system with the help of European advisers.[20] While originally signed to accelerate Siam's economic development, the treaties, moreover, facilitated Siam's further absorption into Britain's informal empire, and by 1932 foreigners controlled over 90 percent of Siam's export economy.[21]

The 1893 crisis also prompted an acceleration of Siam's own modernization efforts, which, as Benedict Anderson has shown, were consciously modeled on European imperial regimes in the region, and these efforts began to operate through the epistemological categories that undergirded Western imperial power.[22] Thongchai Winichaikul has detailed, for instance, how the royal government under the "modernizing monarchs" King Mongkut (Rama IV, r. 1851–1868), King Chulalongkorn (Rama V, r. 1868–1910), and King Vajiravudh (Rama VI, r. 1910–1925) appropriated modern notions of space in negotiations with colonial neighbors, thus enabling the transformation of the flexible tributary relations into a modern system of sovereignty based on the idea of a bounded territory.[23] Most importantly, the reforms instigated by Siamese monarchs at this time began to reflect the modern categories of race and religion that Western imperialism had formed, globalized, and intertwined. Racialized difference that privileged the white Christian West constituted the key condition for the discourse of world religions that divided and investigated the lives of Others in terms of their religious difference; these Others of Western civilization were, moreover, typically characterized as feminine.[24]

In the course of the enforced incorporation of the Islamic sultanate of Patani into the modern Siamese territory beginning at the end of the nineteenth century, these modern categories of difference came to play an important role. Whereas the integration of other tributaries such as the Lao states went hand-in-hand with an official demarcation of their population as Thai and Buddhist, the Patani population was marked as Other. Since the southern *khaek* had a "different religion" and spoke a "different language," the royal government sent an envoy in 1896 to investigate their customs and support the Ministry of the Interior with designing an appropriate policy for governing the South. The envoy, concluding that the *khaek malayu* were living in "semibarbaric states," advised the ministry to implement family law regulations modeled on the British colonial government of Muslims in Malaya.[25] When, in 1902, Patani's Islamic sultan rebelled against the planned Siamese intrusion, Siam engineered a blockade of the Pattani River and imprisoned the raja before integrating the formerly independent principalities into its new administrative system.[26]

In their treatment of Patani, Siamese rulers adopted means typical of modern imperial formations: they merged incorporation with differentiation by completely crushing the sultanate's political and legal authority while narrowing the scope of the Islamic tradition to the private realm of the family. Thus, a population that was regarded as different in modern terms of both race and religion was primarily managed through the feminized notion of the family, and the family law system institutionalized the intersection of these categories of difference, mapped the difference of the Patani population onto the southern provinces, and secured the provinces' marginal status as the geographical periphery. Concurrently, this Othering of southern *khaek* also became a constitutive element of an imperial formation that began to organize itself through a racialized idea of a Thai nation and turned the Buddhist tradition into its official religion while transforming a patriarchal monarchical system into a paternalistic state. The modern category of the Malay-Muslim minority and its geographical counterpart, the three southern provinces, are products of this historical process.

POLICING SIAM: THE COUNTERINSURGENCY ARMY

The instability of Siam's modern imperial formation prompted the establishment of an institutionalized, modern military to engage in what would later be called "counterinsurgency."[27] The military's core function was to fight internal uprisings sparked by the forceful incorporation of former tributary states—those of the Shan and Lao peoples in particular, as well as Patani—into the new state territory.[28] The catalogue on Siam prepared by the royal government for the Louisiana Purchase Exposition, a world fair held in St. Louis, Missouri, in 1904, for instance, glossed the main purposes of the new army as "chiefly the maintenance of order and security in the outlying districts, and . . . to cope with any eventual rising of unruly alien elements whether in the capital or in the interior of the country."[29] Likewise, the preamble to the edict that promulgated conscription in 1905 clarified that "effective, up-to-date government requires trained troops ever ready to suppress rebellions."[30]

Besides internally regulating the emerging state, Siam's armed forces were also important for positioning Siam on a global scale in line with European world powers. Thus, after visits to the Dutch East Indies, Singapore, and the British Raj in the 1880s and 1890s, King Chulalongkorn undertook the first efforts to reform the existing royal forces into an institution that met the military standards of European colonial empires. Like other newly established state institutions, a modern armed force was intended to signal Siam's progress, and initially, many of the senior officers were members of the royal family who had received their military education in Europe.[31]

Remarkably, Siam's modern armed forces were thus not designed to fulfill any external defense function but emerged as a counterinsurgency army, thereby enacting an imperial form of what security studies scholars have called "policing"—a governmental practice that connects the management of the population to the internal order and strength of the state.[32] The analysis of counterinsurgency as policing is based on Michel Foucault's elaboration of "police power" in his governmentality lectures (here, the term "police" does not refer to the constabulary force but reaches back to earlier understandings that Foucault traces to German discussions of *Polizeiwissenschaft* in the seventeenth and eighteenth centuries) and allows for understanding counterinsurgency on a continuum from government to war.[33] As a strategy of unconventional warfare, after all, counterinsurgency locates the local population as the main battlefield and explicitly prefers civilian to military means to fight armed rebellions inside state territory; counterinsurgents foreground methods such as psychological and information operations, economic assistance, and political stabilization to persuade the local population instead of using military force to annihilate the enemy.[34] Since colonial and imperial contexts were key to the development of these population-centric tactics of war, however, postcolonial readings of Foucault's work—which have emphasized the continuity of imperial structures of difference, the function of modern categories of knowledge as imperial technologies of rule, and the fragility of imperial orders—are indispensable to comprehend the work of policing.[35] From this perspective, counterinsurgency, rather than aiming at managing the general population, manages certain populations in specific ways, so that modern categories of difference become central to the operation of police power. Counterinsurgency draws on such hierarchical categories of difference, renders them vital, and thus enables, nourishes, and mobilizes imperial relationships of force.[36]

At the beginning of the twentieth century, Siam's modern military also reproduced these imperial structures of difference internally by excluding certain categories of people from conscription. For instance, the large Chinese population, which had increased dramatically due to Siam's need for labor and was systematically discriminated against, was not allowed to serve in the armed forces. Likewise, the conscription edict exempted "wild tribes"—indigenous populations in mountain and forest areas.

Social status was another critical category of exclusion for senior military positions; in this way, the royal government ensured that the upper ranks were occupied by members of the aristocracy.[37] And although people from the southern Malay provinces were initially included, the Ministry of the Interior regarded them as untrustworthy and eventually refused to arm and train them.[38]

MILITARY COUPS AND THE ALLIANCE WITH THE UNITED STATES DURING THE COLD WAR

Having emerged as a policing rather than a combat force, the Siamese military soon after its establishment started to challenge Siamese rulers in order to strengthen the Siamese state. In 1932, Western-educated elite officers staged a military coup, which abolished the absolutist monarchy.[39] This coup was the first of a series that would haunt modern Thai history, forming what Chai-Anan famously called the "vicious cycle of Thai politics." Until the 1990s, "coups, not elections, formed the norm for changing the government."[40] From 1932 to 2018, the military staged twelve coups; the most recent, in 2014, installed a military government that ruled until the beginning of 2019. By maintaining repressive laws, disbanding an opposition party, controlling the electoral commission, and appointing the senate, the junta has managed to retain power even after official elections in March 2019.[41]

Thailand's alliance with the United States during the Cold War is critical to understanding both the enduring power of Thailand's military and the imperial characteristics of contemporary counterinsurgency in southern Thailand. In the global context of decolonization in the 1950s, the Central Intelligence Agency in the United States began funding academics to further develop theories of anti-guerilla warfare based on tactics of imperial policing, and the John F. Kennedy administration in the 1960s eventually codified the term "counterinsurgency" as the primary method for containing communism and strengthening the power of the US empire in countries considered to be part of the Third World.[42] Fashioning itself as the "epitome of Western power and civilization," the United States thereby attempted to "keep the nations of the Third World within the Western fold," making Thailand the most important regional stronghold in the wake of the Vietnam War.[43]

As in the nineteenth century, a double set of relationships, external and internal, ensured the survival of Thailand's modern imperial formation in the twentieth century. Thus, on the one hand, the Thai state, in general, and the Thai military, in particular, became dependent on the United States as part of the latter's global counterinsurgency strategy, while on the other, they aggressively deployed imperial counterinsurgency strategies to crush political opposition, which was strongest in those geographical border regions that used to be tributary states. In the US-led imperial system of the Cold War, Thailand's civilizational status was now measured in terms of the Thai government's success in anticommunist counterinsurgency, and whereas international advisers had rewritten Siam's legal system in the early twentieth century, US generals completely restructured Thailand's security forces in the 1950s and '60s. Nearly fifty thousand US troops were stationed in a country that had never been colonized—the US armed forces themselves recognized that "the presence of American military men, no matter how benign, tended to confirm the communist contention that the United States had 'occupied' Thailand."[44]

Moreover, Thailand received so much institutional and financial support from the United States to strengthen its security forces that a US officer concluded in

1969: "It is fair to say that there are no major Royal Thai Government counter-insurgency programs in effect or planned that do not receive some kind of US assistance—be it in the form of material, training, or advice."[45] The national military was not only expanded significantly but was also completely reorganized according to US standards, and thousands of Thai troops were deployed to South Vietnam in support of the allied forces.[46] The "distinct American flavor" that US military reports detected in the Thai government's "posture in the realm of counterinsurgency" was also reflected institutionally.[47] To coordinate military civic action in the anticommunist campaign, the armed forces established the National Security Council (NSC) and the Communist Suppression Operations Command (CSOC), later renamed Internal Security Operations Command (ISOC)—both were directly modeled on US military institutions.

In political terms, the US-Thai alliance was based on the United States' backing of the military dictatorship of Gen. Sarit Thanarat and his allies (1957–1973); under his rule, notions of gender, race, and religion gained increasing importance for the counterinsurgency campaign. In direct reference to the imperial ruler of the kingdom of Sukothai (1238–1438), which was promoted in modern Thai historiography as the origin of the Thai nation, Sarit styled himself as the "fatherly ruler" (*pho khun*) of the race of Thai people.[48] Moreover, Thai government propaganda followed US policies by labeling communists as both "un-Thai" and "atheists," proclaiming in the Anti-Communist Law of 1969 that communist activities included "persuading others to lose faith in religion or engaging in activities that would destroy Thai customs."[49] A host of government initiatives that involved Buddhist clerics was eventually centralized under the "missionary monks" program (*thammathut*), which propagated the policing of Buddhist morality as a means to strengthen national security, and sent groups of monks to distant provinces to provide public education.[50] Likewise, counterinsurgency school-building programs focused on teaching Thai to people that were recognized as potentially disloyal to the Thai state—particularly indigenous peoples in the north and northeast.[51] The far south also featured as an area of insurgent activity on the maps of anti-guerilla strategists: recognizing the "unfortunate symptons [*sic*] of colonializm [*sic*] that characterize the southern situation," they feared that "dissident Moslems" might join with "communists" in order to seek "autonomy from the Buddhist-oriented government of Thailand."[52] In fact, the group now suspected to be one of the main drivers of the insurgency—the Barisan Revolusi Nasional (National Revolutionary Front, BRN)—was founded in the 1960s and had intimate connections with the communist parties of both Thailand and Malaysia.[53]

After decades of anticommunist warfare, the Thai armed forces eventually declared themselves victorious in the 1980s—a questionable success, however, which resulted from an internal weakening of the Communist Party and a law granting amnesty to its members; hundreds of cadres gave up their fight and surrendered. Many of the older officers whom I met in southern Thailand had not only participated in the anticommunist campaign but had also learned everything they knew about counterinsurgency during the Cold War, and Thai military discourse still celebrates the Cold War campaign as its main (and only) military success in modern history. In this context, the southern insurgency in the early twenty-first century provided the perfect incentive to revive the Thai forces' main tactics and institutions of unconventional warfare—for instance, the ISOC, which had been lingering for years without a core agenda, has been reinstituted as the main body responsible for coordinating both civilian and military counterinsurgency measures in the southern provinces.

POLICING SOUTHERN THAILAND

The counterinsurgency motto "Understanding, Reaching Out, Development," coined by King Bhumipol Adulyadej (Rama IX, r. 1946–2016) in a speech in February 2004, has guided military operations in the southern region under various governments and juntas, and it encapsulates how counterinsurgency discourse is predicated on and produces the essentialized differences of the southern population.[54] "Understanding" reiterates the official framing of political grievances of the southern population as "cultural misunderstandings"; "reaching out" recapitulates the peripheral location of southern Thailand; "development" integrates a temporal perspective that confines the South to an earlier stage of a teleological history than the rest of Thailand. Most conspicuously, the motto positions Thailand's military as the paternal caretaker of the South and relocates the causes of insurgent violence in the differences of the southern population.

The motto also reflects a depoliticized discourse of military benevolence that has prevailed in official policy toward the southern provinces since the ousting of Prime Minister Thaksin Shinawatra in a military coup in 2006. Thaksin, a billionaire business tycoon who had won the 2001 election with his party, Thais Love Thais (Thai Rak Thai), has widely been seen as having taken a hawkish approach toward the southern insurgency.[55] Following the January 2004 attacks on army bases that marked the beginning of the current conflict, the Thaksin administration imposed martial law in the southern provinces and drafted the Emergency Decree, which was initially designed to replace martial law but ended up being applied in addition to the latter.[56] The resulting legal gray zone allows security forces in the South to detain suspects without warrant, to hold them for a maximum of thirty-seven days, and to be guaranteed immunity if they declare they have acted "in good faith."[57] Moreover, it was under Thaksin's government that two of the most serious cases of abuse by security forces occurred: the incidents of Kru Ze and Tak Bai. At Kru Ze, a small group of men retreated to the historical Kru Ze Mosque, one of the most important Muslim sites in the region, after attacking a nearby Thai security checkpoint; in reaction, special forces stormed the mosque and destroyed it, killing all thirty-two men inside—most of them probably innocent victims. In Tak Bai, the military shot and killed seven protesters marching peacefully outside a police station; seventy-eight additional protestors died after being arrested and tightly packed, hands tied behind their backs, into trucks for transport to an army camp.[58] The widely reported killings were perceived as an embarrassment by military officers opposing Thaksin. When Thaksin was ousted in 2006, coup leaders referred to his mismanagement of the southern problem and promised a more efficient and less brutal counterinsurgency policy.[59]

At that point in time, a number of analysts speculated that Thaksin's approach had mobilized and strengthened the insurgency movement; however, increasing insight into the movement has not only proven such accusations wrong but also, once again, revealed the significance of the imperial context of Patani's annexation for understanding the current conflict.[60] Experts now suspect the Barisan Revolusi Nasional-Coordinate (BRN-C), a successor of the BRN movement founded in the 1960s, to have played a leading role in recruiting and mobilizing a new generation of insurgents since at least the 1990s. The January 2004 assaults had been long planned, and the date of the April 2004 attacks—which in addition to the Kru Ze checkpoint attack involved coordinated incidents in Yala and Pattani Provinces—was likely carefully chosen to memorialize the Thai authorities' brutal suppression of a rebellion in 1948 that had killed over a hundred Muslim militants.[61] The approximately three thousand active insurgent fighters receive support from a number of villages in the southern provinces and make use of a relatively permeable border with Malaysia. Most operate under the banner of the BRN-C, which rallies around the claim to self-rule in an area roughly comprising the former Islamic sultanate of Patani, rather than calling for global *jihad*.[62] While many observers at the start of the conflict described a diffuse network of insurgents, the BRN-C seems to be organized in a structure that includes a military and political wing as well as village-based cells. Operating in secret, insurgents have been able to sustain high levels of violence since 2004: on the one hand through regular small-scale assaults such as targeted shootings, bombings, and ambushes, and on the other by scaling up the violence in certain cases and launching large coordinated attacks.[63]

The military junta that ruled after the 2006 coup presented the counterinsurgency policy in southern Thailand in more depoliticized terms of paternal benevolence than did the Thaksin government. In a peacebuilding policy of 2004, Thaksin had accused certain groups of instigating "war" in the form of "terrorism." By contrast, in October 2006, just one month after the coup, Prime Ministerial Order 206, titled "Policy to Promote Peace and Happiness in the Southern Border Provinces," mentioned neither term and instead assigned the military to deal with "unrest" in the area by "eradicating the factors that facilitate the use of violence." Thaksin's policy had openly invoked the differences in the race, language, religion, and culture of the people in the southern area as grounds for indoctrination; the 2006 order obfuscated such differences by introducing notions of national unity, happiness, and harmony, and using affective language to voice concerns about "feelings."[64] People in the southern border provinces, it asserted, felt (wrongly) that they were not truly part of a unified Thailand. Counterinsurgency, consequently, should eliminate any factors that mobilized such misguided feelings and nurtured an atmosphere of mistrust. In this discourse, Patani's longstanding political problems are collapsed into the subjectivities of people in the three southern border provinces and their feelings, suggesting that the military is dealing with the consequences of minor confusions of identity rather than political opposition. The Thai state thereby emerges as a neutral arbiter offering valuable disciplinary lessons that teach mutual understanding, and the military is called upon to manage the southern population in such a way that its incorporation comes without a need for rebellion. Combining hierarchical differentiation with the eradication of political dissent, this form of policing clearly echoes its imperial forebears.

The post-2006 policy has also authorized the expansion of the military mandate to encompass matters of internal security. Thus, the Internal Security Act, passed in 2007, gave the military the lead role for safeguarding internal security and revived and restructured the ISOC by giving it a new legal foundation and securing powerful posts for elite generals.[65] The ISOC command for the southern region (called ISOC Region 4 Forward Command) became the lead organization for the southern counterinsurgency, and security forces under the southern ISOC leadership became heavily engaged in social development projects and public relations campaigns.[66]

This counterinsurgency strategy has legitimized a military mission in southern Thailand on a previously unseen scale. For an area with a population of approximately 1.8 million, the number of security personnel is huge, and it has been steadily increased, growing from fifteen thousand in 2005 to over sixty thousand by 2015. A large part of the security force is composed of troops from the Royal Thai Armed Forces, the Royal Thai Navy, the Border Patrol Police, and police forces; yet very few of these soldiers are locals. The Royal Thai Armed Forces are organized into four regional armies, and each is in charge of one of the four provincial task forces in the southern counterinsurgency campaign.[67] Soldiers from the Fourth Regional Army of southern Thailand, which includes both the lower and upper southern provinces, are deployed only at Task Force IV, which is responsible for a very small area of three districts of Songkhla. Task Force II in Pattani Province, however, recruited soldiers from the northeastern Second Army. The imperial structure of the Thai state is thus replicated in Pattani. Like the southern Thai provinces, the northeastern states were forcefully integrated into Siam at the end of the nineteenth century and are still considered by the Bangkok elite to be a rural hinterland; the economic conditions in this region are often even worse than in southern Thailand. Manpower from the northeastern margins, in other words, has been dispatched to develop and appease the southern periphery.

Locals recruited by the Thai military, by contrast, are usually paid less, receive less training, and have to work in the most volatile conflict areas. The biggest group is the *thahan phran*—paramilitary forces, also called "rangers," which are largely a legacy of Thailand's anticommunist campaign in the 1960s, '70s, and '80s.[68] The rangers are given only a short forty-five-day training course and earn a relatively low salary of approximately THB 9,000 (around USD 300) per month. Unlike troops who are regularly rotated among different military stations, the rangers are expected to remain in an area of operation for several years, and instead of residing in large army camps, they are stationed in small groups. In the ranger unit responsible for the Saiburi area, for instance, about twenty paramilitaries would usually lodge together in camps located at what were considered to be strategic hot spots, such as opposite a Muslim boarding school.[69] The black uniform of the *thahan phran*, which distinguishes the rangers from the khaki-clad members of the general forces, features prominently in rumors about military brutality in Pattani that often construct the paramilitaries as particularly vicious traitors to the insurgent cause.

Moreover, the security forces have armed and trained civilians to support the counterinsurgency campaign and protect their own villages in southern Thailand. Rough calculations in 2012 estimated there were over eighty thousand members of these volunteer defense forces, a number that has likely increased over the course of a military initiative that has expanded these forces to all districts of the southern provinces (see fig. 2).[70] Due to this large-scale arming of civilians and the easing of firearm regulations, the number of guns in circulation in the southern region has rapidly increased.[71]

Rather than de-escalating the conflict, the counterinsurgency mission has thereby contributed to destabilizing the area; as many rumors and some specialists have it, moreover, the military has profited greatly from its southern mission, using the strengthening of its force in the periphery to repeatedly seize power in the center.[72] Meanwhile, the southern insurgency has continued unabated: by 2018, the estimated number of fatalities had risen to nearly seven thousand, and over thirteen thousand people had been injured since 2004. Victims have included both security personnel and civilians, and although there have been a number of attacks on Buddhist monks and villagers, Muslims account for about half of the casualties. The ongoing conflict has yielded one key result for Thailand's imperial formation: it has, once again, institutionalized the demarcation of Patani as an "exceptional region . . . which is administered and governed . . . visibly differently from other parts of the country."[73]

Figure 2. Thai troops training volunteer defense forces in Pattani, September 2011.
Photograph by the author.

FIELDWORK: THE WORK OF THE MILITARY FIELD

During my stay in Pattani, the ubiquitous military presence constituted a key marker of the region's exceptionality. Throughout the town of Pattani, defense volunteers guarded state buildings and shops in the Buddhist areas of the town, soldiers accompanied Buddhist monks on their daily almsgiving rounds or conducted vehicular patrols and were present at any gathering of people, and military checkpoints controlled the traffic at the main entry points to the town. The locals had adopted the vocabulary of the counterinsurgency campaign. It was entirely common, for instance, to hear people talk about their home village in southern Thailand as red or green—color codes used by counterinsurgents to designate different degrees of insurgent infiltration.[74]

Armed soldiers frequently drove through the campus of the Prince of Songkhla University in Pattani, where I was based, and soldiers in civilian clothing participated in university workshops and courses. In fact, the headquarters of the counterinsurgency task force for the town of Pattani town had been established at a Buddhist temple, Wat Lak Mueang, located right behind the university campus. Inside the temple compound, buildings had been transformed to accommodate approximately two hundred soldiers; the temple had thus become one of many militarized Buddhist spaces across the southern Thai region that Michael Jerryson has researched.[75] Lower-ranking soldiers slept in army tents erected inside various temple buildings (see fig. 3), while makeshift metal huts had been placed on the temple grounds to accommodate senior officers. The task force had also converted the temple's entry gate into a small checkpoint to control access to its headquarters.

Figure 3. Military tents in a temple hall of Wat Lak Mueang, December 2010.
Photograph by the author.

The camp at Wat Lak Mueang also provides insights into the hierarchical organization of troops in southern Thailand. Many of the soldiers I interviewed were conscripts, indicating that their families lacked the connections and the money needed to evade the draft in a highly corrupt system. Often just over twenty years old, they were stationed for a rather short period of time of one to two years, and rotated their positions annually or biennially in October. Most had received only rudimentary training to prepare them for their tour of duty in the South. Conscripts earned a basic salary of THB 4,000–6,000 (roughly USD 115–170) per month and were provided with food and accommodation. At Wat Lak Mueang, many left the temple compound only to carry out the different tasks they were assigned, which included standing guard (at checkpoints, Buddhist temples, or official buildings), going on patrol, and escorting teachers or monks. They worked six- to eight-hour shifts and spent their free time at the temple compound, playing soccer, chatting on the phone, or watching television. After a period of forty to forty-five days, they received a week off to visit their families in the northeast of Thailand; the bus journeys home, centrally organized by the task force, took more than twenty hours.

By contrast, many of the higher-ranking military personnel I met had volunteered for the assignment. For some, gaining one or two years of experience in the southern Thai counterinsurgency was a career move: they could count on professional promotion after their return. A number of them had worked in anticommunist counterinsurgency during the Cold War and were eager to apply their skills and knowledge to defeat the insurgency in the southern provinces. Others had simply decided to stay after their first assignment to the South had ended, having become acquainted with locals in the villages in which they were stationed and having acquired basic Malay language skills. Their tasks significantly differed from those of their subordinates. If they were on one of the task forces, they worked in management and supervision, and they coordinated tasks with other units and state agencies (meetings occupied much of their time). The senior officers, however, also had more specialized assignments in a huge array of military units, including fostering relationships with civil society, intelligence, or socio-psychological operations. Their lives were much more comfortable than those of the lower ranks, even in the southern conflict zone: they earned good salaries, used army cars to travel, and could take one of the frequent flights from Hat Yai back to Bangkok when on leave.

Regardless of their rank, many soldiers expressed that they felt alienated living in southern Thailand. The food was very different—people in the South, as one soldier had it, put "strange herbs" in their curries. Conscripts therefore often cooked their own food in the camp, buying ingredients at local markets where, as another remarked, the smells were unfamiliar. Few soldiers could understand the Malay dialect spoken by people in the South—at Wat Lak Mueang, they preferred to converse in their northeastern Isan dialect. The vast majority of troops I met were Buddhists; some wore protective Buddhist amulets around their necks. Although the soldiers had been told to treat Islam with respect, it proved an enigma to many, especially those who rarely interacted with the local population. As one conscript summarized, "It feels like people here are not from this country."[76] Paralleling the official counterinsurgency motto "understanding, reaching out, development," an unofficial discourse expressed soldiers' experience of alienation from the southern provinces and their inhabitants; in this framing, the policing mission had tasked them with incorporating an area that seemed to be a different country.

My access to these military sites and subjects was eased by a number of factors. Perhaps most important were personal connections that arose naturally given the extensive military presence, even on campus. In addition, three identity categories that marked me as a neutral observer of the conflict likely facilitated the openness of military personnel: I could clearly be identified as a white foreigner from the West, dubbed a *farang* in Thai and invested with an authority that is integrally connected to ideas about the Occidental Other of Thainess; as a woman, I was stereotyped by the military as essentially harmless and potentially vulnerable, and I was thus the welcome subject for paternalistic protection in a dangerous conflict zone; and as a German, I escaped accusations of spying leveled at some US researchers.[77] My accommodation at the well-regarded Prince of Songkhla University, moreover, helped to underscore my status as a researcher, an occupation highly respected in some military circles.

The military's openness to interacting with a foreign female researcher was also based on the close relationship between counterinsurgency and knowledge production: counterinsurgency and its colonial predecessors have long fostered the production of knowledge in the social sciences and area studies, particularly on Thailand, and the policing of information has explicitly formed part of the current military mission in the South.[78] Prime Ministerial Order 206, for instance, advises counterinsurgents to support the dissemination of "real facts about the situation in the southern border provinces" to both national and international audiences. The military not only feared that insurgent propaganda was producing "false images" of the counterinsurgency campaign but also accused human rights organizations of spreading "misinformation."[79] Many officers therefore regarded my research interest as a welcome opportunity to correct such purportedly false information: they hoped to convince me of the "true," "correct," and "good" nature of their mission, and some even assumed that my research would yield military benefits. A paramilitary commander, for example, introduced me to his subordinates by saying, "This is Ruth. She is doing research to help us find the best solution to the conflict."[80] Likewise, at the Army War College in Bang-kok, two colonels started to lecture me about the proper purpose of scientific inquiry after I had explained my research on military counterinsurgency to them: "You have to identify the main problems in terms of culture, history, economy, and so on, and then propose solutions, and tell us where the military has to improve. Research has to have a proper benefit, *na!*"[81] (Military) paternalism here dovetailed with scientific positiv-ism and ideas about the use of science for modernizing progress, exemplifying the powerful work of the gaze "from nowhere" that still characterizes not only research in military academies but also in certain parts of the social sciences.[82] Doing fieldwork in this context therefore meant navigating what Barak Kalir has called the "work of the field"—in this case, the powerful work of a policing mission that itself included a form of knowledge production.[83]

GENEALOGY AND POLITICAL ETHNOGRAPHY

In this book, I combine ethnography with genealogy not only to critically examine such military forms of knowledge production as part of an imperial project but also to trace how notions of difference that constitute Thailand's state formation have evolved and now materialize in concrete encounters. The main body of ethnographic material on which the book is based comprises interviews, observations, photographs, and written documents; most were gathered during ten months of research in southern Thailand in 2010–2011, and some during later short research stays in 2014 and 2016. In total, I conducted over one hundred interviews: approximately half with security personnel and half with locals and experts including journalists, activists, villagers, academics, and high-school students.[84]

Genealogy thereby allows me to practice a form of political ethnography that explicitly entails asking about the politics of the epistemologies that undergird the operation of imperial formations.[85] I begin in chapter 1 by examining a handbook pro-duced for military officers stationed in the South, and I relate some of its central notions to an imperial construction of history in the modern Thai state formation that simultaneously erases the state's conquest of the Islamic sultanate while marking Patani as its Muslim feminized Other. In this narrative, Patani emerges as an ancient Buddhist land incorporated into Siam by mere administrative reform, Siam's crush-ing of the legal and political power of the former Islamic sultanate is elided, and the Patani population is characterized as adhering to a private Muslim culture. Based on this narrative, the handbook constructs state officers as paternal protectors of the southern population.

A genealogical exploration of the Thai imperial formation also underpins the dis-cussion of checkpoint interactions in chapter 2. In general terms, the installation of road blocks from the beginning of the conflict has marked Patani as a different coun-try within Thailand; more specifically, in day-to-day encounters between soldiers and those crossing, racialized ideas have emerged as a key marker to differentiate peaceful from dangerous subjects. The chapter outlines how the racialization of the southern population has historically extended itself to include certain ideas of dress and lan-guage, and it details how these differentiations are drawn in contemporary checkpoint interactions. It also shows the gendering of ideas of the Malay *khaek*, which entails attributing Orientalized and often sexualized beauty to young local girls.

Chapters 3 and 4 are largely located in the contemporary moment. In chap-ter 3, I explore how the difference of young Muslim men is produced in the drug rehabilitation camp Yalannanbaru and discuss how the disciplinary methods deployed by military trainers derive from the Buddhist tradition. I closely follow the different exercises of the camp's program to show how the category of religion is enlisted to serve the disciplined incorporation of potentially unruly Malay subjects. Chapter 4 tracks constructions of gendered and sexualized difference in the Thai imperial formation by examining the more intimate matters of the conflict, including discourses regarding rape and romantic relationships, the establishment of female paramilitary units to police Patani women, and military support for women's groups in the South. I conclude this critical history of the present by examining the politics of the current military junta from the vantage point of the southern Thai counterinsurgency; imperial practices of policing, I argue, are now applied on a national scale.

CHAPTER ONE

POLICING HISTORY

A Military Handbook on the Southern Provinces

"How can I trust you?" A. smiled, but he was staring intently at me. I was caught completely off guard. My housemate had suggested I talk to A., a member of her family: "I think it would be better you ask him, he knows a lot about the situation here!" I could not offer much in response to A.'s question. "Erm . . . here's my card?" He nodded. "Berlin Graduate School Muslim Cultures and Societies," it said under my name. He smiled. "Okay, you can take notes." For A., the conflict in southern Thailand was a conflict about history. The Thai state, he explained, was trying to extinguish the history of the once glorious and independent sultanate of Patani that used to be the center of Islamic scholarship in the region. This history is no longer taught at state schools, said A. Only local *pondoks* keep it alive, yet these traditional Islamic boarding schools have also now come under state control. A. elaborated that what he called the "movement" was therefore determined to fight for the right of Patani people to learn and teach their own history again.[1]

A.'s suspicion reveals how sensitive discussions about Patani's history have become in the context of the southern conflict, and how signifiers of religion—the word "Muslim" on my card—function to indicate support for a certain version of history. According to A., history not only defined the essence of Patani but also determined the cause of the insurgency movement, with which he seemed to identify. His highlighting of Patani's past glory reminded me of the strategies that insurgents reputedly use in recruitment, relaying a similar narrative to convince prospective members that they have to "fight to regain control [of their] history."[2]

The contentions about Patani history have been so fierce that the 2006 report of the National Reconciliation Commission warned, "Violence in the southern border provinces may be regarded as a problem of history." This problem of history is not simply a clash of two nationalisms, but rather characteristic of the Thai imperial formation.[3] As much postcolonial scholarship teaches, the production of history is one of the central discourses through which modern imperial power produces hierarchical difference. Dipesh Chakrabarty has demonstrated that the modern discourse of history—what he calls "historicism"—conditions the project of imperial modernity. The idea of human progress through secular time legitimated the notion of civilizational development. In its spatialized version, history distanced the West from the non-West, placing the latter into the "waiting room of history."[4] This discourse, as Fernando Coronil argues, establishes relations based on disassociations, thereby "separating relational histories, reifying cultural difference, and turning difference into hierarchy."[5] History in the imperial formation thus manages difference by stabilizing its own linear, dominant form of time, and distancing those temporal Others that threaten to disrupt its narrative of homogenizing progress.[6]

In fact, Siam's own imperial entanglement shaped the state-led enforcement of a new practice of historiography at the end of the nineteenth century. The royal elite championed the modern discourse of history to demonstrate Siam's civilized status compared with Western nations.[7] It was thus precisely during the transition of the old Siamese empire to the modern imperial formation that modern historical discourse gained ground. In the course of a relatively short period of time, the elite coined two neologisms that delineated this new field of knowledge: *borankhadi* (literally, "antiquity studies," and later used to designate "archaeology") and its replacement *prawattisat* (literally, "past-science").[8] Significantly, the official endorsement of the modern discourse of history helped to produce a number of disassociations that still centrally structure the narrative of Thailand's civilizational development today. Most important for our purposes here, modern Thai historiography has elided Siam's own imperial encroachment on former principalities and tributary states such as Patani, and has produced a gendered and racialized narrative of a historical Buddhist kingdom wherein a Thai lineage is protected from external (colonial) threats by its paternal royal rulers.[9]

A speech made by King Chulalongkorn (Rama V, r. 1868–1910), who is still revered in Thailand as the great modernizer, to inaugurate the Antiquarian Society in 1907 illustrates the modern narrative of Thai history.[10] In it, the king differentiated the new practice of historiography from the old tradition of writing royal chronicles, and he urged his listeners to collect documentary evidence from proper historical sources instead of following the stories of rulers told in the chronicles. He deployed racialized terms to argue that the written documents available, though few, distinguished the Thai nation from other "negro nations" that only relay their history "by word of mouth." A considerable part of the speech was devoted to a long list of cities and former city-states that he identified as "old settlement(s) of the Thai race" based on archaeological remains of Buddhist temples. These (city-)states were "now joined together as united Siam." Using this evidence, members of the society should help to "compile a history of Siam over the past 1000 years."[11]

The new historiography that Chulalongkorn wanted to establish could narrate the secular progress of modern Siam without relying on old sacred chronicles, and would strive to be as white as the written documents available allowed. The king's speech thereby reveals that the imperial concept of civilization was already ingrained in elite thinking at the time. In colonial scholarship, only peoples with written historical records were seen as capable of civilizing historical progress and as worthy of investigation within the newly established discipline of history, whereas oral historical traditions were left to the discipline of ethnography.[12]

This colonial idea of history became a political program in Chulalongkorn's lecture; he described history as a "discipline" that acted both as an objective norm for ruling the kingdom ("to evaluate ideas and actions as right or wrong, good or bad") and as a means for governing his subjects ("to inculcate love of one's nation and land").[13] Just as he presented Siam as an imperial formation that anachronistically incorporated different city-states into its racialized realm, he imagined an imperial history that absorbed all local histories into one unified, civilized narrative of continuous progress. This history strengthened the power of the state and governed potentially unruly subjects by integrating them into its linear narrative.

Significantly, Chulalongkorn failed to mention Patani in his speech. One reason may be that in 1907, negotiations about Patani between British and Siamese authorities were still underway, and they were only settled with the Anglo-Siamese Treaty signed in 1909. The omission might also reveal the marginality of the history of the Islamic sultanate to the central narrative of modern Siam as a Buddhist kingdom. Perhaps most importantly, it effectively concealed Siam's own imperial conquest of Patani, thus producing national memory based on the erasure of useless historical traces.[14]

PRODUCING KNOWLEDGE ABOUT SOUTHERN THAILAND

A similar method of streamlining history has been deployed by state authorities in the course of the ongoing southern conflict. For example, scholars interested in the history of the southern provinces will find that most of the relevant documents have been rendered inaccessible in the Bangkok National Archives—sometimes whole pages have been removed from the Archives' catalogues. When I visited in 2019, the friendly staff advised me to hurry up and copy the few sources still available because more boxes would likely soon be removed.[15]

While sources on Patani history continue to disappear from the National Archives, counterinsurgents have strategically produced certain kinds of historical knowledge to police the southern population. A prime example is a handbook for military officers that the Internal Security Operations Command (ISOC) published as part of its initiative to win over the hearts and minds of people living in southern Thailand, titled *Handbook of Operational Knowledge for Officers Working in the Southern Border Provinces*.[16] It was published in 2010, with two thousand copies of the first edition, and contains four thematic chapters: "Ethnic History," "Islamic Religion," "Lifestyles and Culture," and "Social Circumstances." It is larger and heavier than similar handbooks, with just over two hundred A5 glossy pages, and it is printed in color. Pictures feature prominently; approximately one third of the book consists of photographs of southern historical sites, cultural practices, and people, some of them interacting with military personnel. Harmony prevails in these photographic representations of Patani past and present, except in the illustrations to a section titled "From the Malay Resistance Movement to Muslim Separatism," which show a group of Muslim men in prayer caps looking skeptically into the camera and, on the next page, police inspecting a motorbike destroyed by a bomb explosion.

The preface by then army commander Gen. Anupong Paochinda leaves no doubt that the ISOC produced the handbook as an integral part of counterinsurgency operations. Recognizing that the southern unrest also has "historical, cultural, religious and ethnic dimensions," he warns that the "perpetrators of violence" use distorted information to win the "hearts and minds" of the local population and to blackmail state authorities, in the end turning people into a "mass" of supporters for the insurgency movement. The handbook consequently is designed, Gen. Anupong explains, to support military efforts to "make people in the area stand on our side" by providing military and civilian state authorities with "accurate knowledge about southern Thailand."[17]

The structure of each chapter reflects how the ISOC envisioned this project of policing knowledge. The first part elaborates the topic. The second part explains the "errors" that circulate in the area, especially among the insurgency movement. The chapters end by instructing officers on what kind of facts they can cite to build understanding and convince the local population of the correct knowledge. The handbook, in other words, not only intends to educate civilian and military authorities about southern Thailand but it also tells these authorities how to use facts to educate the local population.

The epistemological grounds on which the handbook rests are central to the whole military project of building understanding. By referring to a positivistic notion of facts, the handbook aligns the military with objective truth while at the same time eliding the location of these truths. This "view from nowhere" establishes a position of dominance, and "understanding" thereby becomes a unidirectional and paternalistic undertaking of teaching the local population that proceeds from the ISOC's purported objectivity.[18] The military aligning itself with objectivity is especially noteworthy in a conflict region where claims to knowledge—about history, in particular—are among the stated reasons for violence, and in a country where the government restricts open discussions about Patani's history. In this context, the military construction of objective truth furthers the linear narrative of Thailand's progressive imperial formation while marking alternative histories as false.

COUNTERINSURGENCY AND KNOWLEDGE PRODUCTION

Manuals are a common form of knowledge production in counterinsurgency both in Thailand and internationally. The US Army's 2006 *Counterinsurgency Field Manual*, for example, promotes the gathering of "cultural knowledge" as "essential to waging a successful counterinsurgency," and uses anthropological literature to devise different methods for obtaining such knowledge. This cultural turn of counterinsurgency had wide-ranging institutional consequences. Most notoriously, US armed forces in Iraq established the Human Terrain System program, which involved embedding social scientists to conduct sociocultural analysis for military purposes.[19]

The shift in US military policy also had an impact on counterinsurgency strategy in Thailand. After September 11, 2001, the Thai state renewed its historically close military ties with the United States, as evidenced by its dispatching troops to Iraq and participating in, on average, forty joint US-Thai military exercises per year.[20] Thai military personnel regularly receive scholarships to study at US military institutions. As the Royal Thai Embassy in Washington states, "Since 1950, well over 20,000 Thais," including King Vajiralongkorn (Rama X, r. since 2016), have obtained such training, thus "greatly enhancing US access to all levels of Thailand's military hierarchy."[21] Training institutions include the US Army War College and the Naval Postgraduate School, which specializes in studies of unconventional warfare. Many of the theses and reports written by Thai scholarship recipients after the flare-up of the southern conflict in 2004 explicitly deal with questions of counterinsurgency strategy and often directly refer to US examples. One of my military contacts had studied at the Naval Postgraduate School and indicated that the 2006 US manual on counterinsurgency constituted one of the central reference points for developing a counterinsurgency strategy for southern Thailand.[22]

In fact, knowledge production has been at the heart of counterinsurgency ever since the inception of this imperial form of policing and throughout its reincarnations during the Cold War.[23] Thus Montgomery McFate, an important advocate of the integration of cultural knowledge into US counterinsurgency policy, endorsed anthropology as a discipline that had helped to "consolidate imperial power."[24] Thailand itself is a case in point, demonstrating how the gathering of cultural knowledge has been central to military policing projects, particularly with the establishment of the modern military. One of the earliest Siamese ethnographies, published in 1889, for instance, was written by the then commander of the Siamese army responsible for an area in the northeastern part of the kingdom. The article "On Different Forest Races" assembles the commander's observations on people who live "far away from cities" in the "jungle," and the topics included are typical of nineteenth-century anthropology: "villages and housing" as well as "marriage" and "religion, beliefs, seasonal events, and festivals." Although it is unknown how the knowledge was integrated into the military project of appeasing the northeastern region, the mere publication of the text in five issues of the journal *Wachirayanwiset,* a weekly magazine published by the *Wachirayan* Library, is remarkable.[25]

The gathering of knowledge as a counterinsurgency strategy was professionalized in Thailand during the Cold War. The United States, in particular, promoted and financed an array of research activities to save Thailand from the communist threat in the wake of the Vietnam War and the growing popularity of the Thai Communist Party. Under US patronage, the Thai military and government trained and contracted social scientists from various disciplines to gather specialized data, especially in the northern and northeastern parts of the country. Various teams of researchers inquired into village loyalty patterns and socioeconomic needs in the service of stabilizing the area by winning people's loyalty. A joint Thai-US unit, the Military Research and Development Center in Bangkok, controlled much of the counterinsurgency research and produced, inter alia, a handbook on the southern provinces in 1974.[26]

HANDBOOKS ON SOUTHERN THAILAND

There is a second, more local, context important for comprehending the ISOC handbook: handbooks very similar to this one have long been produced as part of efforts to prepare both military and civilian officials for their work in southern Thailand. In fact, most of the soldiers I talked to had received some kind of training in advance of their postings to the South. While the Southern Border Provinces Administrative Centre organized one-week courses for civil servants in Yala, the four regional armies had various ways of instructing soldiers in their home regions.[27] Military units from the Second Regional Army in the northeast, for example, invited members of their local Islamic Committee to teach them about Islam and "the unique way of life in the deep south." Trainers often distributed handbooks and textbooks on the Malay language to sensitize soldiers to "local culture" and "Islam." The military "believed that if the troops were able to conduct themselves properly, conflicts with villagers would be minimized."[28]

The Ministry of the Interior likely published the first handbook on southern Thailand out of a similar concern. In 1922, the Malay-speaking inhabitants of Patani loudly protested the Primary Education Act, which obliged primary schools to teach the Thai language. King Vajiravudh (Rama VI, r. 1910–1925) reacted by promulgating "Principles of Public Policy and Administration for Patani," in which he urged state officers to avoid any kind of conflict with the local population. From now on, the king advised, government representatives should prepare themselves before working in Patani; they should study and gather knowledge—on Islam, in particular—to avoid implementing regulations that contradicted Muslim principles.[29] To this end, the Ministry of the Interior compiled a handbook titled "Handbook for officers of the Ministry of the Interior working in the *monthon* [administrative subdivision] with citizens who believe in the Islamic religion" (1923).[30]

Since then, a wide variety of government agencies have produced numerous handbooks and have even reprinted the 1923 handbook on Patani. These include the Departments of Local and Provincial Administration, the Military Research and

Development Center, the Prime Ministerial Office, the National Identity Board, the Ministry of the Interior, and the Southern Border Provinces Administrative Centre.[31] Although the handbooks vary considerably in the kind of content they present and the order in which they do so, most focus on issues of ways of life, language, and religion, and offer detailed descriptions of various Muslim practices and explanations of the Malay language. The majority present maps of the area (some more detailed than others). Only a few of the handbooks include a chapter exclusively devoted to the history of the region.

Like these other manuals, the ISOC handbook focuses heavily on the topics of culture and lifestyle. Moreover, its appendix is a direct copy of other government handbooks. It includes questions that were posed to the *chularajamontri*, the official head of the Islamic community in Thailand, concerning problems in interactions between Muslims and civil servants in southern Thailand.[32] Recorded in 1982, the interview is reprinted in the majority of handbooks produced to date.

The preparation of officers for their postings in the South and the distribution of handbooks discursively manifest the imperial formation: both assume and generate a fundamental difference of the South, which aligns territory with population and deploys Islam as an overarching signifier.[33] Reminiscent of colonial handbooks of information that were produced to prepare prospective settlers for life in a foreign place, the handbooks on southern Thailand reiterate a construction of the region as different and distant in terms of culture, history, and religion. Temporally speaking, the reprinting of old editions and interviews furthermore invokes a common Orientalist stereotype: it suggests that progressive officers from different parts of Thailand must prepare for their encounters with southern Muslims supposedly mired in tradition.[34] At the same time, however, the handbooks are clearly constructed as tools of policing to manage the consent of the population so that they willingly retain their hierarchically lower position within the Thai imperial formation.

Administrative Reform

The introduction to the ISOC handbook chapter "Knowledge about Ethnic History in the Three Southern Border Provinces" begins by again glossing the relevance of learning the truth about the history of the region. "The Kingdom of Thailand," it clarifies, "was established on territory that used to be different states and city-states in the past." According to the handbook, these states "merged together" to form the modern state. Because these (city-)states used to be independent, the kingdom sometimes faced conflicts over power and authority both inside and outside the royal realm. However, even after a clear-cut agreement regarding the status of different states in the southern region had been reached during the period of Western colonization, some political and ethnic groups remained dissatisfied and in a constant state of rebellion. It is therefore all the more important, states the introduction, to teach people in the area the truth about the history of the region, because "historical facts can serve as starting points for building a common understanding." Another section of the same chapter deals with "misunderstandings" promoted by insurgents, such as their insistence that the territory of the state of Patani was conquered by Siam. Yet "in actual fact," the handbook explicates, "this [incorporation of Patani] was an administrative development during the Western colonial period."[35]

A number of narratives are interwoven in the history of Thailand that the handbook sketches. One tells a story of the kingdom's civilizational progress: conflicts with (city-)states were resolved through agreements with Western powers, resulting in a peaceful unity (only questioned by certain political and ethnic groups). Linking up with this narrative of progress is another one that describes the incorporation of Patani as a seemingly natural administrative process devoid of politics. A third narrative shines through in both cases: Western colonialism figures as an external context that somehow helped to accelerate administrative reform and the fixing of boundaries. Taken together, these narratives are particularly potent because they maintain one of the central pillars of the discourse of modern Thai history: the externalization of imperial agency onto the West allows for the disavowal of Siam's imperial ambition toward Patani.

The handbook's assertion that the kingdom of Thailand arose on a unified territory projects a national map onto the premodern empire of Siam, where rule was not bound to the modern category of territory.[36] Instead, in this premodern setting, Patani was a tributary state to different kingdoms in the region that scholars have called *mandalas* or "galactic polities"—polities structured around hegemonic centers, headed by "rulers with imperial ambitions [that] expanded by force of arms."[37] Patani's status as a tributary of multiple kingdoms was a survival strategy: it paid gifts to a range of overlords to guarantee protection from different centers of power. Depending on the strength of the Siamese ruler at any given time, the Patani sultans either yielded to their Siamese overlord or rebelled against him.[38] In other words, the notion of a unified territory in the handbook depicts Siam's incorporation of Patani as a natural rather than political process, erases the violence of that process, and creates Siam as an entity that has been able to continuously travel on the historical path of linear progress.

The handbook, moreover, suggests that the formal incorporation of Patani into the modern state of Siam was a harmonious exercise already under way during the period of Western colonization in the nineteenth and twentieth centuries. This official narrative performs a number of disassociations that further help to obfuscate the imperial nature of Siamese state formation. First of all, it omits the eighteenth-century wars that ensured Siam's dominance over the sultanate and paved the way for its later inclusion. In 1785, Siam attacked Patani, which had been weakened by internal political strife, after the tributary failed to support Siam's campaign against the Burmese kingdom. It deployed "slaughter, forced expulsion, and capture" in this and four subsequent wars "to depopulate Patani as a measure of establishing political dominance once and for all," and it used captured slaves to construct "the emerging Siamese political center of Bangkok" (in fact, many of the Muslims who live in central Thailand are descendants of former war slaves).[39] Thus, the dominance that the premodern Siamese empire established over Patani through brutal warfare, depopulation, and slavery enabled Patani's subsumption into the modern imperial formation; Siam's modern politics of benevolent inclusion continued a relationship of force by other means.

The handbook's description of the process of Patani's formal incorporation as an administrative development reflects official Thai historiography, which holds that, in the face of great imperial threats in the second half of the nineteenth century, Siam "owed her survival as an independent nation . . . to her accommodating diplomacy and to the modernization of her government and administration."[40] This narrative both projects Siam's own imperial action onto European colonial powers and obfuscates how central Patani figured as a showcase for Siam's own imperial modernity, particularly vis-à-vis Siam's British colonial neighbors.[41] Tamara Loos shows that

King Chulalongkorn's adviser on Patani, Chao Phraya Yomarat, "never expressed a fear of extinction" by neighboring colonial powers in reports to the Ministry of the Interior "but revealed instead a desire [for Siam] to be considered an equal to European colonial states in the region."[42] In fact, many of the administrative measures Siam used to strengthen control over the southern region built directly on models of British colonial government in Malaya. After forcefully removing the last Patani sultan in 1902, the royal government divided Patani into seven different principalities and used a system of indirect rule. It stripped local rulers of any political and fiscal powers while restricting judicial autonomy to customary or Islamic matters of family and inheritance.[43] Rather than merely demonstrating Siam's capacity for colonial conquest, Patani represented the ability of Siamese leaders to benevolently rule a foreign population by protecting what they considered native customs; it was through policing Patani's (religious) difference that leaders hoped to prove Siam as civilized as other imperial powers in the region.

In this context, the Anglo-Siamese Treaty of 1909, which stipulated formal boundary negotiations with British Malaya, can be seen as a result of Siam's own imperial ambitions rather than as the starting point of an administrative process initiated by Western colonial threats that resulted in Patani's harmonious inclusion. The negotiations eventually prompted the territorial demarcation of an area that would only later be subdivided into the three provinces of Pattani, Yala, and Narathiwat. With the drawing of a permanent border on the national map, Patani was thus formally incorporated as the lower south of Siam's modern imperial formation; its history and the history of its violent inclusion, by contrast, were systematically erased.

After all, the creation of a new system of controlling the provinces through a modern administration went hand-in-hand with the formation and policing of a new kind of centralized imperial history that was to evidence Siam's civilization. No one better personifies the merging of the two projects than Prince Damrong Rajanubhab (1862–1943), son of King Mongkut (Rama IV, r. 1851–1868). As the head of the newly created Ministry of the Interior, Damrong became one of the chief authors of this reform of provincial administration. Moreover, he has been glorified as the father of Thai history.[44] Damrong, in other words, is an exemplary figure of the modern imperial formation because he fundamentally shaped the system of imperial domination of the former tributaries while helping to authorize a historical narrative that disassociated Siam from its own imperial agency. Moreover, he championed a paternalistic discourse that claimed historical evidence to support the superiority of what he called the "Thai race" and the "Buddhist religion," thus helping to inscribe into official historiography the system of differences that continues to structure Thailand's imperial formation today.[45]

As the Minister of the Interior, Damrong was predisposed to contribute to the elite's civilizing mission of compiling the proper history of Siam. His government service, similar to that of colonial officials, provided him with the power and the access to gather knowledge in the provinces, centralize it, and produce authorized versions that accorded with the government's demands. When the new National Library was created in 1905, a royal proclamation ordered provincial officials of the Ministry of the Interior to collect all books and Buddhist manuscripts from the provinces and transfer them to the National Library. Damrong himself had already started collecting government documents on his ministerial tours to the provinces at the end of the nineteenth century, where he oversaw the reorganization of administration; after his retirement from the Ministry of the Interior in 1915, he had all government documents transferred to the National Archives.[46]

Once appointed director of the National Library in 1915, Damrong proceeded to produce an official version of what came to be designated as Thai literature and history. The library not only gathered manifold manuscript versions of a particular story—written in different scripts, languages, and narrative styles—that existed throughout the former tributaries but also transcribed them into Thai and edited them to construct a single source that was printed and disseminated as part of the National Library editions. These library editions often included a preface by Damrong himself and a seal that indicated the origin of the text. The library labels on a number of the manuscripts that Damrong had officials gather in southern Thailand identified them as "gift[s] from Prince Damrong," not only underscoring his sense of ownership of the past but also masking the often enforced appropriation of manuscripts from local people.[47] Damrong also edited royal chronicles and introduced certain elements characteristic of modern historiography.[48] His revised chronicle of Ayutthaya has since been officially regarded one of the most authoritative sources of Thai history.[49]

In a famous text, "The Nature of Government in Siam since Antiquity," Damrong used the evidence he claimed to have gathered from the royal chronicles to argue for the supremacy of the "Thai race" and "Buddhism," explaining that the Thai possessed the moral virtues of what he described in English as "Love of National Independence, Toleration and Power Assimilation" that had assured their power over the land of Siam for almost three hundred years. This notion of a Thai race, probably introduced in the Thai elite's discussion with Western Orientalists and Indologists, provided the discursive key to the ruling elite's claim to historical continuity. That elite's racial roots could supposedly be traced back to the Nan-Chao kingdom in southwestern Yunnan, from where the Thai were said to have migrated into Sukothai, established Ayutthaya, and eventually arrived at Bangkok. The Pali term Damrong uses for "toleration" in the text can be translated as "non-oppression" or "nonviolence" and designates one of the ten virtues that kings ought to possess according to the Theravada Buddhist tradition. Indeed, an implicit idea of natural Buddhist tolerance surfaces when Damrong explains that Thai rulers have always aided people of other races and religions to practice their religion since ancient times—for instance, by supporting the building of Christian churches and Muslim mosques. Following a logic central to modern imperialism, Damrong thus maintains the supremacy of Thai-Buddhist rule on the basis of the benevolent inclusion of its inferior Others such as Muslims.[50]

Patani figured in this racialized history of an ancient Buddhist kingdom as a tributary under the suzerainty of Siam from the time that the Sukothai kingdom expanded southward. Damrong coined the phrase "Patani has belonged to the Thai kingdom since time immemorial" as part of a linear history that completely sidelined any struggles over power and authority.[51] By referencing the trope of administrative reform, counterinsurgency efforts now, much like Damrong's initiatives then, seek to redraw a historical line of continuity of time and space that incorporates Patani as inferior Other into the progressive narrative of the modern Thai imperial formation while eradicating any traces of its imperial conquest.

Muslim Culture

The fourth and longest chapter of the handbook is devoted to the lifestyles and culture of people in the southern region. In the section of supposed facts, the handbook explains that Islam determines the Muslim way of life from birth until death, from waking until sleeping. In the subsequent sections, the handbook elaborates a remarkable variety of customs. These include birth, giving names, and fasting, as well as food, festivities, and dress. Studying culture in general and Islam in particular, the handbook clarifies, is indispensable for officials who want to build understanding with the local population.

By extension, the handbook's information is to equip military officials for fighting certain misunderstandings that circulate in southern society: "The officer must point out clearly that the Thai state does not have a policy of cultural assimilation. If there ever was any policy of assimilation, that is the story of the past. . . . But in the present moment, the state policies documented in the peacebuilding strategy, other strategy plans, and the special development plan clearly show that they accept cultural diversity and absolutely support everyone in practicing their beliefs according to their own way of life and culture." The handbook further explains that Muslim culture should be considered a local part of Thai culture. Thailand, it asserts, "is not a Buddhist society" but a "plural cultural society"; "Muslim culture, Khmer culture, or Isan culture are part of Thai culture."[52]

A number of issues are worth highlighting in the handbook's gloss of Muslim culture and its recipes for building understanding. Although another chapter is devoted exclusively to Islam, Islam here figures as the single decisive factor determining people's way of life and culture in the southern region. In many cases, consequently, the handbook identifies regionally specific customs, such as a type of handshake used in southern Thailand, as Islamic, and in the summary of the essentials of the "Islamic way of life," it lists Melayu as the spoken language of Muslims.[53] By contrast, other local cultures that the handbook compares to Muslim culture belong to different categories: "Isan" is a regional expression referring to the northeastern part of the country, whereas "Khmer" denotes both a language and an ethnicity. "Muslim" is the only designation that deploys the modern category of religion to specify one of these local cultures, thus, in a typically Orientalist move, defining the life of the southern population primarily through the lens of religion.[54] Moreover, the handbook's assertion that all of these different cultures are part of Thai culture parallels the imperial logic of absorbing local histories into a unified Thai history. It marks parts of the population as particular and different while subsuming them under a dominant universal Thai culture.

Amalgamating the Patani population under the overarching signifier of Islam, the handbook also homogenizes an extremely diverse community of Muslims in the South that includes, besides the Sunni majority, a Shi'a minority and Sufi orders, students of traditional *pondoks* (traditional Muslim boarding schools) and Salafi-reformist schools, a large group of followers of the missionary movement Tablighi Jamaat, and migrants returning from places like Meccah and Cairo.[55] In this context, the practice of the Islamic tradition is in no way uniform, and it is subject to constant negotiation and even conflict in the southern communities.

Most crucially, the notion of Muslim culture normalizes a secularized and privatized understanding of the Islamic tradition of the southern provinces, concealing the violence necessary to curb its political and legal power at the beginning of the twentieth century. Siam's establishment of Islamic family courts in Patani to regulate issues of marriage, divorce, and inheritance instituted this privatization and secularization of Islam, and is therefore worth tracing in more detail. In the imperial context at the end of the nineteenth century, King Chulalongkorn sent an adviser to investigate the British system of jurisdiction for Muslims in Malaya and designed a similar Siamese version, which was formally promulgated in 1901. Mirroring the practice in

British Malaya, Islamic courts in southern Siam were to protect Malay customary law, which was equated with Islamic family concerns. The court regulations consequently included a mixture of Quranic law and Malay customary regulations, also known as *adat*.[56]

An emerging policing discourse of the modern state that operated on the secular distinction between public and private shaped the family law jurisdiction that Siam implemented in Patani. In continental Europe, the family became an administrative and legal category that prepared the ground for state intervention while featuring as the most private unit tasked with the physical and moral reproduction of individuals in society. The first proponents of an explicit family law in nineteenth century European legal thought consequently applied a binary distinction that replicated the public/private dichotomy: they juxtaposed contract law as "universal" with family law as "local," the latter supposedly expressing the particular "spirit of the people" that varied from place to place.[57]

These conceptions of family law came to operate on multiple registers of imperial discourse, thus becoming relevant for Siam. Dovetailing with the idea that the family represented the spirit of the people, family law regulations facilitated an imperial construction of native culture. Orientalist researchers of various disciplines, such as legal anthropology, often closely cooperated with imperial governments to collect data on the legal systems of those cultures they considered primitive, static, and endangered by Western colonialism.[58]

An important temporal element also fed into this discourse, positioning traditional legal practices on an evolutionary scale of development with Europe at its apex. Non-European laws in this scheme represented Europe's—and therefore universal humankind's—past; their collection, so scholars hoped, could enable mapping of the steps of universal legal progress.[59] Colonial representations of courts in the British Malay states illustrate the use of such language of civilizational advance and historical comparison.[60] In an address to the Royal Colonial Institute in 1899, for instance, the colonial administrator Sir Hugh Clifford remarked that "the laws which are administered by the native courts, and are carried out by these men, are a strange medley of the legislation of Muhammad and of the Law of Custom, the traditional code of the Malays. By the law of Muhammad many barbarities are permitted such as no European Government could countenance, but these are by no means repugnant to the Malays."[61]

Clifford, moreover, analyzed the Malay system of government as a feudal one that bore "a startling resemblance to the European models of a long-passed epoch," and he thus concluded that "to live in independent Malaya is to live in the Europe of the thirteenth century."[62] Capitalizing on the imperial discourse that cast the Islamic legal system as barbarous, Max Weber would later coin the term *Kadijustiz* (*kadi* justice, *kadi* designating Islamic courts) to characterize legal systems that lacked rational reasons for judgement, and he clarified that these arbitrary systems had long since been overcome in continental Europe.[63] In this sense, the institutionalization of family law in the colonies became an integral part of the European imperial discourse of history. Expressing a non-European culture that was equated with Europe's past, colonial family law simultaneously served to demonstrate Europe's own civilizational progress.

Key to understanding the construction of Muslim culture in Siam, however, is an additional element in imperial family law discourse: the category of religion centrally shaped ideas of a traditional native culture supposedly encapsulated in the family. Thus, Talal Asad argues that family law jurisdiction was effectively a "secular formula for privatizing religion and preparing the ground for the self-governing subject."[64] Asad's analysis is helpful to upend the often-voiced claim by colonial governments that they were reluctant to intrude into matters of the family because they were at the heart of religious traditions. On the contrary, Asad argues, it was actually the very family law policies of colonial governments that formed the family as a legal category while simultaneously reducing religious traditions to governing certain aspects of this supposedly private realm. In this way, imperial policies such as the British policy of non-interference created the family as the site of private morality shaped by religion. These policies also had significant political effects: local religious authorities, who had been stripped of their political functions and wide-ranging juridical powers in the traditional Islamic system, were left with legislating matters of marriage, divorce, and inheritance. They became, in other words, guardians of a culture that was defined through privatized religion—whereas matters of real politics were left to colonial powers.

A very similar process can be observed in the case of Siam's imperial policies toward Patani. Toward the end of the nineteenth century, the royal elite mobilized a colonial-style discourse of cultural advancement that cast the people in the outer provinces as less developed. Authors including royal officials, ministers like Prince Damrong, and even the kings themselves wrote travelogues that often included ethnographic notes describing the strangeness of people they had encountered and temporal distinctions characteristic of civilizational discourse. Tellingly, for instance, Prince Damrong entitled his account of his travels throughout the royal realm *Nithan borankhadi* (Tales of the past).[65] Loos argues that royal officials applied a similar Orientalist language of barbarity when it came to the southern region in particular. King Chulalongkorn's adviser Chao Phraya Yomarat, for example, called the southern provinces "semibarbaric states," while other officials described local rulers in Patani as "abusive, inefficient, corrupt, nepotistic, and oppressive to the 'people.'" Concentrating in particular on the local legal system, Yomarat highlighted punishments as excessive and despotic, urging the Siamese government to intervene.[66] In this discourse of civilizational advance, Patani was placed in an inferior position that simultaneously promoted the civilized modern status of Siam.

The construction of religious difference played a crucial role in the discourse of Patani's legal reform. Remarkably, it was only in Patani that the authorities implemented family law jurisdiction. Other former tributaries such as the Lao states in the Northeast, where Siamese centralization efforts were met with fierce resistance by local leaders, were marked as Buddhist despite their often varying practices of the Buddhist tradition; in these areas, the government proceeded by streamlining particular interpretations and customs they regarded as part of proper Buddhist religion—for instance, by labeling certain traditional practices as superstitious, by prohibiting the performance of traditional tales, and by centrally organizing the Buddhist monkhood (*sangha*).[67]

By creating a system of Islamic family courts, the government thus simultaneously curbed the public political power of the local sultans while fortifying the difference of the southern area in terms of privatized religion. Muslims had for centuries lived in various parts of Thailand, but the new legal system helped to demarcate the southern provinces exclusively as Muslim, while defining other parts of the country as Buddhist. Real juridical and political power was now transferred into the hands of Siamese authorities. The explication of Muslim culture in the ISOC handbook clearly resonates with this imperial construction of religious difference that still centrally structures the contemporary imperial formation.

BUDDHIST LAND

The long discussions of both Islam and Muslim culture in the handbook are noteworthy for another reason: they completely sideline other religious practices in the southern region. The Buddhist tradition of Patani, however, suddenly appears in a section discussing how historical evidence shows that "Islam is not the traditional religion in this area" and that "Patani has never been an Islamic state."[68] The handbook lists several claims to prove these points. Earlier kings of Patani, it states, were Buddhist, and therefore, it argues, Malay people used to follow a range of different religions, including Buddhism, Hinduism, and Brahmanism. Buddhist temples and statues of the Buddha are the most important evidence that the handbook presents to demonstrate that Patani was originally part of the larger Buddhist world. Among these, the handbook names Borobudur in Indonesia, the reclining Buddha in the city of Yala, and the Choeng Khao Temple in Narathiwat, and it emphasizes that some of these historical Buddhist sites are more than thirteen hundred years old.

At first sight, the handbook seems to usefully complicate its simplistic construction of Islam as the overarching signifier defining life in the three southern provinces. Both historians and anthropologists have, in fact, highlighted the vast diversity of religious practices past and present in the region. Patani most likely replaced the Hindu-Buddhist kingdom of Langkasuka (second to twelfth century AD) in the thirteenth century, and it was probably not until the sixteenth century that Patani's royal family converted to Islam. Subsequently, people were allowed to continue practicing other religious traditions and maintain their own traditional spaces such as Buddhist temples. Moreover, anthropologists have argued that the long cohabitation of Muslims and Buddhists helped to produce shared cosmologies that have manifested in common practices such as healing ceremonies unique to the southern Thai region.[69]

However, the handbook is not geared toward illustrating the religious and cultural diversity of the southern provinces; it rather uses Buddhist temples to undermine any political claims for Patani independence. The handbook's policing of history in this instance works through establishing a narrative of origins that enmeshes the category of territory with the category of religion to maintain that Patani was part of the Thai imperial formation from the beginning. As in King Chulalongkorn's speech to the Antiquarian Society, Buddhist temples in this historiography have acquired the epistemological status of documentary sources that seem to inherently connect religious sites to political rule. Patani, the handbook appears to suggest, might now be culturally Muslim, but politically it has been part of a Buddhist empire and a Thai polity for over a thousand years.

The genealogy of the kind of knowledge claims that came to be attached to Buddhist temples and that resonate with the way the handbook seeks to police Patani's history today dates back to the end of the nineteenth century. We might start with King Chulalongkorn's frequent official trips to Patani (in 1888, 1889, 1890, 1896, 1898, and 1901) before it was officially incorporated into the modern Thai imperial formation. His itineraries were explicitly designed around the Buddhist temples of the area, deliberately ignoring important Muslim sites on the way. During these visits, Muslim officials had to demonstrate their loyalty to the king by performing a traditional royal Buddhist ceremony—drinking the water of allegiance—in a Buddhist temple.[70]

Chulalongkorn's visits to the Buddhist sites of the Malay Peninsula occurred at a time when the very concept of travel was undergoing a complete transformation in Siam. The idea of traveling for enjoyment was new; up until this period travel was arduous and dangerous, undertaken only by traders for business and monks for religious pilgrimage. Both socioeconomic change and increasing interaction with Westerners, however, helped to revolutionize the notion of travel, and a new term, *pai thiao* (to go on a trip), was introduced toward the end of the nineteenth century. In 1894, Prince Damrong devoted a whole book to this new concept, explaining that its two main aims were pleasure and knowledge.[71]

The royal elite embarked on knowledge-finding expeditions both within and beyond the royal realm, visiting, for example, colonial administrations in Burma, the Dutch East Indies, and India, and traveling to Europe to investigate matters like education. At home, such travels engendered knowledge of the different peoples that inhabited the kingdom, but the main focus was on Buddhist sites and artifacts. Prince Damrong and interior ministry officials collected these objects for exhibition in a new museum in Bangkok that paralleled the new central library. The initial plans for the new museum (never realized because of funding problems) took the British Imperial Institute as their model, aiming to feature exhibits from the different provinces that would equal exhibits of the different colonies of the British Empire.[72]

Reflecting the elite's engagement with Western knowledge regimes, these efforts to collect Buddhist objects were fueled by the modern discourse of archaeology, which transformed such objects into antiquities of unique historical value and was strategically deployed by colonial regimes in the region to support their claims to territory. Archaeology at the beginning of the twentieth century relied on the emerging disciplines of racial science and religious studies, utilizing specific sites and objects to distinguish different civilizational lineages. For instance, French Orientalists and explorers conducted excavations of Angkor Wat on Siamese territory, determined the racial origin of collected artifacts to be Khmer, argued that they belonged to the former Khmer empire, and pursued "territorial claims vis-à-vis Siam." In 1907, Siam eventually ceded the administrative district of *monthon* Burapha, the location of Angkor Wat, to French Indochina, in exchange regaining sovereignty over two Siamese provinces and jurisdiction over Asian protégés.[73]

By this time, the royal elite had started to deploy archaeology in ways similar to European colonizers. Under Chulalongkorn's predecessor, Mongkut, royal authorities had undertaken archaeological expeditions to particular sites, seeking to use temples as historical evidence "to demarcate the borders of Siamese territory." Perhaps most importantly, Mongkut himself toured the country and discovered the now famous inscriptions by King Ramkamhaeng (r. 1279–1298), who had ruled the ancient Sukothai kingdom (1238–1438). In the official historiography promoted by the royal rulers, the Sukothai inscriptions came to figure as expressions of an original civilization that was ostensibly both Thai and Buddhist.[74] Sukothai still features in contemporary historiography as the earliest Thai kingdom and capital and as the name of the historical era of the supposedly first Thai dynasty.

King Chulalongkorn continued to elevate the significance of archaeological history in Siam by establishing the Antiquarian Society in 1907, modeled on newly founded colonial bodies in the region. The British had established the Archaeological Department of Burma in 1899, the Dutch Colonial Antiquities Commission was established in 1901, and in the same year, the French transformed the Permanent Archaeological Mission in Indochina into the École française d'Extrême-Orient.[75] Chulalongkorn's opening speech to the society, in which he emphasized that Buddhist temples could serve as evidence for settlements of the Thai race, has to be understood in this imperial context. Archaeological inquiries into past civilizations that were seen as expressions of different races were deployed to support claims of territorial expansion.

In fact, the ISOC handbook's reference to the temple Borobudur in contemporary Indonesia as material proof of the region's Buddhist history also has to be seen in this discursive context of ideas of imperial expansion. In the nineteenth century, Borobudur became one of the central sites in elite attempts to establish a civilizational history of Siam as an ancient greater Buddhist empire. It was an important stop on King Chulalongkorn's 1896 tour of Java, which, like his travels to the Malay Peninsula, resembled a pilgrimage to different Buddhist sites. At Borobudur, in particular, the king performed as an Orientalist archaeologist. He left his signature in one of the stupas and ordered it to be engraved in gold, and he selected a large number of tokens from the temple to take back home. These included Buddha statues and relief fragments, many of which were exhibited in different temples, with some later moved to the newly founded museum.[76]

Moreover, in Orientalist discourse, Borobudur represents one of the final traces of a lost Buddhist civilization and an Aryan race that were later polluted by Islam and Malay blood. The Siamese elite knew of and participated in this discourse prior to Chulalongkorn's visit to Borobudur. The 1867 *Kitchanukit* (Elaboration on major and minor matters), written by a royal official close to King Mongkut and now considered an important source of nineteenth-century Siamese intellectual history, contends that Buddhism was the original religion of Java, now only traceable through deserted temples left in the jungle.[77] It is quite likely that Chulalongkorn's travels to the South operated on a similar imperial rationale of uncovering an ancient Buddhist civilization supposedly lost to a different race (the Malays) and a different religion (Islam). The modern discourse of archaeology thereby fed into the emerging discourse of Thai history and laid the groundwork for the political claim about territorial belonging that the king could attach to visiting Buddhist temples.

Another, more affective, dimension constituting the modern imperial formation surfaces in the official designation of Patani as Buddhist land. At the moment of demarcating Siam's territorial boundaries through colonial treaties at the turn of the twentieth century, royal rulers established Siam as a wounded entity, asserting they had lost territories of Siamese origin to neighboring colonial powers after the 1893 Franco-Siamese crisis.[78] This historical narrative that projects a national map onto the former *mandala* formation is still officially endorsed and replicated—a military informant, for instance, explained to me that "Thailand was bigger eight hundred years ago"—and it has consequently also shaped official perceptions of the southern insurgency movement as seeking to "tear apart the land."[79] The reactivation of Siam's constructed wound once again evacuates Siam's conquest of Patani territory by externalizing the imperial threat to Western colonial powers; likewise, it elides Patani's history as an Islamic sultanate and instead establishes a threatening future characterized by the loss of territory to Muslim extremists.

These insights also add another dimension to the military occupation of Buddhist temples in the course of the southern conflict.[80] At Wat Lak Mueang, one of the reasons that soldiers of different ranks gave when asked why they were residing at the temple was protection. They were in a win-win situation, one captain explained; for the Thai military, the temple provided free shelter in an area where it would be hard to find land suitable for military purposes. At the same time, the military could help to protect the temple and the monks.[81] Read within the broader framework of military constructions of history, protecting the temple also worked toward policing the

history of an ancient Buddhist civilization that has structured the modern Thai imperial formation and marked the Muslim minority as people without history.

Consequently, Patani's demarcation as Buddhist land denies any kind of political
contestation in the South by projecting modern coordinates of political rule onto an
imagined ancient Buddhist civilization that has ostensibly moved linearly through
time. If the Buddhist civilization is portrayed as ancient, traditional, and original,
then the practices of Muslims in the South can only be temporary. And if temples
alone provide the evidence of an ancient civilization, mosques are merely religious
buildings without any historical value according to the military's construction of
history. In this imperial narrative, the past that temples and mosques share on the
Malay Peninsula is erased. This history, moreover, incorporates Muslims through
excising the political part of their tradition and denies their contemporaneity, with
clear racializing and gendered implications. After all, on the positivistic scale of
progress to which the military subscribes, those possessing and writing history are
more advanced than peoples like those King Chulalongkorn called "negritos," and
this linear narrative simultaneously constructs a powerful male position that works
to feminize its Others.[82]

Paternal Benevolence

The first two pages of the ISOC handbook feature a series of photographs of the
army commander general Anupong Paochinda. On the left-hand page, Anupong is
shown in three pictures at what seems to be a major public-relations event—giving
a speech, admiring local snacks decorated by Thai flags, and examining artworks. In
contrast, a single composite photograph takes up the whole of the right-hand page.
Against the background of the central mosque of Pattani, Anupong is shown offering
a gift to a young Muslim girl and smiling. Because she is standing with her back to the
camera, her face cannot be seen. The image is given the familiar counterinsurgency
motto as its caption: "Understanding, Reaching Out, Development."

This picture is indicative of the style in which soldiers are depicted in the following pages, where they are mostly shown in what might commonly be seen as unusual
postures for the military. They are shaking hands with local people, offering a basket
of gifts to Islamic authorities, and presenting children with large bags of presents in
front of smiling mothers. The benevolent military agents are always male, whereas
the passive recipients are mostly the local Muslim population and, in the majority
of cases, women or children. The photographs clearly celebrate soldiers as powerful,
although their potency is grounded in charitable acts of giving rather than martial
acts of shooting; the only two pictures that show military personnel with guns are
hidden in the last chapter on social circumstances. The images thus reproduce a trope
of paternal benevolence that has become key to the modern discourse of Thai history
and resonates with both colonial metaphors and constructions of the Thai monarchy.
In its military adaptation, the active Thai military father contrasts with the passive
and feminized Muslim population; the kind military patron provides paternal care for
his offspring, who is placed in the waiting room of history.

Such parental metaphors are, of course, familiar to students of European colonialism and imperialism. Colonial regimes frequently referred to the people native to the
colonies as "untutored children," implying that Western powers could provide powerful parental guidance.[83] Possibly influenced by Christian missions, this parental rhetoric not only located colonial subjects hierarchically but at the same time suggested

they were naturally bound to the colonial regime by familial ties—a relation of love that sometimes required violence.[84]

More significantly, in the Thai context the trope of paternal benevolence is integral to a historical discourse that revolves around the continuity of fatherly virtues guaranteed by the succession of Chakri monarchs. In fact, Prince Damrong's initiation of modern Thai history involved fashioning the kingdom of Sukothai as Siam's real origin and promoting the Sukothai stone inscriptions by King Ramkamhaeng, which King Mongkut had discovered in 1833, as documenting the original tolerance and benevolence of paternal Thai rulers that led to the flourishing of this ancient Siamese civilization.[85] Articulated within the modern categories of race and religion, paternal benevolence was thus marked as both originally Thai and Buddhist, and embodied in Chakri monarchs into the present.

Under the influence of US imperialism during the Cold War, the notion of paternal benevolence acquired additional political significance. The United States favored a paternalistic regime to self-determination, backing a military dictator, Gen. Sarit Thanarat, who referred to himself as a "fatherly ruler." In addition, during the Cold War counterinsurgency the reigning monarch, King Bhumipol Adulyadej (Rama IX, r. 1946–2016), transformed traditional rituals of Buddhist kingship such as the *kathin* ceremony (a traditional Buddhist festival held to celebrate the end of the rainy season) and publicly promoted development projects to perform his royal generosity and aid the project of securing national stability.[86]

This supposed benevolence of the Chakri dynasty also makes a direct appearance in the ISOC handbook in praise for the policies of King Vajiravudh. It was Vajiravudh, the handbook clarifies, who inaugurated an exemplary policy of carefully selecting the state officials to be sent to the southern region. The implicit reference here is to Vajiravudh's 1923 decree "Principles of Public Policy and Administration for Patani." Had subsequent governments continued to follow its benevolent principles, the handbook seems to suggest, they would not have encountered the kind of resistance that has now escalated into violent conflict. References to the 1923 decree also appear in other publications of the military administration of southern Thailand. In 2012, for instance, the Southern Border Provinces Administrative Centre reprinted all six regulations of the policy under a color portrait of Vajiravudh on the last page of every issue of its monthly magazine.

It is worth briefly dwelling on these royal principles, because they constitute such an important element in the historical discourse of the military in southern Thailand. Academic historiography on Thailand portrays Vajiravudh as Thailand's first official nationalist. Having studied history and law at Oxford University, he coined the slogan "Nation, Religion, King" after the British "God, King and Country," and he popularized the word *chat*, which is still used to mean "nation."[87] Vajiravudh's decree illustrates, however, that his creation of the nation depended on the construction of the imperial difference of the Patani population. The regulations explicitly called the southern subjects *khaek*, using the racialized term that connotes "guest" and "foreigner" and has long been used to describe Muslims in the Thai language.[88] The principles' most important aim was enshrined in the first regulation: officers should refrain from any action that might "make citizens feel that the Islamic religion is being suppressed." Rather, they should enforce policies supporting "the religion of Muhammad." Through this positive reiteration of religious difference, in particular, Vajiravudh seemed to be at pains to emphasize that *khaek* citizens should not feel excluded from the kingdom. In the explanations of Regulation 3, for instance, the decree clarified that officials should be friendly, not act rudely, and highlight that there is no difference between "us and them."[89] The decree does not promote comradeship in a national, all-Thai fraternity, but rather manifests a paradoxical discourse of inclusionary exclusion that uses paternal benevolence to reify the difference of the Patani population. Once again, Islam figures as the determining factor in the lives of *khaek* citizens in Patani.

The military has intentionally connected itself to the royal discourse of benevolence that elevates soldiers to paternal caretakers of the Muslim South. After all, the junta of 2006 was endorsed by the royal family, and the post-coup government conveniently tapped into royalist discourse.[90] Thus one of the stated reasons for choosing the counterinsurgency motto "Understanding, Reaching Out, Development" was that King Bhumipol coined it. The official counterinsurgency strategy, moreover, highlighted that it followed the royal principle of "sufficiency economy."[91] The ISOC used the motto and the principle to describe its own vision of policing the South. Accordingly, the ISOC stated that it wanted to "help people in different ways, for example by helping people to solve the drug problem, by improving their quality of life, by improving the building of infrastructure, by giving suggestions on different issues in order to win over the hearts of the people and, on the other hand, using military force for protecting and taking care of the safety of the people and for helping people only—this force is not to be used for suppressing or subjugating people."[92] The dominant verbs "helping" and "improving" are of a piece with the photographs of the soldiers in the ISOC handbook; the military is the active agent taking care of the passive local people in need of multiple forms of development.

In practice, the soldiers I talked to saw themselves in a similar manner. Most of them told me that they were contributing to solving the problem in the South by helping the local population. They said that they implemented the royal motto "Understanding, Reaching Out, Development" by "giving things to villagers" or "helping them whenever they needed help"—for instance, "helping them to build a house after the floods."[93] In fact, one of the busiest times at Wat Lak Mueang was after heavy flooding had severely affected a number of villages in Patani Province. Soldiers were constantly called to help with reconstruction work in different villages, and the military also gave flood-relief money to villagers whose homes had been completely destroyed.[94] The flood, in other words, provided the perfect setting for the military to enact its core mission of paternal benevolence. As one colonel put it, "We take better care of them [the local population] than of our own brothers and sisters."[95]

There is a part of Thai history that is markedly absent in the ISOC handbook: the military's own Cold War history. Implicitly, however, there are traces of the anticommunist fight throughout. Photographs show military generals who have advanced their careers through fighting communism in northeastern Thailand, and the language throughout the book strongly echoes Cold War counterinsurgency discourse. In particular, the motto "Understanding, Reaching Out, Development" reads as a direct reference to Cold War rhetoric; in projects and publications of the Thai anticommunist campaign both the notions of "reaching out" and "understanding" were pervasive. In 1963, for instance, counterinsurgents established the Program to Reach the People, which was led by the Ministry of the Interior and included governors and district officers in all Thai provinces. According to an internal counterinsurgency report, the program worked on the assumption that communists had encouraged innocent villagers to "hate and misunderstand the government" and represented "an attempt to provide a bridge to link government officials with the populace" and unite them under a "common understanding" so that they would not "be easy prey for communist propaganda."[96]

Likewise, the idea of development, initially popularized under the regime of General Sarit, gained greater importance under the US-guided counterinsurgency campaign that sought to capitalize on the nexus of security and development.[97] Fashioning "economic development" as the "preferred path to achieving security in Thailand," US policymakers supported massive aid programs for Thailand, many of them channeled through the Thai armed forces.[98]

Significantly, the fight against communism still constitutes the only success story of the Thai military. When asked about their approach to counterinsurgency, soldiers would often answer by citing a phrase that directly invokes the anticommunist campaign: "Politics Leading the Military" (*kanmueang nam kanthahan*). In Thai military parlance, this phrase refers to a policy coined by Gen. Prem Tinsulanonda. His 1980 Policy of the Struggle to Win Over Communism had prescribed that in the "struggle to defeat the communists, political actions must prevail and military actions must basically be supportive of these political actions."[99] The military's narrative of its own history has hailed Prem's policy as the ultimate key to success, securing victory in an internal war that had raged for over thirty years.

This self-referential Thai military narrative overlooks, however, that political action constitutes a core part of the definition of counterinsurgency as an unconventional form of war. Scholars mostly attribute the construction of counterinsurgency as a political offensive to David Galula, a veteran of the French colonial war in Algeria.[100] According to Galula, the objective of counterinsurgency is "of a political nature": winning over the population. Consequently, "political action remains foremost throughout the war," and "so intricate is the interplay between the political and the military actions that they cannot be tidily separated."[101] What Galula means by "politics" is what Michel Foucault calls "policing": a form of managing the population that secures internal order and increases the strength of the state. The blurring of boundaries between political and military action that Galula highlights thereby inadvertently confirm Foucault's revision of Clausewitz; politics become "the continuation of war by other means."[102]

This chapter has shown that the recalibration of military violence in southern Thailand included the policing of historical knowledge, bearing striking resemblance to projects of the royal elite at the end of the nineteenth century. Prince Damrong had traveled the country to collect manuscripts and produce a single centralized history that was supposed to absorb all provincial histories of the new imperial formation. The military policing of history reproduces this project in the opposite direction. Citing the positivistic notion of "facts," the ISOC handbook promises to represent the single universal narrative of Thai history that is to convince the southern brothers and sisters of their inferior place in the imperial Thai family. In this light, the phrase "politics leading the military" that soldiers in the South often cited assumes yet another meaning. The military is adopting instruments of imperial rule to win over the southern population, and it is constantly reproducing the difference that supports the basic structure of the imperial formation.

CHAPTER TWO

CHECKPOINTS

Racialized Practices of Suspicion

Checkpoints were the most obvious signs of the militarization of southern Thailand when I arrived there in 2010. In that year, an ISOC spokesman estimated that about five hundred permanent checkpoints were in use, together with an additional two hundred flexible roadblocks that could be moved to different areas according to need.[1] Permanent checkpoints were located on the main roads into the towns of Yala and Pattani and at sites within them that the army had identified as potential targets, including Buddhist temples, government schools, and army camps. In rural areas, the majority of checkpoints were located in villages believed to be infiltrated by insurgents.[2] Their official purpose was to heighten security by curtailing insurgent attacks.[3]

My perception of these military roadblocks changed considerably in the course of my stay. The first time I crossed a roadblock, I was shocked to see soldiers armed with automatic rifles at the side of the road. Wanting to document them but afraid that the soldiers would be suspicious of my camera, I dared only to take a picture out of the car window. The shot shows nothing but a red and white fence barely recognizable as part of a military checkpoint. I soon learned, however, that there was no need for me to be afraid; the soldiers rarely stopped me, and I never had to show my ID card. I clearly stood out as a *farang*—the Thai word for a Western foreigner with white skin. The people who the soldiers stopped, in contrast, were *khaek*—the colloquial Thai term for foreigners that connotes both a religion—Islam—and a distinct phenotype— "a dark complexion, an aquiline nose, and, in men, facial and/or body hair."[4] Racialized notions of religion determine the difference between a *farang* and a *khaek*.

Checkpoints in the South manifest a racialized problematic. Soldiers' practices of suspicion often inadvertently reproduce the racialized hierarchies that constitute the inner structure of the imperial formation.[5] Checkpoints operate on a constant anticipation of violence. They announce by their very presence that certain sites, such as official buildings, are potential targets, and soldiers are constantly required to identify and unmask suspicious people in the flow of traffic.[6] The bias in profiling people as suspicious and potentially violent at roadblocks was subject to frequent debate by locals during my research in southern Thailand. Soldiers often justified their practices of mainly stopping local Muslims by referring to the distribution of the population in the southern provinces; likewise, a local journalist cautioned, "It's important to see that 80 percent of people here are Muslim, so if you check ten people, eight are surely Muslim."[7] Yet the data from a student survey conducted at a checkpoint in Pattani provides some contrasting evidence; although approximately one fifth of the southern population is labeled "Thai-Buddhist" on the Thai census, Thai-Buddhists constituted only 1 percent of the people stopped at the roadblock over a one-week period. By contrast, the students concluded that the vast majority of those held at checkpoints were Malay-Muslim.[8]

Although the historical construction of "Thainess" has featured prominently in scholarship on Thailand, the southern conflict reveals how Thailand's racialized Other sustains the modern imperial formation—the production of Thainess goes hand-in-hand with the production of Malay-Muslimness.[9] To be clear, imperial modernity was not the beginning of what we would today call "racialized distinctions." The premodern empires of Thereavadin Southeast Asia, for example, were "polyglot institution[s]." Distinct communities were often listed as part of the king's titles, signifying the successes of military conquest. Because sovereignty rested entirely in the ruler himself, rather than the people of a nation, there was no need for a concept of racial homogeneity. Rulers expanded their realms through a system of polygyny and were themselves "mixed-bloods."[10]

What distinguishes the mobilization of race in imperial modernity is its role in the emergence of the nation-state. In this context, the discourse of race has provided naturalized truth claims for measuring, enumerating, and dividing up populations in accordance with central state-building practices such as maps and statistics, locating those populations' differences in physical properties such as skin color.[11] In nineteenth-century Siam, the notion of Thai as the language of a discrete race was consolidated through writings of both Orientalists and the Siamese royal elite. Most importantly, after the Franco-Siamese crisis in 1893, royal authorities adopted racialized terminology to describe people in the northeastern Lao states, changing their official designation to "Thai" to fortify Siam's claims to former Lao territory. As Siam's first census of 1904 explained, "It has been definitely ascertained by learned men that the people who are called Laos at the present day are really of the Thai race, and they also consider themselves to be such."[12] The census also drew racialized distinctions among the population of Siam, however. It not only identified different races such as Thai, Chinese, and Malay but also included detailed explanations as to how the differentiations between them were made.[13]

These 1904 census explanations exemplify another conceptual point: race has always been the offspring of categorical *métissage*. Although race grounds difference in biological markers and naturalizes exclusion, these biological "signifiers have always also been used, by discursive extension, to connote social and cultural differences," and vice versa.[14] The notes to the 1904 census detailed not only the difficulties involved in clearly identifying people of different races (intermarriage, among other factors, had led to categorical confusion) but also mentioned the shortcuts used to secure identification. With regards to Cambodians, for instance, census officers were directed to "to classify them racially according to their style of dress and the language commonly spoken among themselves." Traces of a "Chinese race" were found hidden in hairstyles: "All males who wear the 'queue,' whether they be full blooded Chinamen or only mestizos of whatever degree," were to be categorized as "Chinese."[15] As Stuart Hall has put it succinctly, "Biological racism and cultural differentialism . . . constitute not two different systems, but racism's two registers."[16]

In 1904, the director general of the Royal Survey Department contributed an essay titled "General Description of Siam" to the catalogue on the Kingdom of Siam prepared by the royal government for the Louisiana Purchase Exposition, remarking on Siam's inhabitants: "From the north down to the southern limits of Singora and Trang, the indigenous population is Siamese; south of that it is Malay. There are, of course, many Malays north of this line, and Siamese south of it, and also a certain amount of a mixed breed; but this is the main ethnological division. Besides these two settled races, there are the Negritos, who are found very sparsely inhabiting the jungle-covered mountains of Lakon and all the country south of it."[17]

Other sources confirm that the director general was up to date with the findings of European racial science at the time. The "Map of Thai Races" included in a 1903 book on Siam by French honorary resident Charles Lemire, for instance, clearly excludes the southern peninsula as "Malay." Likewise, an ethnographic world map of the "distribution of human races" from an 1885 German lexicon distinguishes between the Malays and the Indochinese. Geographically, the racial dividing line runs directly through what is today southern Thailand (see fig. 4).[18] Consequently, the category of race in nineteenth-century Siam was not merely deployed to mark the inhabitants of Siam's emerging state territory as Thai; rather, and more significantly for southern Thailand, it helped to draw up new distinctions. Patani was now seen as overwhelmingly inhabited by the Malay race.

The British encroachment on the peninsula further shaped ideas that mapped the people of purported Malayan racial descent onto the political entity governed by the British.[19] Where the Malay term *bangsa* had meant "genealogy" or "lineage," it came to be translated as "race" in the eighteenth and nineteenth centuries; where *Melayu* had been used to describe the descendants of a specific dynasty, it slowly came to refer to "both royalty and their subjects not just in Malacca but in many regions of the Malay Peninsula, Sumatra and the surrounding islands." Indigenous intellectuals in the nineteenth century adopted this racialized language to advance their reformist demands against the sultanate, promising to make the *bangsa Melayu* "great" and "clever."[20] The racialized construction of Malays also entered the discourse of early generations of Patani

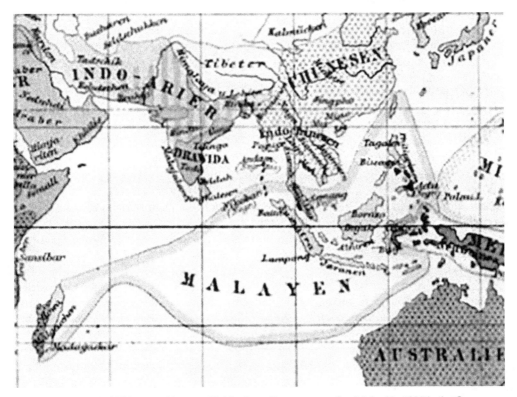

Figure 4. Detail of "Ethnographic map: Distribution of human races," published in 1885 in the German encyclopedia *Meyers Konversationslexikon*.

independence movements, which propagated a distinct Patani Malayness as the basis for self-rule.[21] During a campaign for Patani independence in 1948, for instance, resistance leaders demanded: "Give us back our race as Malays and our religion as Islam."[22] The resolutions and recommendations of the first Asian Islamic Conference held in Pakistan in 1978 concluded that "religiously, racially, ethnically and linguistically [the people of Patani] are entirely different from the Thai people."[23]

Concurrently, in twentieth-century Siam, the construction of a Thai race was not only reinforced but also conflated with Buddhism, the Thai nation, and the Thai state. Indicating the links to the Buddhist tradition, the Siamese translation of the term "race" in the nineteenth century was *chat. Chat* originally derived from the Sanskrit *sati*, which designates belonging to a certain caste in the Buddhist cycle of rebirth.[24] As noted in the previous chapter, King Vajiravudh (Rama VI, r. 1910–1925) officially translated *chat* as "nation," whereas "race" became translated as *chuea chat*, signaling the affinity between the two terms. Vajiravudh popularized the racialized insights of religious studies of his time. He located the origins of the Buddhist religion with what he called the "Aryan people," contrasting them with those he termed "black people" of less intelligence and less sophisticated beliefs. Referring to insights of European scholars, he explained that "religion and race cannot be separated." Buddhism was the religion of the "yellow race" of the Siamese, and a "change of faith" would require, first, a change of "skin and flesh." He established Siam as the last fortress to "defend Buddhism" and lectured his scout soldiers (the "Wild Tigers"), a national paramilitary corps, to "preserve Buddhism" to "the honor of [their] race." Both Islam and Christianity appear in these lectures as negative opposites to Buddhism. Whereas "the word of our Buddha speaks of no punishment," Vajiravudh clarified, Christianity and Islam sought revenge against unbelievers, and taught their followers a blind dependence on God.[25]

Eventually, in 1939 the official name of the country was changed to Thailand, mapping the name of the ruling "Thai race" onto the territory of the state.[26] "This was not a change," Luang Wichit Wathakan, main intellectual authority of the dictator Field Marshal Plaek Phibunsongkhram (1938–1944 and 1948–1957; hereafter Field Marshal Phibun), explained; rather, the Thai people had finally adopted the indigenous name of their race, a civilization he described as more ancient than that of the Chinese.[27] Likewise, the lyrics of the new national anthem, which are still in use, poetically deploy this overlap of the Thai race with nation and state: "Thailand unites the flesh and blood of the Thai race" (*prathet thai ruam lueat nuea chat chuea thai*).

The people of southern Thailand, racialized as Malay, became citizens of a state that bears the name of another race in its official title and that celebrates the Thai race as the embodiment of the Thai nation. As in other modern imperial and colonial settings, the hierarchies of rule that clearly structure the relationship between the central government and the southern population are undergirded by a hierarchy of racialized difference.

At the heart of the mission of the modern state military is a racialized opposition between civilized warfare and savage violence. In colonial and imperial settings, it has functioned to rationalize the violence of colonial rule, while at the same time condemning the violence of the colonized. Military discipline, for instance, still remains an important racialized marker distinguishing the reason of military force from the violence of what colonizers viewed as barbarian hordes. Likewise, in southern Thailand, checkpoint practices depended on continually drawing racialized boundaries that positioned the military on the civilized side of violence, echoing a discourse that has fused military discipline with the essence of the Thai race.[28]

The association of racialized difference with violent potential has also figured prominently in counterinsurgency. As late as 1940, the US Marine Corps' "Small Wars Manual" advised counterinsurgents to study the racial psychology and racial origin of the enemy, invoking imperial classifications that connected racial characteristics with warrior qualities.[29] Although couched in the language of culture, the advice that the current US counterinsurgency field manual gives clearly resonates with this more explicit interest in the racial character of a population.[30] The literature on the Cold War counterinsurgency mission in Thailand likewise illustrates how policing practices are racialized. Thus, the government labeled communists "un-Thai," both for their dissident status and because many were descendants of Chinese and Vietnamese immigrants; moreover, it marked the highland people of northern and northeastern Thailand as ethnically different and feared that foreign powers such as France and Vietnam could easily mobilize them on the grounds of their apparent lack of national allegiance. Counterinsurgency programs were thus designed to civilize the borderland people by making them more Thai—by, *inter alia*, teaching them Buddhism and the Thai language.[31]

Racialized distinctions often also play a direct role in policing practices at checkpoints, which are, according to the current US counterinsurgency manual, part of population and resources control measures undertaken to separate insurgents from the civilian population by controlling the circulation of people and goods.[32] In Iraq, for instance, checkpoints were constructed as the gates to fenced-in neighborhoods in the cities of Baghdad and Ramadi, which U.S. forces had divided along ethno-sectarian fault lines. Historically, Palestine has constituted a significant site for the global transmission of counterinsurgency knowledge and techniques such as the construction of fences and watchtowers to restrict people's movement. In fact, the Israeli military has made extensive use of checkpoints and roadblocks in the Palestinian territories, particularly the West Bank—here, 705 permanent checkpoints and roadblocks were recorded in September 2018, excluding the hundreds of flying checkpoints installed on demand. As a host of critical literature has documented, these checkpoints function in a gendered and sexualized way to imprint the racialized inferiority of the Palestinian people onto their bodies.[33]

The Thai southern counterinsurgency was likely strongly influenced not only by the US military, as elaborated in chapter 1, but also by Israeli models; as early as the 1960s an Israeli delegation visited Thailand to discuss possible Arab involvement in the Patani conflict.[34] Although Thailand and Israel have signed multiple agreements since the start of their official relations in 1954, the first two bilateral treaties on cooperation in matters of defense and security were signed in 2006 and 2017—after the renewed flare-up of the southern conflict in 2004. More explicitly, the Thai and Israeli defense ministers signed an intelligence pact in 2012 that included a nondisclosure agreement on classified military, security, and intelligence information and the exchange of antiterrorism technologies designed to support the southern counterinsurgency.[35] Thailand has become one of the most important customers of Israel's expanding arms industry; the first ever Southeast Asia–Israel Security Summit was hosted in Bangkok in 2017 and brought together companies and government officials to foster long-term cooperation in the fields of cybersecurity and homeland security, the latter designed to secure the "homeland against a hostile environment" through the "proper management of borders."[36]

CHECKPOINTS IN SOUTHERN THAILAND

Nevertheless, checkpoints in southern Thailand in 2010–2011 were hardly comparable to those in Iraqi and Israeli counterinsurgency missions. In the southern provinces, roadblocks were neither constructed as entrances to gated communities nor effectively connected with measures of territorial control. Rather, their setup resembled a militarized version of the traffic checkpoints that have long been used all over the country. Most lower-ranking soldiers I talked to openly doubted that the army checkpoints could serve effectively to capture insurgents. In a group interview, young conscripts admitted: "If you ask me, what criminal would ever drive through a checkpoint? [*laughs*] . . . If you build a checkpoint, then they know where it is and try to avoid it."[37] Indeed, at none of the checkpoints I visited had soldiers ever arrested any insurgents. Rather, they had arrested people for petty crime, disregarding traffic regulations, and possession of drugs. In these cases, the army cooperated closely with the police.[38] As conscript S. outlined, "Mostly, it's only normal petty thieves who are caught, and then we have the police come here to arrest them properly. So we mainly just contact the police and tell them when a criminal has tried to cross the checkpoint and that we are holding him."[39]

Other features also sharply distinguished the southern Thai checkpoints from roadblocks in other conflict contexts. Military roadblocks in southern Thailand seemed to be designed to displace what we would conventionally associate with force. Although dressed in full army uniform and armed with automatic rifles, the soldiers checking people stood on the road rather than sitting on tanks, and tanks were parked out of sight. Soldiers were tasked with performing friendly interactions—they would, for instance, often smile and greet people. Military force here smiled at passersby through the friendly faces of waving soldiers—their weapons were always present, but barely visible on their backs.

The outward appearance of the checkpoints was relatively mundane. Roadblocks were built unobtrusively to control vehicles rather than pedestrians and therefore often had two lanes, separated by red and white traffic cones: one for bicycles and motorcycles, and one for cars and trucks. The majority featured speed bumps consisting of materials such as ropes, forcing vehicles to slow down. Many also involved obstacles like concrete blocks around which vehicles had to maneuver or that forced them to wait for oncoming traffic. Simpler roadblocks had movable red and white iron barriers with sandbags or old tires at the base to fortify them—in some cases, soldiers put potted plants in front of them for decoration (see fig. 5). At the permanent checkpoints at central entry points to the town of Pattani, the barriers were made out of wood painted red and white and fortified by concrete blocks. All featured signposts that looked like traffic signs—they were round in shape and also painted red and white—with two simple words: "Stop, check" (*yut, truat*). At night, neon lights illuminated the signs.

Unlike U.S. checkpoints in Iraq, many checkpoints in southern Thailand were not permanently manned but were only used to perform checks at times of high alert after an insurgent attack. Even without soldiers carrying out inspections, however, checkpoints constituted important symbols that contributed to marking the southern territory as a different country incorporated into Thailand. Thus, individual army units often decorated checkpoints with national and royal flags. One soldier clarified his mission of standing guard at checkpoints as demonstrating to people that they were living on Thai land (*phuen thi thai*) and therefore had to behave according to

Figure 5. Soldier guarding a checkpoint on the road between the town of Pattani and the village of Tanyong Luloh, December 2010. Photograph by the author.

Thai law. He called the southern population "Thai brothers and sisters" (*phi-nong thai*) and explained that the army's mission was to secure peace in the area, invoking an association of civilized peacefulness with Thailand typical in military discourse, and one often coupled with references to the essential peacefulness of Buddhism.[40] In this way, checkpoints reinforced ideas of the South as a violent and uncivilized territory; in fact, simulating the document checks carried out at international borders, the ID checks positioned soldiers as rightful inhabitants of peaceful Thailand while casting into doubt the identities of the people crossing.[41]

Checkpoints were also sites of suspicion, arbitrary arrest, and fatal encounters. At permanent checkpoints, the soldiers' primary task was deciding which vehicles to stop. They used either orange sticks or their hands to signal "pass" (if held straight) or "stop" (if held crosswise). Drivers had to slow down significantly and wait for the sign. Some drivers, especially of cars with dark or mirrored windows, also wound down their windows to look at the soldiers. The soldiers had a very short amount of time to decide whether there was any cause for suspicion. Such cause necessitated further investigation, which usually included examining the vehicle, checking ID cards, and sometimes also conducting personnel searches.

What made these interactions particularly precarious were the legal grounds on which military checks were conducted; martial law allowed soldiers to detain suspicious subjects for further interrogation without an arrest warrant. Although at checkpoints I visited soldiers had not detained anyone on national security charges, arbitrary detention—which was also permitted—was one of the main issues that human rights organizations dealt with in the southern provinces. When I visited the Pattani branch of the Working Group for Justice and Peace, for example, the local coordinator was concerned with the case of an Islamic teacher who had not returned from a school trip with his students because he had been held at a checkpoint. A volunteer at the Muslim Attorney Centre confirmed that there were many cases of arbitrary arrest at checkpoints.[42]

Under these conditions, friendly encounters could turn deadly. For instance, one of the most controversial incidents occurred at a checkpoint administered by paramilitary rangers (*thahan phran*) in Pattani's Nong Chik district in January 2012. In this case, the rangers had received an order to stop and check certain types of vehicles after a recent attack on a military camp. When halting a suspicious pickup truck, they mistook unexpected sounds for gunfire and directly shot at the vehicle, killing four civilians and wounding another four. All of the victims were later found to be innocent.[43]

Even more frequently, encounters at checkpoints turned deadly for soldiers themselves. Precisely because checkpoints operated as markers of Thai land, the soldiers operating them were prime targets for insurgent attacks—particularly in rural areas. In one such attack that occurred in May 2012 at a checkpoint in Chanae District of Narathiwat, four alleged insurgents on two motorcycles shot dead two defense volunteers, seized their weapons, and disappeared. Some soldiers expressed to me not only their frustration at the ineffectiveness of checkpoint searches but also their fears about standing guard dressed in full army uniform. As a sergeant described the situation, the army uniform made soldiers highly visible. Insurgents, by contrast, were "hidden in the dark." He himself had been shot during an insurgent attack on a rural army checkpoint.[44]

Most people who had to cross these checkpoints, in contrast, had become used to them as part of their daily routine. In one instance, a friend from a nearby village immediately identified a driver who took the wrong lane in the checkpoint obstacle course as an outsider to the southern provinces. Checkpoints had become so ubiquitous in the area that, for him, knowing how to drive through checkpoints was essentially equated with being from Patani. Regardless of the routine, however, many were unhappy about the roadblocks. For example, a schoolteacher told me about how her son, on holiday from his university in Chiang Mai, had gone out on his bike one night to get a *roti* at one of his favorite shops in the area and was stopped at a checkpoint on the way. He was very upset and told his mother that he felt like his home had been transformed into a different country.[45] The story that a young student at the Prince of Songkla University told about her experience with checkpoints echoed this perception:

> If I am at home, I have to get up at 5:30 a.m. and go out to sell snacks, and it's quite dangerous anyways because it's still quite dark. . . . There was one time when I was passing a checkpoint, with my motorcycle full of snacks, and they made me stop at the checkpoint, and asked: "Where are you going?" "I am going to sell snacks at the teashop!" And then the soldier [said]: "Do you have your ID card?" And I was like: "Well, my ID card is at home in the village." And it was okay then, but it's sometimes difficult, and then the next morning when I did bring my ID card they did not check me at all. Sometimes it's uncomfortable and scary, especially when it's still dark.[46]

A number of people I met shared similar feelings: they simply wanted to be left in peace within their own homeland instead of feeling like they were entering a different country every time they visited a neighboring village.

The insurgency movement frequently sought to exploit these feelings by spreading rumors about the real purpose of roadblocks and portraying checkpoints as symbols for the overall failure of the counterinsurgency mission. I was confronted with such rumors when attending the funeral of an *imam* who had been shot in a tiny village in the district of Rueso in Narathiwat. The head of the subdistrict administration and another official had also been killed in the incident; the three had been on their way to a meeting with members of the local army taskforce. The shooting had taken place just three hundred meters from a military roadblock. People told me that the fleeing perpetrators passed another three checkpoints without provoking any significant reaction; the soldiers had either been indifferent or scared. In another version of the story, the perpetrators themselves had dressed in ranger uniforms, and their car had turned into the army camp after the shooting. The implication of these stories was clear; checkpoints were useless, and the counterinsurgency mission was a complete failure—or, in the darker version, the military was behind the attacks.[47]

Khaek Masculinity under Suspicion

Given these contestations, the military was at pains to emphasize that it determined grounds for suspicion according to standardized processes, underscoring the soldiers' neutrality and objectivity. Soldiers commonly replied to my asking how they identified suspicious persons and objects by stating that they simply followed military orders; they looked out for certain vehicles or people, for instance, that had been identified in recent incidents of violence.[48] Moreover, they frequently mentioned that they sought to identify criminal suspects depicted on police posters, which were hung inside the huts that were constructed beside most checkpoints; they noted that they could run an online check of ID numbers, which would reveal if a person was officially listed as suspect.[49] Others also highlighted the need to search people for objects such as hidden weapons.[50]

Weapons, however, provide a good example of the futility of such standardized processes. By 2010–2011, when I was conducting my research, the proliferation of small arms in the southern provinces had progressed to a stage where a large number of civilians were carrying arms for self-protection. State regulations had been eased to facilitate access to firearms, especially for people working for state institutions and paramilitary organizations, and weapons were readily available on the black market.[51] Indeed, though the army expressly avoided distributing weapons, the military played an important role in providing arms training to members of certain paramilitary organizations.[52] Thus the notion of armed civilians had become entirely accepted, and many people carrying weapons were state officials or paramilitaries who were supporting the counterinsurgency mission. The possession of weapons could not, therefore, effectively function as a determinative ground for suspicion.

Soldiers highlighted another dilemma in identifying suspects at checkpoints; they could only access people's appearances and never knew what they were really thinking. "There are some people whom we cannot access. . . . I mean, mostly, they talk to us in a nice way, but we don't know what is in the back. We can only see the surface." As another conscript put it, "They will talk to us as if they were saying the truth, but we don't know what they really think inside their hearts." If anything, the fact that soldiers were tasked with performing friendliness and respectfulness at checkpoints further exacerbated this situation. Many people reacted to the frozen smiles of military personnel with frozen smiles of their own. When counterinsurgents needed information after an insurgent attack, people would just "smile without telling anything," another conscript complained.[53] In other words, soldiers were alert to the risk that the friendly surfaces of civilians could not properly indicate their insurgent potential.

In this situation, discourses that attached the potential for violent threat to certain categories of people fed into determining grounds for suspicion. The power of such categories can be explained by what Judith Butler calls "performativity," a "reiterative and citational practice by which discourse produces the effects that it names."[54] The repetitive enactment of suspicion at checkpoints revealed how soldiers were impli-cated in discourses that connected certain kinds of people and certain ways of being with potential threats of violence. At the same time, through constantly checking certain categories of people, counterinsurgents contributed to "making up people" by producing the effects that they named.[55]

Perhaps most crucially, the suspicion that soldiers practiced at checkpoints against those labelled "Malay-Muslims" has to be related to a historical discourse that has constructed the *khaek* as a violent threat in Siam's Buddhist imaginary. *Khaek* derives from Sinitic vocabulary and originally meant "guest" or "visitor." In a second, more specific, sense, *khaek* even in its premodern usage described foreigners (other than close neighbors such as Khmer and Vietnamese) who did not fit into the categories of *farang* or Chinese.[56] This second sense seems to have become more closely associated with racialized differentiations of religion in the nineteenth century. The first diction-ary of Thai compiled by Bishop Jean-Baptiste Pallegoix translated *khaek* as "moor, mahometan, stranger, passenger"; another missionary dictionary by Dan Beach Brad-ley further emphasized racial characteristics when providing a gloss of *khaek* that translates as "one particular race, of dark (black) physique and with curly hair."[57] The 1867 *Kitchanukit* (Elaboration on major and minor matters), one of the first books printed in Thai and published in 1867 by an official close to King Mongkut (Rama IV, r. 1851–1868), borrowed heavily from this discourse and included lengthy descriptions of the strange customs of the *khaek* that equated the "religion of the *khaek*" with the "religion of Mohammad." At the same time, it cast "the religion of Buddha" as "the traditional religion of Thailand," thus constructing a racialized connection between Buddhism and the Thai people that excluded the southern *khaek*.[58]

This historical Othering of the *khaek* has also involved anxieties that the expansion of Siam's Buddhist empire would be threatened by their propensity for violent aggres-sion. A mid-nineteenth-century mural in a Buddhist temple in Songkhla, for instance, depicts *khaek* as demonic attackers of the Buddha led by the fearsome demon-king Mara. Contrasting with the Buddha's white skin are fearsome warriors distinguished by their dark skin, their facial hair, and their large noses. The historical context of this mural is telling; in the course of re-establishing the Siamese empire after the fall of Ayutthaya in the late eighteenth century, the first king of the Chakri dynasty, Rama I (r. 1782–1809), gave Songkhla administrative authority over the southern Malay states that his troops had reconquered. By the mid-nineteenth century, Songkhla had become "an important outpost of the Siamese empire" on its southern periphery.[59]

Racialized and religious distinctions similarly intersect in late twentieth century official definitions of the term *khaek*. The current edition of the dictionary of the Royal Institute (1982), the authoritative governmental body determining the standard use of Thai language, explains: "*Khaek* can refer to people from India, Sri Lanka, Pakistan, Bangladesh, Afghanistan, Nepal, to Malay people, Asian people from the Middle and the Near East, but it excludes Jews in Northern Africa and Negroes." The negative exception at the end of the sentence is particularly revealing in that it exempts both the racialized categories of "Jews" and "Negroes" from the category of the *khaek*.[60]

Moreover, traces of the framing of *khaek* as potentially violent persist in a well-known Thai saying: "If you meet a snake and a *khaek*, hit the *khaek* first."[61]

At checkpoints in southern Thailand, however, not all *khaek* were seen as suspicious. Soldiers stopped men almost exclusively, mostly citing practical reasons. Only male soldiers were normally stationed at checkpoints, unless the army was specifically searching for female perpetrators and asked female defense volunteers, paramilitaries, or police officers for temporary support, and many of them highlighted that in the cultural and religious context of the southern provinces it was not considered appropriate for male soldiers to check female subjects. Counterinsurgents were particularly cautious about cross-gender interactions at checkpoints given rumors about the sexual exploitation of local women by soldiers (see chapter 4). Most crucially, the army suspected that the majority of insurgents were men from Patani, so that soldiers at checkpoints were asked to be specifically wary of this group.

Yet in stark contrast to stereotypes of male Muslim terrorists that often convey ideas of monstrosity and hypermasculine aggression, suspects at checkpoints were largely constructed as effeminate, weak, misguided, and potentially indoctrinated males victimized by their socialization in the underdeveloped South, reflecting typical imperial characterizations of the colonized as feminine.[62] Practices of suspicion were thus both shaped by and productive of a racialized hierarchy of masculinities that undergirds the Thai imperial formation, with Buddhist soldiers performing civilized superiority vis-à-vis racialized and feminized Muslim subjects.

CREATING UNDERSTANDING

A guiding idea in counterinsurgency strategy was the creation of understanding (*kao-chai*), the first term in the tripartite counterinsurgency motto. The ISOC website included a subsection that laid out a strategy to build understanding that illustrated the notoriously broad use of the term. Counterinsurgents were charged with ensuring people's correct understanding of their own history and identity. To this end, counterinsurgents could use handbooks such as the one discussed in chapter 1. The army sought to make residents of the border provinces understand government policy to curb potential resentment, and to make international organizations understand the conflict to avoid negative press coverage. On the basis of proper understanding, moreover, people in the southern provinces would be motivated to provide intelligence information that authorities needed to arrest insurgents.[63]

For soldiers at checkpoints, in practice, the task to build understanding with the local population translated into efforts to talk with people passing through. Indeed, the training that prepared paramilitaries for working at checkpoints included an exercise in which they had to practice talking politely to civilians. Moreover, whereas military officers often visited villages in the region to fulfill a range of different tasks and therefore also frequently conversed with villagers, many younger conscripts and privates were not allowed to leave their camps. Checkpoints therefore constituted the only places where they could interact with and get to know the local population. One soldier also mentioned that his conversations with people passing through had helped him to overcome his anxiety about working at checkpoints.[64]

However, I rarely observed any in-depth conversations with civilians during operations at military roadblocks. In particular, if the volume of traffic was high, soldiers tried not to stop or hold people any longer than necessary, and the conversations I overheard were short and to the point. If soldiers stopped drivers, they asked them where they were coming from and where they were going, and then proceeded to examine ID cards, vehicle papers, and number plates. Only in a handful of cases did these interactions exceed the usual process of question and answer.[65]

Even more challenging was the question of language. Army personnel usually communicated in Thai when halting people at checkpoints and could not understand the Malay dialect spoken by the majority of the southern population. Many soldiers noted that some basic Malay language instruction had been included in their preparatory training, but not enough to enable them to communicate properly with people in Malay. Although most members of the younger generation in the South speak basic Thai, soldiers reported communication problems especially with people from rural areas and members of the older generation; their accent, even if they spoke Thai, was often hard to comprehend. Conscript C., for instance, admitted that soldiers and civilians sometimes had "difficulties in understanding each other." People in the South, he glossed, "talk to us as if they were talking in a different language." Private N. described the communication difficulties similarly: "I mean, I really don't understand them if they speak *yawi* [the Malay dialect spoken in southern Thailand] here. It's like Cambodian. I don't have a clue." Soldiers, in addition, signaled the foreignness of the local Malay dialect by using a common Thai expression; people in the South, they said, "speak Islam" (*phut islam*).[66] Once again, a signifier of religion is used to express the difference of Patani people, now in the realm of language.

Both a lack of facility with the Thai language and unwillingness to engage in conversation with soldiers elicited suspicion at checkpoints. Many soldiers deemed people suspicious if they gave only short answers to questions. Likewise, a conscript at the checkpoint in Yala explained that his colleagues identified suspects based on whether people were willing to talk to soldiers.[67] In this way, the ability to speak Thai became the condition for what the army called "creating understanding"—a one-sided process that in practice meant properly answering the questions posed by soldiers in Thai. In turn, a lack of Thai language skills connoted a potential threat, undergirded by a racialized fear of darker-skinned subjects who "spoke Islam."

The weight attached to language at checkpoints has an important history; distinctions of language have come to signify distinctions of race in the Thai imperial formation, and this history more generally relates to the role philology has played in the modern construction of race. One of the leading paradigms of comparative philology in the eighteenth and nineteenth centuries was the idea that language, especially grammar, could express "the genius of each people" and provided the key to their history, not least in terms of their racial and religious origins.[68] Scholars like Friedrich Max Müller (known as the founding father of the science of religion) identified people's racial descent through grammatical rules, and grouped them into a universal taxonomy of language families and races that distinguished the Aryan from the Semitic and the Turanian.[69]

The malleability of the construction of such language families is illustrated in Müller's work on Asia. He asserted that "the grammatical fibres of the Taï and the Malay languages hold closely together" and proved his point by listing their shared grammatical rules. The "numerical affixes" used in both languages, for instance, led him to conclude that both races were "incapable of conceiving quantity in the abstract; a defect in their logical powers more suggestive to the ethnologist than any peculiarity in the anatomical structure of their skull."[70] Müller's conclusions exemplify the overlapping constructions of race and language in philological discourse; he deduces not only the commonality of the Thai and Malay races from their common grammatical structure but also "a defect in their logical powers" that indicate their low status, and argues that this cultural differential trumps the biological variant of racism that ethnology favored in the nineteenth century.

Colonial and imperial politics in the region contributed to separating Malay from Thai in terms of both race and language. As Rachel Leow has traced, British colonial rule helped to fix the label "Malay" as indicating a distinct language and race.[71] At the same time, the construction of the Thai language as an expression of a constructed Thai race gained currency in the kingdom of Siam; and Tai (without the *h*, and sometimes spelled "Taï") became a referent for a greater language group that encompassed other peoples, such as the Lao, but excluded the Malay.[72] The 1904 census report, for instance, seeks to substantiate its claim that the Lao belong to the Thai race by referring to their spoken language and arguing that the Lao and the Thai languages are identical except for pronunciation and a few words or phrases.[73] However, as the first director of the newly opened State Library of Siam asserted in 1904, "The affinity of the Tai group with other languages is not certain, but there is no connection with . . . the Malayan family."[74] Whereas Müller, in the mid-nineteenth century, had postulated a racial and grammatical similarity between the Thai and the Malay, the British and the Siamese elite used these categories to determine clear racial distinctions that fit the new political borders of both the Kingdom of Siam and the British Malay States by the twentieth century.

Southern Thailand was, of course, located on the fault lines of this distinction, which became even more pronounced when the royal government sought to standardize Central Thai as the national language and script. The government introduced formal Thai language textbooks in the 1870s and had the first prescriptive Thai grammar book prepared by 1905. Whereas the southern provinces had initially been exempted from educational reform, the Primary Education Act of 1921 made the teaching of Thai language compulsory—albeit still allowing instruction in Malay. The act prompted one of the first major rebellions in Patani, and the question of teaching language in schools remains controversial to this day. Currently, the overwhelming majority of students in the South attend Islamic private schools, where the standard Thai curriculum is combined with instruction in Islam as well as the Malay and Arabic languages.[75] Despite their multilingualism and fluency in different scripts, students from southern Thailand still rank low in the central university examinations because of their comparative lack of Thai language skills. Given its political salience, the issue of language is also significant to the current insurgency, which "enjoys its widest support . . . where loyalty to the Malay language is greatest."[76] Thus perhaps the most contentious suggestion made by the National Reconciliation Commission, an agency tasked with working out policy solutions for the conflict, was the proposition in 2006 to grant Malay the status of a working language in the South.[77]

The fact that the Commission's proposition was highly controversial demonstrates the degree to which Central Thai has become the quintessential linguistic expression of Thainess, standing at the top of a hierarchy that combines language with racialized difference in the modern imperial formation.[78] This racialized taxonomy of language was central to the security discourse at the military checkpoints in southern Thailand and helped to transform non-Thai languages into an anti-Thai threat; soldiers compared the Malay-speaking southerners to people of a foreign country such as Cambodia. Speakers of Central Thai, in contrast, were positioned on the civilized side of the state. Distinctions of class also fed into these hierarchies; in the southern provinces, fluency in Central Thai signals more education and urban origins. Religious signifiers also came to bear; as encapsulated in the Thai expression to "speak Islam," speaking the Malay dialect of southern Thailand connotes a Muslim identity, whereas speaking Central Thai implies Buddhism.[79]

Ironically, once off duty, many soldiers themselves relaxed into a different language. In Pattani, most troops were from Isan, the northeastern part of Thailand, where, as noted previously, the former Lao languages had been subsumed within the Thai language family to engender the Lao peoples as Thai. Thus, what the soldiers spoke in their free time, though incomprehensible to me, is classified as a regional Thai dialect. In the South, however, the racial distinctions drawn in the course of nation-state formation had impeded the absorption of Malay into Thai. At checkpoints, therefore, the soldiers' practices of suspicion were based on identifying the speaking of Malay as the sign of a violent, racialized threat.

THE DANGER OF DRESS

The only time I observed soldiers undertaking a body search at a checkpoint, the subjects were two young men on a motorcycle who were each wearing a sarong, a knotted skirt typically worn by both men and women, particularly in the rural areas of the southern provinces. While men in the border provinces usually wear plain, checked or striped sarongs in duller colors like white, brown, and grey, women often dress in brightly colored floral patterns. The soldiers stopped the men and ordered them to dismount and push the bike to an area beside the checkpoint. There, the men first had to open the seat of the motorcycle. Then two soldiers, who had positioned themselves in front of the men, ordered them to lift up their shirts and show their bare stomachs (see fig. 6). Finally, the men also had to untie the knots of their skirts. As another soldier explained to me, they had to make sure the young men were not hiding anything under their sarongs. When the soldiers did not find anything, they let them drive away.

For males in the southern provinces, wearing a sarong was a marker that could arouse military suspicion at checkpoints; a soldier explicitly referred to the sarong as a garment worn by suspected insurgents. Members of the southern population, in turn, frequently complained about the military practice of identifying danger through clothing. School students pointed out that they were never checked while wearing their school uniform, but they risked being stopped when they wanted to pass a roadblock in their village dress.[80] Another interviewee suggested that I myself try to cross a checkpoint while wearing a sarong—but then admitted that the skirt alone might not suffice to overwrite my *farang*-ness. In combination with other racialized markers such as skin complexion and language skills, however, the sarong appeared to imply a potential for violence to soldiers at checkpoints. An important gendered element was involved here, too; whereas women in sarongs were rarely stopped, men in sarongs seemed to fit ideas of a suspicious masculinity.

The practice of policing people according to clothing stands in an imperial tradition of reading dress as the outward sign of a racial essence; more specifically, the sarong has long signified un-Thainess. Although dress was an important marker of social status in a variety of premodern empires through sumptuary regulations, it became key to establishing a "categorical separation between dark subjects and fair-skinned rulers" in the politics of modern Western imperialism. British colonial rulers, for instance, made the turban the objectified sign of the racialized warrior qualities such as fierceness and courage that they believed to be inherent in Sikhs.[81]

Figure 6. Soldiers undertaking a body search of young men at a checkpoint in Yala, September 2011. Photograph by the author.

Early accounts of the Thai and Malay races by missionaries, Orientalist scholars, and foreign advisers attest to the significance of dress in outlining racial characteristics. J. G. D. Campbell, a British adviser to Siam's Ministry of Education at the beginning of the twentieth century, for example, deliberated over the Siamese *phanung*, a traditional garment consisting of a long piece of cloth wrapped around the waist, in his account of what he called the "inferior physique" of the Siamese race (especially the upper classes).[82] Likewise, Siamese census administrators differentiated between races on the bases of dress and hairstyles, explaining after the first census of 1904 that "races which could not be determined with certainty by other criteria had to be classified in general by the dress of those races." In particular, there were difficulties identifying the Chinese population as racially distinct. The surveyors consequently decided that "all women wearing Thai style clothes were counted as Thai."[83]

In Western imperial discourse, dress also signified a racialized degree of civilization. Nudity, in particular, was a sign of a barbarism, and nineteenth-century commentators on Siam frequently outlined how nudity figured in the costumes and manners of the Siamese. The royal elite's project to make Siam more *siwilai* (civilized), therefore, also became one of refashioning styles of clothing—first and foremost, those of the elite themselves, but slowly also those of the Thai population.[84] Field Marshal Phibun, whose dictatorship deliberately aimed to civilize the Thai people and assimilate the Muslim minority, went as far as legally enforcing specific styles of dress in a series of decrees. A royal decree that he countersigned and executed banned improper dress and explicitly equated wearing a sarong with damaging the prestige of the country (in the decree, the wearing of a sarong was compared to wearing only underwear or wearing sleeping garments). Properly civilized styles of dress for men, in contrast, included trousers, shirts, and hats.[85] As the decrees under Phibun demonstrate, the sarong became a sartorial marker of both a lack of civilization and a lack of Thainess in the modern imperial formation.

Members of the Patani independence movement soon protested this enforcement of dress, and in response to Phibun's policies framed the sarong as integral to Malayness. In the 1940s, one resistance leader, who had been fined and arrested for not wearing a particular kind of hat, refused to leave his house without his sarong.[86] In a petition to the British Southeast Asia Command after the Second World War to grant independence to Patani, one of the grievances listed was that the Siamese government forced "the Malays to dress like the Siamese."[87]

The danger that soldiers at checkpoints in the southern provinces saw in civilians wearing sarongs must be placed in this political context of racialized *khaek* masculinities. Southern men wearing sarongs connoted a dangerous lack of civilization to members of the Thai armed forces. Body searches thus operated performatively through the "foreshadowing of an accusation" that detected danger in male *khaek* bodies, justifying a subjugating and feminizing act that stripped them of any (political) agency.[88] The military uniform of the soldiers, in contrast, regardless of their ranks or backgrounds, signified the orderliness integral to the construction of Thainess that distinguished civilized force from terrorist threat on sartorial grounds. As a symbolical marker of a civilized Thai-Buddhist masculinity, the uniform thus helped to legitimize the violence that soldiers enacted in body-searching *khaek* suspects.

The forced undressing of male bodies at southern Thai checkpoints, moreover, reenacted some of the cruelest episodes in the history of Thai counterinsurgency. Pictures of shirtless young men have become iconic markers for the massacre that ended a leftist student uprising on October 6, 1976 in the course of the US-supported counterinsurgency campaign against communism.[89] In the southern conflict, security forces at Tak Bai in 2004 removed the shirts of protesters at the local police station before literally piling them up in trucks for transportation to an army camp, killing seventy-eight of them. Consequently, in southern Thailand, representations of the bare upper bodies of men have come to symbolize the excess of Thai state violence exerted on Muslim bodies.[90]

Religious Dress

Wearing sarongs was also grounds for suspicion because soldiers categorized them as part of what they called "religious dress," which often referred to clothing that Muslim men in the South wore for prayer. Although there are varying opinions about what exactly constitutes the correct dress for prayer, some men in Pattani wear a sarong and a prayer cap (*kapiyoh*, or *piyoh* in Malay), and others also add an Arab-style loose white cotton shirt. Many do not change their ordinary clothes except when going to Friday prayers at one of the larger mosques in the area.[91]

A young man in the village of Tanyong Luloh, for instance, had almost no experience of being questioned at checkpoints. The only exception, he told me, was when he was riding his motorcycle to prayers at Pattani's Central Mosque. He was wearing what he called "religious clothes"—a sarong and a white shirt—and carrying a small bag. The soldiers at the roadblock stopped and questioned him and had him open his bag, which revealed only that he was carrying his prayer mat. A high school student likewise remarked, "Do you know the shirt that we wear for going to prayer? It's our culture to wear it to the mosque. And they [the soldiers] normally check people wearing that."[92]

In a similar vein, a former head of a local *tambon* (subdistrict) administration outlined how religious dress seemed to elicit suspicion: "There are a number of local authorities who have travelled on their motorbikes in religious dress and wearing a *kapiyoh* [prayer cap] who were all stopped at checkpoints. One of them explained to the military that he was working at the local Islamic court, the *datoh* court. But they still had to check him. So once the checking was over he went home and changed his clothes, like wore a tie and trousers and went to exactly the same checkpoint. And they let him pass. Why didn't they check him?"[93]

A number of soldiers confirmed that they not only identified a certain style of dress as religious but also thought that such clothing could hint that certain individuals were suspect. As one soldier said, he worried that people could easily hide weapons under their "big white religious shirts." Another young conscript explained that the men they suspected were mostly those who wore a sarong or sometimes their "*dawah* outfit." *Dawah,* an Arabic word literally translated as "invitation," in this context is often associated with the South Asian missionary movement *Tablighi Jamaat,* which has gained large numbers of followers in southern Thailand. In military parlance, however, *dawah* was invariably used to refer to all Muslims, regardless of their affiliation, and often connoted ideas of religious threat. Soldiers feared, in particular, that young men had been indoctrinated by Muslim authorities. An essential part of this religious indoctrination, one soldier explained, was that the young men were taught to hate soldiers.[94]

MONKS' ROBES

The stopping of subjects in religious dress at checkpoints is remarkable for another reason; the very term "religious dress" as it was used by both soldiers and civilians referred only to the dress of Muslim people in the region and clearly excluded Buddhist monks' robes. This exclusion once again demonstrates a racialized operation of the category of religion in the Thai imperial formation, which clearly functions as a category of difference that overdetermines Muslims while excepting Buddhists.

The saffron robes that monks wear in Southeast Asia are distinct to the Theravada Buddhist tradition.[95] In Thailand, the robes grant monks a privileged position, which is related to the higher status of merit that monks have attained according to the Buddhist tradition. On public transport, for instance, signs for priority seating include symbols of monks in yellow robes.[96] In the southern provinces, however, the privilege that monks are granted in the rest of the country has heightened the danger of attacks; insurgents target monks precisely because they embody one of the pillars of the Thai state.[97]

Consequently, monks in southern Thailand can only travel with military protection, particularly during their daily alms round. Soldiers stationed at Wat Lak Mueang told me that one of the advantages of living in the temple was that they could always accompany monks who had to leave the compound. The soldiers woke at 5:30 a.m. in rotation to escort the monks, and they used different routes to reduce the chances of insurgent attack. Nevertheless, an insurgent bomb that exploded near the university compound during my fieldwork injured four soldiers and one monk from Wat Lak Mueang who had been conducting the morning alms ritual.[98]

The establishment of an army camp inside the temple of Wat Lak Mueang, which housed seven monks and twenty novices, more generally epitomizes the role of Buddhism in policing southern Thailand. The soldiers for the most part felt at ease living at a temple—most of them were Buddhists themselves. Some placed Buddhist statues inside the huts beside the checkpoints. Many also befriended monks and novices. After their morning rounds, the monks would share the food they gathered with the soldiers—once, for instance, a young conscript offered me a package of soy milk that he had received from a monk.[99]

Perhaps ironically, given that they had been trained to kill people, a number of soldiers also cited a stereotypical equation of Buddhism with peace. A ranger captain was explicit in this regard; for him, Buddhists all over the world were "peace-loving." In contrast, Islam was "scary" because it was a "religion of violence." If there were fewer Muslims in Patani, he concluded, a violent conflict like the southern insurgency would never have occurred. In this military discourse, monks function as the harbingers of peace—despite their documented involvement in paramilitary activities.[100] For soldiers at checkpoints, consequently, a saffron robe clothed the noble patriot, whereas a sarong or a *kapiyoh* concealed a potential terrorist.

POLITENESS AND THE FREEDOM OF THE THAI

Given that they often had to struggle with language barriers as they promoted understanding, many soldiers emphasized the significance of smiling as an alternative way of reaching out to the population. One private explained that a central element of soldiering in the South was to "keep smiling" even "if you don't understand what they are saying." Smiling was also seen as the correct reaction to people who did not want to talk to soldiers. Young conscripts described the practice of smiling at people and "getting along with them" as a crucial part of their counterinsurgency mission in the southern region.[101]

The practice of smiling was indeed codified as part of the professional conduct of soldiers in the southern provinces. All soldiers were technically required to carry with them a small plastic card that spelled out the regulations for military officers in the southern border region. The first instruction on the card enjoined soldiers to "interact with civilians with respect and honor." As it has become encoded in the Thai context, smiling for many soldiers functioned to demonstrate friendly respect for civilians and at the same time to signal to their superiors that they were obeying the rules for policing the South. Even in the eyes of many people living in the southern provinces, soldiers behaved very politely. Students often compared the politeness of Thai soldiers with the rudeness of the Thai police and paramilitaries.[102]

In turn, a lack of politeness could arouse suspicion at checkpoints; suspects, for many soldiers, were those who did not behave according to Thai codes of propriety, which included such behavior as smiling and chatting with soldiers. A case in point is a remark of Private Ch. When asked about how he determined who was suspect, he suggested that if he looked "at people's eyes" he could see that there were some people who "look at [soldiers] in a strange way." He also mentioned that he deemed civilians suspicious if they did not want to talk, and he hastened to add that, as a soldier, he nevertheless had to "keep smiling" despite an unfriendly reception. A sergeant similarly described a typical suspect as someone who behaved unusually, such as giving only short answers to questions. Put differently, from a military perspective, the transgression of certain codes of conduct seemed to mark specific people as dangerously un-Thai.[103]

Such racialization of codes of conduct has significant precedents in Thailand and is more generally related to the construction of race in modern imperialism. Perhaps the most prominent modern example is the regime of Field Marshal Phibun, which, as noted previously, enforced certain ways of acting that were deemed both civilized and authentically Thai in a series of decrees. Phibun's National Cultural Maintenance Act (1942), for instance, obliged Thais to display "proper dress, behavior, and etiquette in public places." Another decree specified that Thai citizens should refrain from a "forceful acquisition of space on buses or at ticket windows or at theater entrances."[104] The notes to one of Phibun's state edicts clearly extend these cultural practices to a racialized idea of embodiment; every Thai citizen should be compelled to embody Thainess. More broadly, such notions are related to an imperial practice of cultivating codes of conduct to define the racial and class boundaries of white colonial society. Ann Laura Stoler shows, for instance, how whiteness in the Dutch East Indies was demarcated through bourgeois codes of conduct (see chapter 3).[105]

Likewise, for the royal government in late-nineteenth- and early-twentieth-century Siam, etiquette was key to attaining the *siwilai* status of the white Western world, not least because some foreign advisers had claimed the Siamese lacked certain traits of character that indicated civilization. For instance, J. G. D. Campbell mused in his writings that the "races" of Europe had overcome the savagery of their character that still prevailed in the eighteenth century "with its slave trade, its noisome prisons, and its barbarous penal code" because "their character contained in itself the germs from which alone such growth could take place." The "Siamese race," by contrast, for him contained a "general character" that was unchangeable: "No European adviser," he warned, "can alter . . . the fundamental qualities of the Siamese character." Campbell repeatedly claimed that the Siamese conducted themselves like children; on the surface, they had acquired the "manners of grown-up people," but they still required the tutelage of the adult colonial nations of Europe.[106]

In such a context, the urgency with which the Siamese royal elite addressed the teaching of proper manners toward the end of the nineteenth century is comprehensible. Manners, after all, seemed to determine the status of their race and the fate of their country. The first modern school curriculum, designed in 1892, consequently included a subject that was later termed "the study of proper behavior" and became compulsory for all students. One of the first school textbooks, published in 1901, was *Sombat khong phu di* (The qualities of a gentleman), a handbook on proper conduct that remains widely influential to this day, indicating how manners have come to bear on notions of civilized Thai masculinity.[107]

The model of masculinity encapsulated in the notion of the gentleman has distinct colonial connotations and became integral to military codes of conduct in the modern Siamese army. In nineteenth-century Europe, the idea of the gentleman was used to legitimize the colonial rule of white men in a discourse that championed their alleged moral refinement and superiority. Likely transferred to Siam by British-educated royal officers, this ideal also became encoded in the first military regulations of the modern army, which translated "gentleman" as *yaentalimaen*. Gentlemanly codes of conduct were also inscribed in the regulations of the military cadet school and the Royal Guards; both were modeled on European armies that were designed to function as schools of manliness by, for instance, teaching cadets reliability and respectfulness.[108] Staff at these modern Siamese military institutions were to exhibit "politeness both in manners and in speech," and distinguish themselves not only by military dress but also by moral virtues.[109] The practice of smiling became a recognized part of military good manners.

Besides functioning as a racial marker of the Thai in the southern context, the performance of good manners also operated in an international context that became obvious over the course of my own field research. Contrary to my initial expectations, and in marked contrast to the experiences of researchers at police checkpoints in Bangkok, I was not only allowed to conduct research at checkpoints but often even welcomed to do so.[110] Many soldiers saw me as a window to the international world and were grateful that they could demonstrate their good intentions toward and their polite interactions with the southern population, because one of the main concerns of the counterinsurgency mission was to correct the allegedly false representation of the military in the international arena.[111]

This concern points not only to the politics of representation that formed an important part of policing the South but also, more broadly, to the political saturation of ideas of Thainess with the notions of freedom and independence, which again needs to be understood in the context of modern imperialism. Counterinsurgents often equated insurgent propaganda with the work of nongovernmental organizations; both, they charged, were manufacturing false images of the military in order to discredit the policing mission. Armed forces were, moreover, anxious about insurgents using their contacts to gather support from international organizations—in particular, they suspected the Organization for Islamic Cooperation of supporting the insurgent cause.[112] Perhaps the army's greatest fear was that such an increased international awareness would eventually lead to an intervention authorized by the United Nations, like that in East Timor in 1999, which some officers themselves had supported as military delegates. In an interview in 2010, General Anupong Paochinda, then the army commander, expressed these worries clearly. Insurgents, he claimed, wanted to internationalize the conflict and gain the support of both the Organization of Islamic Cooperation and the United Nations in order to create a situation similar to East Timor.[113]

This military anxiety is most telling for what it reveals about ideas of Thainess and of the Thai military. In etymological dictionaries, the original meaning of the word "Thai" is often given as "free."[114] As Thanet Aphornsuvan has demonstrated, however, the association of the word "Thai" with a liberal ideal of freedom was forged in the course of nineteenth-century debates about slavery in Siam. The word "tai" in premodern inscriptions referred to non-slave subjects who were still in the service of the king. However, when Western observers took slavery as a proof of both the despotism of the Siamese government and the inherent servility of the Siamese people, the royal government slowly abandoned slavery and supported a translation of the word as "free."[115]

The most ardent promoter of this redefinition was Prince Damrong Rajanub-hab (1862–1943), who, significantly, added the construction of the Thai race to the equation. Using historical material, he argued that slavery was un-Thai, because "originally in the Thai race there was no place for slavery."[116] As noted in the previous chapter, he defined the quintessential character of the Thai race as consisting of "Love of National Independence, Toleration and Power Assimilation." From the royal chronicles, Damrong inferred that the strength of the Thai derived from their unwillingness to submit to other races; they had sacrificed their lives for the independence of the nation in a number of wars—in particular, by fighting "wars of liberation" against their "archenemies," the Burmese.[117] The essence of the Thai race in Damrong's writings emerges as the opposite of servility and despotism; an inherent quest for freedom and independence, Damrong suggests, has determined the fate of the Thai people.[118] Field Marshal Phibun's renaming of Siam as Thailand built on Damrong's redefinition of the Thai. On the one hand, "Thailand" matched the name of the country to the name of the ruling race. On the other, given that "Thai" connoted freedom, it characterized the country as one of the great powers, its historical independence marking it as one among other civilized countries.[119]

These notions of Thai independence and freedom underpin the military's anxiety about the remote possibility of UN intervention provoked by misrepresentations. An armed intervention would not only allow foreign forces to operate on Thai territory but also seriously undermine the essential freedom of the Thai. In military discourse, the UN peacekeeping operations in East Timor stood for modern forms of colonialism; even the thought of a similar intervention in Thailand shattered the self-image of the army as safeguarding Thai independence.

KHAEK FEMININITY AT CHECKPOINTS

Practices of suspicion at checkpoints were highly gendered. Women were often coded as harmless and became the preferred target group for friendly trust-building exercises. Women in headscarves were treated with greater respect than men wearing religious dress, who, as previously noted, aroused suspicion. Indeed, though most women I interviewed reported instances where soldiers had talked to them, none of them had ever been subject to a full body search by a female volunteer or paramilitary. Some female informants themselves wondered about the reasons for their privileged status.[120]

My conversation with soldier P. illustrates this point. As he elaborated, "Women sometimes drive their motorcycles past here. If they are women that we know, we talk to them. It depends on the person. Yet mostly the women come past with their children. And the kids would normally wave their hands, so we also smile at them. But usually they are not stopped." Soldier P.'s collapsing of women into mothers exemplified a gendered construction of armed conflict in which motherhood typically embodies peacefulness.[121] In this context, however, the conflation also highlighted that an important generational component was at work. Like soldier Y., the military generally depicted mostly the older women of the Patani region as generally "not really having any role to play," which significantly reduced their potential danger in the soldiers' eyes.

Some soldiers explicitly connected these gendered stereotypes with racialized ideas about the backwardness of Islam as practiced in the southern provinces. According to this narrative, fathers and husbands in the region were putting women into an inferior position. Soldier S., for instance, said that "the women here are pressured back into their traditional cultural role. It's like they are second-class citizens. The man is the head of the family, and they have to step back. Some people go to work and leave their wife at home. And men here can have four wives." In soldier S.'s view, the religious tradition of Patani ensured that women could only play secondary roles because men were the heads of families. To him, Islamic family law as it applied in the southern provinces further entrenched women's oppression, because men were allowed not only to practice polygyny but also apparently to force their wives to stay in the private realm of the home while they themselves enjoy working in the public sphere. Consequently, southern Muslim women were deprived of their political agency as citizens. This theme of polygynous Muslim men in the South was frequently cited by military respondents; it often functioned not only to discredit men in the region but also to highlight the lack of modernity of the region's Muslim tradition more broadly.[122]

Racialized ideas are also part of this discourse about the harmlessness and backwardness of Muslim women in the southern provinces. First, it resonates with an imperial discourse that Gayatri Spivak, analyzing the abolition of sati by British colonial rulers in India, has aptly described as "white men saving brown women from brown men." Using gender to draw civilizational divides, this imperial trope has helped to legitimize military interventions such as the US-led intervention in Afghanistan in 2001.[123] In the southern Thai case, which I will discuss further in chapter 4, the notion of soldiers acting as proto-feminists saving Muslim women from Muslim men similarly fed into legitimations of the counterinsurgency mission.

In a related way, these stereotypes about Muslim gender relationships echo Orientalist taxonomies that ranked races according to the perceived status of women. At the Louisiana Purchase Exposition, for instance, Siamese representatives declared: "The position of women is high in Siam."[124] Describing the Lao people, the missionary John Freeman more explicitly drew the connection between gender relations and race at the beginning of the twentieth century: "This unique position of women, and the high moral standards that accompany it, cannot be attributed to Buddhism or to any outside influence; they are a part of the racial inheritance of the Laos people."[125] By contrast, "Mahometanism" was seen as placing a "stigma" on women that "cast a blight on . . . social institutions" of the southern Malay states.[126] The military discourse at checkpoints likewise intertwined notions about Islam as misogynist with the alleged victimization of Malay women, both pointing to an un-Thai lack of civilization that supposedly marked the Malay race.

Some soldiers, however, expressed insecurity and ambivalence about female civilians at checkpoints, and recognized that a potential danger might be hidden under a supposedly harmless female disguise. When elaborating on who might be suspicious, for example, a conscript explained that in some cases there "might also be a guy wearing a headscarf like a woman." Similarly, another soldier warned that insurgents might use headscarves to produce a "female image," allowing them to cross checkpoints without being checked.[127] Significantly, in these narratives, the notion of women as harmless and innocent subjects was again reproduced. Male insurgents could apparently use both women themselves as well as their image—symbolized by the headscarf—as instruments of mobilization and disguise, but the danger beneath the headscarf was still projected as male.

FLIRTATIOUS ENCOUNTERS

Entwined with the idea of male danger was an idea of exoticized female beauty concealed beneath the headscarf. The generational distinction between women was once again key in this context, as were perceptions of dress. Whereas soldiers tended to read older women as harmless, they often associated images of sexualized beauty with younger women, and a number of soldiers described the traditional way young Muslim women dressed in southern Thailand in positive terms as *riaproi*, a Thai word connoting the propriety of gender and sexuality. Interestingly, some soldiers also highlighted the women's difference from the women in their northeastern home region; the latter would not cover up but liked to wear "short trousers" and "shirts with very short sleeves." While northeastern women mostly played more central roles in society that did those in the South, they would also, one soldier cautioned, do "just about anything for money." Consequently, as his colleagues suggested, the covered-up style of Malay-Muslim women was "good in another way."[128] In these stereotypes, the perception that women in the southern region were less modern than their counterparts in the Northeast took on a favorable bent, contrasting with negative ideas of Muslim men's traditional practices as signifiers of religious indoctrination that often served to explain their potential deviance (see also chapter 3).

This sexualization of young Muslim women also translated into flirtatious encounters at checkpoints. Although the soldiers whom I observed remained strictly professional while interacting with women, in interviews some openly admitted to flirting. P., for instance, provided a playful account of meeting women at checkpoints, describing his interactions with them as teasing. More explicitly, another young conscript admitted that he would sometimes ask young women for their phone numbers when they crossed his roadblock. Many women I talked to confirmed such flirtatious practices. A nineteen-year-old student described how she was sometimes addressed at checkpoints: "When I drive my motorcycle home, they would say something like: 'Oh, you are cute!'" Other young women likewise elaborated that soldiers would usually only question men at the roadblock in their village. "But if we pass there, they ask us for our phone numbers." Soldiers would, they explained, ask whether they could chat, or ask for their email addresses.[129]

The power differentials on which such flirtatious encounters operate are exemplified in the following account by a seventeen-year-old student from the village of Tanyong Luloh: "I have had incidents when soldiers stopped me and had me open the flap of my helmet. And then the soldier said: 'Okay, very beautiful.' Like at that checkpoint over there. At this checkpoint here there are never any incidents, but at that checkpoint over there, there are. Sometimes we are afraid that if we don't open the flap of the helmet they will check us, and then if we open it they look at our face and let us go."[130]

In the student's description, the playful atmosphere of smiling interactions between military men and civilian women is lost; although she clarifies that she is never afraid to pass checkpoints, the flirting here is clearly one-sided. Interestingly, a number of normal processes of checking are repeated in this account; she has to stop and receives orders from the soldiers. Yet what the soldiers examine once she opens her helmet is not any ground for suspicion but the beauty of her face. The soldiers use the checkpoint to undertake a beauty check—a game that is not played with the female civilian, but at her expense. The student's uneasiness regarding her relatively helpless position and dependence is palpable in her account; if she refuses to play the beauty game, a stricter or more thorough check might follow. Although, as many young women cautioned, flirtatious interactions at checkpoints were not necessarily such one-sided affairs, they could never occur independent of this power relationship that made young women the objects of soldiers' sexual desire.

Asked about the reasons for the attractiveness of young Muslim women, some soldiers described them in Thai as *borisut,* which means "innocent" and "harmless" but also connotes virginity. It was this perceived sexual purity that made young women into objects of military desire. The sexualization of young Muslim women is also, in more general terms, connected to Orientalist notions of female Muslim dress. The veil, in particular, has long been a prominent symbol for the mysteries of the Orient and, in its sexualized version, for the cover of an untouched sexual object that invites unveiling. In these fantasies, colonial occupation was translated into sexual possession.[131] In the southern Thai context, moreover, the significance of female Muslim sexuality in military discourse has to be seen in light of family law regulations that have made sexuality into one of the main markers of the difference of the southern population (see also chapter 4). This difference, of course, promised sexual excitement for soldiers usually lodged in all-male environments.

Racialized stereotypes about *khaek* femininity also play a role in incidents like those described by the schoolgirl above. Soldiers would sometimes casually mention that they regarded *khaek* women as beautiful; they had, soldiers said, perfect skin (not too light, not too dark) and beautiful faces. Beautiful noses, in particular, seemed to mark young women as *khaek.* The soldier forcing the student to open her helmet has to be understood in precisely this racialized context. He reenacted the typically Orientalist unveiling of Muslim women in order to examine her face, which instead of affording further identification of a potential suspect revealed her stereotypically *khaek* beauty.

Owing to the racialized rendering of their religion in military discourse, young women in the South were not criminalized but sexualized. Whereas young men became feminized objects for soldiers to check, young women became sexualized objects for them to check out at checkpoints.

Handsome Soldiers

As noted above, flirtatious interactions at checkpoints were not always one-sided affairs. Using the verb *len,* which translates as "playing" but can also mean "playful flirtation," many young local women emphasized that they themselves sometimes had an active role in the game. One student put it like this: "They smile at us. Some ask for our phone numbers. But if we are not interested in them, they don't play with us. . . . I think it has to come from both sides, if the woman is not interested, nothing happens."[132] The game was immediately over, she implied, if the young women did not respond to the soldiers' advances.

Some young women however, did find soldiers attractive, and a number of the racialized notions discussed in this chapter were reflected in their accounts as positive features that constituted their attraction to soldiers. One positive stereotype about Thai soldiers was that they could speak in a polite and sweet way. As one female interviewee explained, one could gauge from the way soldiers talked whether they were good people. Others used the Thai expression *phut phro* (talking in a pleasant or harmonious way) to describe the refinement of the soldiers' speech. A young male journalist shared his observation that soldiers at checkpoints would alter their tone when talking to women—instead of investigating them, they would talk to them in a "sweet voice." This way of talking furthermore figured as a key part of what young women highlighted as the soldiers' "good" and "proper" manners.[133]

For many young female students, the soldiers' politeness and propriety were identified with their military uniform, which was often described as *tae*, meaning "smart," "handsome," or "trendy." The uniform, one of them elaborated in English, looks "*smart*, you know. Even someone who is not handsome but wears the uniform looks *tae*. Like 'ohooo!'" Another student noted that some of her female classmates did not just admire the uniform but became "crazy" about it. Some soldiers held similar views and regarded their dress as symbolic of their propriety and gentlemanly manners; it showed, one soldier explained to me, that the wearer followed the rules and would speak in a refined way.[134]

Other young women generally emphasized that they found soldiers handsome; they had beautiful faces, and they had light skin. Therefore, one girl explained, it was *tae* for a girl to have a soldier as a boyfriend. One respondent highlighted that flirting with soldiers was a welcome excitement for female adolescents who were often subject to tight social control, especially in the more rural areas of the South, where "we don't really have many opportunities to talk with boys, and we cannot go out that much." This excitement also stemmed from the fact that few of the women had traveled to other parts of Thailand—it was new for them to interact with soldiers from other Thai provinces.[135] Some also explicitly compared a positive image of soldiers to a negative racialized image of local men; the latter were often impolite, they would neither speak nor dress properly, and they tended to have darker skin.

Many of the cultural registers of race analyzed in this chapter reemerge in the young women's perceptions of soldiers. For example, a positive notion of propriety is attached to the central Thai dialect that soldiers have to speak in professional interactions. The racialized taxonomy of languages that structures the Thai imperial formation is clearly replicated by the young women in the southern provinces. Central Thai, in their descriptions, figures as a more civilized and proper language than the local Malay dialect. The standardization of Central Thai in the public-school system has likely contributed to this normative hegemony of Thai language.

The young women's appreciation of military uniform and the idea that soldiers in uniform embody gentlemanly manners likewise relates to the politics of dress and the performance of manners that have become central to constructions of Thainess. The military uniform is a particularly interesting case in this regard. The monarchs who spearheaded Siam's transformation into a modern imperial formation liked to be portrayed in military attire to demonstrate to outside observers that Siam had acquired the civilized status of the Western world. When the modern army was established, military cadets not only had to learn gentlemanly manners but also had to follow strict rules about how to dress and keep their uniform clean.[136] The uniform, which had been a vestimentary prop marking Thai civilization for the royal elite, became an important means to differentiate the gentlemanly soldier from the "dishonest and unprincipled ruffian" in modern Siam.[137] The racialized subtext of this contrast becomes especially clear in the context of military perceptions of the sarong outlined above. Whereas the sarong epitomizes the local dress of the Malays and often connotes ideas about the danger of Islam, military uniform has become the hegemonic standard that signifies the essential civilized qualities of Thainess.

For women who have been racialized as *khaek*, the soldiers come close to *farang*. Whereas *farangs* are constructed as white, economically powerful, Western foreigners, soldiers at least seem to offer lighter skin, more economic security, and a non-local origin—in contrast to local men stereotyped as dark and lazy. If the *farang*, as Pattana Kitiarsa has argued, features as the Occidental Other of Thainess, Thai soldiers in the South seem to gain their attraction from operating as the civilized Other of Malayness.[138]

CHAPTER THREE

THE NEW PATH TO PEACE

Disciplining Religious Subjects

The first time I heard about the camp Yalannanbaru was during my first research visit to Pattani in March 2010. I had become acquainted with a high-ranking colonel at a workshop and told him about my interest in counterinsurgency projects. He was eager to help—after all, he said, journalists and researchers would often write distorted accounts of the military in southern Thailand. He introduced me to the director of a project that he described, in English, as a "drug rehabilitation camp" that was called Yalannanbaru. He pronounced "Yalannanbaru" in Thai but glossed its origin as a Malay term (*jalanan baru*) translating to "The New Path."[1]

The camp director, Colonel S., explained how he had helped to design Yalannanbaru as a measure to reduce drug abuse among young men in the southern conflict region. To this end, camp instructors recruited Muslim men aged fourteen to twenty-five from the southern provinces for a one-week training course. He was open to my conducting research at the camp and described it as one of the most successful and popular counterinsurgency projects; by 2011, fifteen thousand young men had already attended Yalannanbaru, according to a military source. My subsequent interviews with students confirmed that Yalannanbaru was well known throughout the area of the southern border provinces.

The project is still ongoing, albeit having undergone significant changes. When I visited again in 2016, the strategy had been altered and broadened to include mosques and religious teachers in the purported fight against drugs, and a new program for young women had been instituted. The main training site had also changed. Originally located on a hill opposite Camp Sirindhorn, which houses the headquarters of the southern-region ISOC command, the main body responsible for coordinating counterinsurgency measures in the South, Yalannanbaru was moved inside Camp Sirindhorn in 2016. This change of location is a material reminder that Yalannanbaru operates within a counterinsurgency rationale. In fact, as the material I collected in 2010 and 2011 demonstrates, the project of teaching young men to stay on the new path was designed to prevent them from getting onto the wrong path of insurgency.[2]

Religious practice played a pivotal role in this counterinsurgency effort.[3] In contrast to Cold War programs that employed missionary monks to fight the communist insurgency, Yalannanbaru does not aspire to convert participants to Buddhism; rather, Muslim practices occupy a prominent place in the training schedule. As outlined in an internal strategy report, the topic of Islamic education was considered an important entry point for recruiting young men for the seven-day training camp. The report also repeated often-voiced military fears that a misinterpretation of Islam was driving the insurgency. In response, Yalannanbaru was to teach young men the "correct understanding of Muslim religion" and instruct them to "conduct their life according to correct Islamic principles."[4]

The modern concept of religion is not only central to the Yalannanbaru report but also key to understanding how power at the camp operates within the larger structural context of Thailand's imperial formation. Thus, the strategy report reveals the military's assumption that the southern population, especially its young men, not only identifies as Muslim but is also saturated by Islam, and is therefore susceptible to a training program that highlights Muslim practices. This supposition mirrors common Orientalist and racialized notions about Muslim identity. In this stereotype, Muslim subjects are governed by their religious rituals and therefore lack the capacity for rational thinking. In the Thai context, more specifically, the stereotype is integrally connected to the homogenizing construction of the southern provinces as Muslim, and to the merging of Malay customary practices and Islamic law in family law.[5] Both have decisively grounded the contemporary imperial formation. The legal reforms have stripped the Islamic tradition of its legal and political components and mapped Islam onto the southern provinces, thus enabling the incorporation of the southern Muslims as the Other of Buddhist Thailand (see chapter 1). Furthermore, the Yalannanbaru training exhibits the military's paternalistic approach; counterinsurgents, many of whom are Buddhist, teach young Muslim men the supposedly correct practice of Islam.

While the Yalannanbaru training mobilizes a normative category of Muslim religion, it also implicitly relies on practices and norms central to the Theravada Buddhist tradition. In particular, the correct understanding of Islam as defined by the military is grounded in ordering principles that the Thai state supports and that the insurgency challenges. Power here operates through disciplining young Muslim men into religious subjects willingly incorporated into the Thai imperial formation, which depends on the imbrication of Buddhism and statehood. Yalannanbaru thus illustrates how the category of religion is deployed as a primary device by the military to police the southern population, managing it in such a way that the imperial order of the state cannot be contested.

Studies of state and military practices in southern Thailand focus for the most part on how the counterinsurgency campaign and other state programs have enlisted Buddhism and Buddhist institutions; they challenge the association of Buddhism with peacefulness by outlining Thai-Buddhist nationalism as a state ideology that has fueled the conflict.[6] Yalannanbaru, however, requires a different conceptual approach to the military's framing of religion because counterinsurgents, rather than propagating Buddhist religious warfare, mobilized a positive construction of Islam.

Critical secular studies have exposed the Western Christian history of the modern category of religion and shown that, in the process of globalizing the imperial project of modernity, the category of religion was simultaneously universalized and abstracted from Western Christianity's precepts. These studies have also demonstrated that religion has itself functioned as a normalizing category for other traditions and helped to reframe some of them as "world religions," a hierarchical discourse codified in nineteenth century scholarship that distinguished primitive religions from those with a larger group of followers, a recognized founder, and a canon of ancient texts, such as Islam and Buddhism.[7] Moreover, they have shown that this universalizing project has enabled certain forms of rule and subjection in modern nation-states.[8] Supposedly abstracted from power and politics in modern secular states, religion has served not only to classify and differentiate populations but also to regulate subjects. Crucially, the supposed secularist separation between the religious and political spheres has in no way eliminated their imbrication. Secular state projects have, for instance, appropriated forms of disciplinary regulation from religious traditions and constructed them as a seemingly neutral and secular standard. In Western European states, disciplinary practices of Christian monastic orders have decisively shaped the very concept of discipline.[9]

In Siam, the metamorphosis of the Buddhist tradition into Buddhism as a religion played a central role in transforming the premodern empire into its modern incarnation, and Siam's interaction with modern European empires is central to this reconceptualization of the tradition. Imperial encounters among missionaries, Orientalist scholars, and the royal elite contributed to strengthening a movement that framed the Buddhist tradition as a modern religion indigenous to the emerging modern state. King Mongkut (Rama IV, r. 1851–1868) instigated a new monastic sect that advocated purifying the Buddhist tradition by returning to original Pali scriptures in a way reminiscent of Christian Protestantism's push to return to original scripture after the Reformation, and his heir, King Chulalongkorn (Rama V, r. 1868–1910), supported Orientalist scholars in their efforts to translate Buddhist manuscripts.[10] Sources from nineteenth-century Siam, moreover, indicate that the notion of *sasana*, the living practice of teaching and learning in the Theravada Buddhist tradition, was stripped of its traditional context, translated, and abstracted as a generalized notion of religion.[11]

This epistemic shift toward defining Buddhism as a religion enabled new forms of power and subjection that undergird the modern imperial formation of Siam. At the beginning of the twentieth century, the royal court prohibited popular Buddhist practices such as spirit possession, converted the Buddhist monkhood (*sangha*) into a state agency under state authority, and mobilized the newly formed army to fight against millennialist movements in the Northeast. The abstraction of Buddhism as a religion also enabled it to be mapped onto the modern state of Siam as a geographical entity.[12]

Less well researched, although occurring simultaneously and integrally connected to these processes, is the demarcation of the southern provinces as Muslim during Patani's incorporation into Siam, which similarly created a secular split between the religious and political spheres. In instituting the family law system in Patani, Siam's royal court mimicked the British imperial policy of noninterference in religious affairs, thus initiating the regulation of the Patani population through the privatized notion of religion while forcefully eradicating the public, political part of the southern Islamic tradition.[13] The application of this imperial model of rule elevated the status of the Buddhist kingdom to that of a modern secular state.

This equation of a Buddhist kingdom with a secular order lies at the heart of the contemporary Thai imperial formation, and the first constitution, written in 1932, illustrates this paradoxical construction of a Buddhist secular order. It redefined a central element of the Buddhist tradition that obliged the king to promote and protect the teachings of the Buddha by stipulating that the king was both a Buddhist and the patron of all religions in Siam. Concurrently, it allowed religious freedom, a secular principle that was to demonstrate the modernity of the Siamese state.[14] The king's status as the patron of Thai Muslims was further spelled out in the Royal Patronage of Islam Act of 1945, which instituted a model of governing the Muslim community that directly reproduced the state-led administration of the Buddhist monkhood. Note the hierarchy implied in this construction of Buddhist patronage; it transformed elements from the Buddhist tradition into a universal state law that was to incorporate all other religious communities as particular entities. Buddhism, a tradition made a religion, became the universal legal standard of the modern imperial formation of Thailand.

ENTERING THE NEW PATH

This secular construction of Buddhism has also historically played a role in the Thai military's counterinsurgency practices. The Cold War counterinsurgency campaign defined communism as an antireligious ideology and held that communists threatened Buddhism and Thai customs. As a consequence, the government instigated a program of Buddhist missions, the *thammathut*, whereby groups of monks traveled to different Thai provinces to educate villagers, strengthen their Buddhist morality, and increase their trust in the Thai state in the name of national security.[15] Counterinsurgency operated through the conflation of a particular version of Buddhism with the Thai state.

The founder of Yalannanbaru, Colonel S., is a pious Buddhist and an experienced counterinsurgent. A graduate of the prestigious Bangkok Cadet School, he worked on counterinsurgency projects in the northeastern province of Loei in the 1980s. In the wake of the new counterinsurgency policy implemented after the 2006 military coup, he came to the southern provinces, motivated by an ambition to solve the southern problem through development work rather than armed intervention. He began collaborating with the Office of Narcotics Control Board, the national agency responsible for narcotics-control strategy, to fight drug addiction in the southern provinces. He emphasized that religion played a major role in this effort.[16] Consequently, what discursively framed the Yalannanbaru project was not only an emphasis on drug abuse but also, and more importantly, a definition of drug abuse as a religious problem.

Certain drugs are widespread in the communities of southern Thailand. Particularly in rural areas, smoking tobacco and drinking a relatively harmless substance obtained from boiling local *kratom* leaves, which is sometimes mixed with cough syrup and cola, are quite common.[17] Moreover, given that the border area is a longstanding regional hub for criminal networks that engage in the drug trade, methamphetamines and marijuana are readily available throughout the provinces.[18] Owing to high rates of unemployment and low rates of education, most drug users are lower-class men.[19] Many village officials and Islamic authorities I talked to therefore saw drug abuse as a significant social problem and often understood Yalannanbaru as principally a good project. In the words of a local journalist, hardly anyone objected to the military's New Path initiative because everyone knew "that many people take *kratom*, and it might be better to send them to the camp than have them stay at home."[20]

It thus made sense for counterinsurgents to employ drug abuse as the overarching theme for a reeducation camp and to use a broad definition of drugs; for Yalannanbaru instructors, both smoking and drinking *kratom* counted as gateways to drug addiction. In addition, the issue of drug prevention, which many local village authorities deemed critical, provided counterinsurgents with direct access to local communities. Given that the boiling of *kratom* leaves is not widespread in southern Buddhist communities, it also offered a justification targeting the Muslim part of the southern population. Moreover, whereas heavy drug users or criminals were imprisoned or sent to special hospitals for treatment, the military fashioned attending the camp as a fun activity that would help young men overcome a number of problems, such as lack of religiosity and discipline, that could lead to future drug addiction. This preventive rationale enlarged Yalannanbaru's target group to potentially encompass all young Muslim men.

According to military sources, participants were recruited on a voluntary basis. However, it is clear that a central condition of recruitment was what Mrinalini Sinha, in a different context, has called a "patriarchal compromise," forged in this case between the military and particular members of the southern communities.[21] My observations suggest that men of a certain age, class, and educational background were targeted by the military's disciplinary project. Many of those I met, for instance, had difficulties correctly speaking and writing Central Thai, which suggested a low level of standard Thai education. Their style of dress hinted at a lower-class status. Some had been sent to attend the camp by their teachers, heads of villages, or heads of local mosques. In a number of instances, parents hoping for positive educational effects had brought their sons to attend the camp.[22]

Yalannanbaru thus exemplifies the counterinsurgency logic applied by the military in the South: the program allowed the military to work against the insurgency without using direct military force. Counterinsurgents cooperated with local village authorities, who persuaded young men from their communities to participate and who thus provided the army with relatively easy access to targets who would otherwise have been difficult to reach. To quote a soldier working at Yalannanbaru, preventing drug abuse offered a useful "bridge" between counterinsurgents and young men. Counterinsurgents thereby hoped to "win their hearts" and to "pull their parents and relatives" in local villages onto the side of the military.[23]

The framing of drug abuse as a religious problem, moreover, is consistent with the depoliticizing discourse of the counterinsurgency campaign, which circumvents any questions about state structures driving the insurgency. A common official narrative suggests that young men have been systematically drugged by insurgent cadres and forced to commit attacks. This narrative eliminates any agency or political motivation.[24] Adding religion to the equation, furthermore, relocates the problem of the insurgency inside the southern Muslim community, and Yalannanbaru staff often invoked stereotypes of southern men as lazy and undisciplined in explaining that members of their target group were not practicing Islam correctly and were therefore in danger of falling prey to both drugs and insurgent ideology.[25] Moreover, this framing of drug abuse and insurgent violence as a religious problem enabled counterinsurgents to represent Yalannanbaru as a camp that strengthened young men's religious discipline and thus facilitated counterinsurgents' access to members of the Muslim community.

The organizers of Yalannanbaru were indeed well connected with certain *imams* in the southern provinces, with whom they held regular meetings and workshops to ask for advice on the Yalannanbaru strategy and to plead for their support in recruitment.[26] Even more importantly, the organizers had gained the support of the *chularajamontri*, the administrative head of the Muslim community in Thailand.[27] An article published in the magazine of the *chularajamontri*'s office, for instance, reported positively on a meeting between the *chularajamontri* and the commander of the ISOC Fourth Army Region to discuss military projects against drug abuse. In the article, the *chularajamontri* also directly appealed to the local *imams* in the southern provinces to cooperate with the military. This cooperation, he clarified, was not meant to provide the security forces with intelligence information. Rather, he argued, supporting the military to combat drugs should be part of the spiritual leadership that heads of mosques were expected to display.[28]

Besides gathering the official support of high-level members of Thailand's Muslim community, the Yalannanbaru team also tried to directly integrate Muslim authorities into the training. At least one Muslim religious authority was present at every camp session and was usually referred to by the military as the *ustadz*, the Malay word for an Islamic teacher. However, none of the *ustadz* I met at different Yalannanbaru sessions had a classical education in the Islamic tradition that would qualify them to teach at an Islamic school. One had studied public administration at the Yala Islamic University, for instance; another had studied Islamic Studies at the Prince of Songkhla University in Pattani before working in environmental development projects administered through the university.[29]

Colonel S., the director and inventor of Yalannanbaru, had never formally studied the tradition of Islam. He started to engage with Islamic teachings when preparing the Yalannanbaru project and studied with a contact who would later become one of the *ustadz* at the camp. Elaborating the significance of religious instruction at Yalannanbaru, he outlined to me how he wanted to use the young men's own culture and religion to bring them back onto the right path. In addition, one of the *ustadz* referred to a worrying trend in the moral development, or lack thereof, of young men in the southern provinces. Many of them, he warned, were neither practicing Islam correctly nor familiar with its true teachings. Therefore, his aspiration in supporting Yalannanbaru was to teach young men the correct ideas and practice of Islam, so that they would abstain from the antinational separatism he identified with the insurgency.[30] Although this religious framing of Yalannanbaru functioned to depoliticize the insurgency, such instruction itself was highly political. Its implicit normative goal was to discipline young men into accepting those structures and tenets of the Thai state challenged by the insurgency.

THE WRONG PATH

The camp's core exercise, which the staff handbook called the lesson on virtuous life, was structured around a poster that depicted what it called the "wrong path" and the "new path" (see fig. 7). Yalannanbaru trainers usually introduced the exercise on the second day of the training and repeated it several times during the week. After the instructor had presented the poster and its narrative, small groups of participants redrew the poster themselves, elaborated their posters in front of the whole group, and explained the concept of virtuous life. As part of the presentation, participants outlined the danger of the wrong path and the steps necessary to get back onto the right path at this important crossroads in their lives.

The narrative of the poster provides insight into some of the conceptual underpinnings of Yalannanbaru. It begins in the upper left corner with a depiction of human birth that defies biological explanation. Beside the sperm and the ovum is a third factor supposedly necessary for the process of conception. Depicted as a question mark, this factor is described in Thai as *chit winyan*, a term originally derived from Buddhist ideas of rebirth that has now taken on a more general meaning of "spirituality." The result of this process is the birth of a pure, innocent, and virtuous human being, whose subsequent development is described, through four different age ranges, in the lower left of the poster. The crucial juncture is located from the ages of fifteen to nineteen. As the poster proposes, the independent thinking reached at this stage can lead to the development of a good or a bad personality.

The little figure on the poster has clearly taken the wrong turn toward the development of a bad personality. The path it has chosen is colored red and points downward to a destination designated as "hell." No longer innocently white, the figure on the wrong path is painted black. Fortunately, however, the figure encounters a blockade, which stops it from proceeding farther down. It turns around and walks on a new

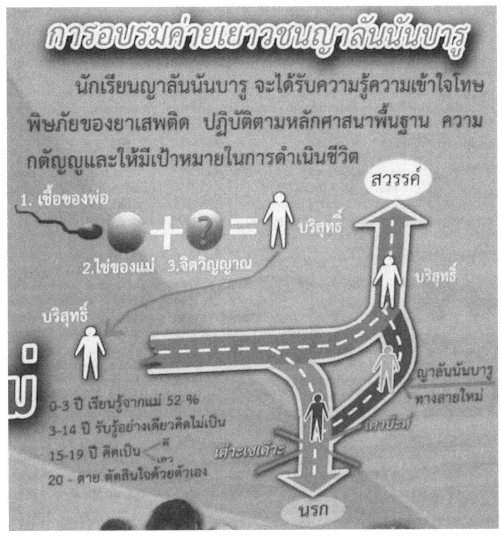

Figure 7. Core instruction poster at the Yalannanbaru camp, October 2011.
Photograph by the author.

path, which is painted blue and labeled in Thai script as both Yalannanbaru and the Thai translation of "new path" (*tang sai mai*).

The poster's emphasis on different stages of development according to age ranges reverberates with behavioral psychology—an important influence on counterinsurgency practices in general, and on the Cold War counterinsurgency campaign in Thailand in particular. Characteristic of these approaches are ideas of insurgency prophylaxis, which concentrate on the psychological status of individuals. Potentially toxic emotions that purportedly animate insurgencies are subjected to immediate treatment. The emotional disorder of individuals thereby becomes an explanatory factor for political rebellions, while psychological therapy is transformed into a means of policing the population.[31]

The poster's simplistic and teleological narrative, in fact, connects ideas of individual downfall and progress with the danger of insurgency and the prospect for peace. Thus, it is no coincidence that the wrong path on the poster is painted red, and that the figure walking toward hell at the bottom of the poster has darkened to pitch black. Counterinsurgents use a color code to designate the degree of insurgent infiltration in the southern provinces, with green signifying secure areas and red the most dangerous ones. In addition, insurgents are commonly associated with darkness and dark influences.[32] In short, the red path on the poster clearly also depicts the danger of deficient and disoriented Muslim subjects taking the wrong turn toward the insurgency. Yalannanbaru not only offered those subjects the possibility of returning to a new path of individual progress but also connected this offer with the prospect of peace in the southern provinces. Thus, after successful completion of the training, participants were given T-shirts bearing the happy proclamation "Yalannanbaru . . . to peace!" The green lettering mirrored the green figure on the new path of the camp poster and matched the counterinsurgency color code for those villages free from insurgents.

At Yalannanbaru, however, religious practices rather than psychological treatment were enlisted to choreograph Muslim subjects' return to national progress and peace. The introductory explanation written at the top of the poster states that participants are to learn to practice their lives according to the basic principles of "religion" (satsana). The poster contains one obvious reference to Islam; the decisive barrier that hinders subjects from walking farther down the wrong path is described by the Malay terms tawba and tak se dok, which designate two steps in the practice of sincere repentance, with the latter entailing the obligation to never repeat the sin.

More prominent on the poster, however, are notions from the Theravada Buddhist tradition, the most obvious being the concept of the path itself. A metaphor central to many Buddhist traditions, the path generally prescribes a soteriological regimen of personal training that leads toward Buddhist awakening.[33] In the Thai context, more specifically, the notion of the Buddhist middle path has been prominent in royal propagations of sufficiency economy, a moralizing project that calls on Thai citizens to practice moderation instead of following the uncontrolled consumption of greedy capitalists.[34] Most importantly, it has also appeared in formulations of the counterinsurgency strategy for southern Thailand. For instance, Prime Ministerial Order 68, issued under the Thaksin government in 2004, invokes the path as a metaphor for the deradicalization of insurgents. The government, it states, should embark on a political offensive to fight radical mindsets (of insurgents, that is) and bring radicals back onto the middle path.[35]

The fact that a counterinsurgency training camp is called the "New Path" and uses the path metaphor as a central motif for instruction neatly illustrates the hegemony of Buddhism in the Thai imperial formation. The Buddhist path at Yalannanbaru is part of a discourse that refers to Buddhist principles to define the proper and virtuous individual behavior of Muslim subjects and implicitly conjoins these normative ideas of a proper religious subjectivity with the stability and peace of the state. As is typical of secular states, the precepts of one religion are universalized and unmarked as the hegemonic standard, with Buddhism here occupying the powerful position usually reserved for Christianity, implying that the peacefulness of Muslims is measured by their alignment with the Buddhist path.

Another illustration of the use of this secular Buddhist discourse to discipline Muslim subjects is the significance of the notion of gratefulness in the Yalannanbaru training. The introductory text of the core poster describes one aim of the camp as training students to practice gratitude, which ranks as one of the most significant moral emotions in the Buddhist tradition. The word for gratitude used on the poster, *katanyu*, etymologically derives from Pali and literally means "knowing what was done" and "acknowledging past services." In the Theravada Buddhist tradition, *katanyu* is instilled through the telling of Buddhist histories and, in particular, through the histories of the past self-sacrificing lives of the Buddha; it is "then embodied in a moral subjectivity that is understood to condition devotional acts."[36] Central to the notion of gratitude in the Buddhist tradition is an ethic of dependency on past benefactors that recognizes the necessity of a moral community for a felicitous future. Emotions like gratefulness are consequently considered productive of virtuous persons, compelling them to practice ethical reflection and acts of ritual that are beneficial to individual moral development and progress along the Buddhist path. This emphasis on the notion of gratitude opens an affective register in the secular production of proper religious subjects at Yalannanbaru and enlists moral emotions key to the Buddhist tradition to incorporate Muslim subjects into the Thai imperial formation.

Although not apparent at first sight, a racial referent also significantly shapes the notion of gratitude in the Thai context. Luang Wichit Wathakan, chief ideologue for Field Marshal Plaek Phibunsongkhram and his racial policies in the mid-twentieth century, dedicated a long section to gratefulness in his well-known book *Thailand's Case*. Wichit constructed gratitude as both part of Buddhist teachings and an essential quality of the Thai race. Thai people, he wrote, "have this quality not by education but by instinct: the Thais are born grateful."[37] The Yalannanbaru training illustrates a similar racialized construction of gratefulness. If Thais were born grateful, the young Malay men of the southern provinces were not naturally grateful; they required military training to educate them in an essential moral trait that characterized the Thai race.

Of course, what lurks behind efforts to bring subjects back onto the new path is the danger of them continuing downward along the wrong path, commonly understood by the training staff as the danger of religious indoctrination. A paramilitary soldier working at the camp, for instance, outlined that insurgents were instilling in poorly educated youth wrong ideas about Islam in order to deploy them as instruments for the insurgent cause.[38] Another military staff member expressed his fear that insurgents were brainwashing young men by filling their heads with what he called "wrong ideology."[39]

Legitimizing the Yalannanbaru training intervention, in other words, was a discourse that positioned its young Muslim participants as vulnerable subjects already walking on the wrong path. One internal document characterized these subjects with a series of lacks: a lack of self-esteem, a lack of purpose in life, and a lack of religious discipline.[40] Violence emerged in this discourse as the result of victimized Muslims too weak to defy instrumentalization. In this sense, what the military called the "wrong" understanding of Islam threatened the overall stability of the state. The vulnerability of young Muslim men also precipitated the vulnerability of the imperial formation. Against this background, the teaching of what counterinsurgents described as the proper understanding of Islam was of central importance at Yalannanbaru.

THE COMMON GOOD

Directly linked with the poster on leading a virtuous life was a poster used for a camp lesson called the "Exercise on the Common Good," which was particularly important because it negotiated the difference of the southern Muslim population. The key message of the lesson was that both Muslim and Buddhist traditions were principally good religions that eventually met on a common path of good morals. That is, this lesson strived to produce Muslim subjects as commensurably different, a commensurability that would enable them to be incorporated into the imperial formation. Crucially, the normative yardstick used to measure moral goodness was again based on Buddhist principles.

In contrast to the projected universality of the exercise on the new path, the narrative of the second poster starts with asserting the particularity and difference of Buddhist and Muslim traditions. On the bottom of the poster, the different countries of origin, languages, and main scriptural sources of Buddhism and Islam are described. Buddhism emerges in India and Islam in Saudi Arabia; Pali and Thai are designated as belonging to Buddhism in contrast to the Arabic and *Yawi*, which are connected to Islam; and the Buddhist canon is distinguished from the Quran.[41] These two paths eventually intersect, however, in terms of their common moral principles, described in Buddhist terms on the poster as *dharma*.

The staff handbook had instructors explain that there was only one direct path to goodness, and that this path was common to both Buddhist and Muslim traditions. When asked about the exercise, the camp director further clarified that it was important to teach "them" (Muslim participants) that "they are all part of our nation, they are all Thai" and that "they are not different."[42] Thus instructors encouraged participants to draw the national flag under the common path of morality, and explained that misunderstandings between different communities of Thailand were wrong and unnecessary.

At the same time, however, the two paths at the bottom of the poster depict the underlying assertion of difference that constitutes the imperial formation. By attempting to overcome this difference, the poster reinscribes religion as the core distinction between Muslim and Buddhist subjects. Moreover, the collapsing of this difference into one common path echoes ideas of the secular universality of the state—with one decisive alteration. As noted above, the common path here is openly configured in Buddhist terminology as *dharma*. Buddhist ideas of morality thus become the normative benchmark for what counts as commensurable Muslim religiosity and for what should be excluded from it. In addition, given the emphasis on self-development at Yalannanbaru, the journey depicted on the poster also operates on a subjective level. The training aspired to produce correct Muslim subjects who believed in a common religious morality transcending religious differences. Such an understanding of Islam does not challenge the Buddhist moral principles structuring the imperial formation.[43]

Both signs and trainers at the camp frequently referred to a generalized notion of religion. A sign at the main camp site, for instance, prohibited smoking with the additional statement that smoking was against "religious regulations." Likewise, one of the senior staff members explained that she did not need to study Islam in detail because it was more important to learn about moral messages and religious prohibitions so that counterinsurgents could use Islam to teach participants how to abstain from bad deeds.[44] All Thais, she thus implied, shared common moral norms regardless of their respective beliefs. In addition, her instrumental approach to Islam as a local variety of universal religion carried traces of the depoliticizing counterinsurgency rationale, which reduces Islam to a disciplinary framework designed for governing Muslim subjects.

Importantly, the poster and the instructors used Central Thai to teach participants about the common path to goodness. Thus, an implicit connection between the Thai language and Buddhist morals oriented the common path, again hinting at the racialized subtext of Yalannanbaru. As discussed in the previous chapter, Central Thai has been positioned at the apex of a racialized taxonomy of languages that places Malay at the bottom. This normative hierarchy was conveyed by trainers to camp participants as a subjective deficiency; it was they who supposedly lacked proper language skills and required tutoring. Instructors would, for instance, frequently support participants in writing posters in Thai and correct their spelling mistakes.[45] At the same time, in their role as tutors, military instructors could display benevolence and understanding; they were not trying to convert young men but rather to bridge differences through reference to a common overarching Thai morality.

DISCIPLINE AND PRAYER

The training at Yalannanbaru was clearly a form of discipline in Foucault's sense of the word: it worked through norms that classified individuals hierarchically and that relied on notions of religion and morality drawn, however implicitly, from the Theravada Buddhist tradition to position individuals on the correct or the wrong path. Furthermore, epitomizing one of the core modes of disciplinary power, Yalannanbaru followed a temporal model of linear development that was oriented towards an ideal final destination.[46] The posters discussed above exemplify this linear structure.

Two other Thai models of disciplinary practice reverberate with the Yalannanbaru program: Buddhist monastic ordination and military conscription. In Thailand, Buddhist ordination still constitutes a central rite of passage for young men. As well as allowing individual families to organize ordinations throughout the year, Buddhist temples across Thailand also hold popular summer ordination programs for young boys (aged from ten to seventeen) every year during the summer holidays. This practice of ordination thus connects a certain notion of masculinity with ideas of religious discipline. In line with ascetic traditions, it teaches renunciation of the world, mindful spirituality, and bodily control as Buddhist principles central to male maturity. Military conscription in Thailand occurs at a slightly later age and has an analogous function. Like Buddhist ordination, military training aims to promote self-control and self-discipline as ways to heighten masculine authority. Consequently, military-monastic regimes of discipline undergird ideas of male maturation and strength in the Thai context.[47]

EMBODYING GOOD HABITS

Yalannanbaru instructors framed the setup of the camp as a disciplinary lesson. Using a typical means of disciplinary enclosure, they required camp participants to leave their family homes and stay for one week in an unfamiliar and often uncomfortable environment in order to accommodate themselves to a different way of life. In addition, participants had to learn to submit to specific camp regulations that entailed performing the virtues of respect and patience. The term used for rules and regulations in the staff handbook, *rabiap winai*, is used in military parlance to describe soldiers' duties, hinting at direct overlaps with the discipline taught in military training.[48]

The overall framework of the camp also in some ways resembled that of a Buddhist monastery. Thus, in contrast to military training camps, participants were not allowed to have contact with the outside world during the training; they had to leave their cell phones with the staff at the beginning of the camp. In addition, the spatial setup and the simplicity of accommodation were reminiscent of Buddhist forest temples in Thailand. The central hall used for group activities had a function similar to the main communal building of a monastery, while the sleeping huts dispersed around the area resembled the "small houses," simple huts where monks live on a temple compound. The seven-day stay at the camp, although much shorter than the usual three months that young Thai men spend in Buddhist temples to be ordained, was a set period of time during which participants were, as discussed previously, supposed to undergo a change of subjectivity and learn to follow a new path to moral improvement.

Yalannanbaru was temporally organized according to a strict disciplinary regimen. The first day of a session began around 10:30 a.m., when participants arrived at the camp with their families or in vans organized by the military, but the wake-up time on all other days was 5 a.m., and participants performed morning prayer as the first scheduled activity. Aside from regular breaks to eat meals, activities usually ran until 10 p.m. Moreover, instructors were keen to teach young men to be on time. Thus, the facilitator of an exercise would regularly refer to a large clock hung in the central meeting hall when designating a certain time for group work or a lunch break. Participants who were late were singled out and warned to be on time in the future. The strict temporal regimen echoed both assumptions about southern Muslim men's lack of self-discipline and ideas about the southern provinces as underdeveloped; it aimed at directing those subjects lagging behind back onto Thailand's national path of progress.

On the first day, instructors divided participants into groups distinguished by differently colored kerchiefs, which were reminiscent of those used by boy scouts and in paramilitary training.[49] They functioned both to symbolize a new camp identity and group loyalty and to discipline participants. Trainers referred to different color groups, for instance, to organize group activities such as drawing posters, and participants had to perform various small-group tasks throughout the camp, so that they learned to react whenever their color group was asked to perform an exercise such as standing up or clapping hands. These tasks were meant to train young men to develop quick physical reactions and had a militaristic flavor. The central clapping exercise, for instance, involved a succession of three rhythmic claps building up to shouting the slogan "We fight!" (rao su). Participants had to raise their right hands and repeat the exercise if the clapping was not performed in the proper rhythm or the slogan was not shouted loudly enough.

What was being fought at the camp was an internal, moral battle. On the fourth day, one of the instructors gave a lecture titled "Life Is Fighting," which, according to the staff handbook, was to support participants in their moral struggle toward a new goal in life. Instructors usually showed short videos of people who were physically disabled living full lives despite their disabilities. In one clip, a man who had lost his hands was shown living a relatively normal life using only his feet and legs.[50] Fighting, in this context, clearly linked disciplined and strong bodies to notions of moral strength and goodness and thus to the correct path of virtuousness and peace that structured the whole Yalannanbaru camp.

Foucault's notion of discipline is helpful to understand this focus on the embodiment of good habits at Yalannanbaru. In Discipline and Punish, Foucault explains that discipline emerged as an art of the human body that joined its productivity with its submission. Discipline functions by making bodies more obedient as they become more useful, "so that they may operate as one wishes, with the technique, the speed, and the efficiency that one determines." It is through this subtle relation, rather than through an openly violent appropriation of bodies or unlimited domination, that discipline produces bodies as docile.[51]

To unravel the operation of discipline at Yalannanbaru, however, it is necessary to grasp discipline's function in religious traditions. As Talal Asad elaborates, disciplinary practices at medieval Christian monasteries aimed to form and transform moral dispositions, in this case especially true obedience to God. Discipline here was not instrumentally deployed by an authority but rather worked as a habituated body practice that made obedience to God an individual virtue of the monk. Similarly, discussing a Muslim mosque movement in contemporary Egypt, Saba Mahmood argues that disciplinary practices serve to form those "pious dispositions" necessary for the realization of a "pious self." Likewise, one of the key text collections of the Buddhist tradition, the *vinaya*, functions as a disciplinary code by which Buddhist monks and nuns conduct an ascetic life in line with the Buddhist path to awakening. Covering areas such as diet, comportment, and exemplary behavior, the *vinaya* code prescribes how to disengage from the world and how to govern both the body and the mind. As in practices of Christian monasticism and Muslim piety, disciplinary practices in the Buddhist monastic tradition thus aim to refashion the self and develop particular virtues. The embodied practice of the *vinaya* code itself carries moral value within the framework of the Buddhist tradition.[52] In all three religious traditions, crucially, the docility of the body is not necessarily linked to submission to an authority but increases the virtue of the disciplined practitioner.

Combining techniques of the monastery and the military camp, instruction at Yalannanbaru deployed a counterinsurgency version of general morality to highlight the value of participants embodying specific disciplinary practices. On the one hand, linking embodied discipline to the achievement of moral virtues seems to reverberate with Buddhist monastic tradition. On the other hand, however, the deployment of a generalized idea of morality in a counterinsurgency context aims to create a relationship of submission that echoes the kind of discipline that Foucault elaborates. In other words, the camp deployed a secular appropriation of Buddhist monastic disciplinary practices for counterinsurgency purposes that grounded lack of discipline in the difference of Islam.

The teaching of hygiene, which formed a constitutive part of the camp schedule, provides a good exemplification of this point. The different color groups at Yalannanbaru were also organized as teams for cleaning camp facilities. Cleaning was usually scheduled for the morning and involved the dormitories as well as the bathrooms. Groups were also assigned to clean up the kitchen area after each meal. Camp assistants verified the cleanliness of facilities and checked whether each of the camp participants had properly washed themselves and dressed appropriately. In one instance, an instructor summoned a participant to the front of the group, removed his kerchief, and tied it around his neck in the correct manner.[53]

One of the military instructors at the camp, soldier Sa., explained in an interview the significance of hygiene and propriety as part of the Yalannanbaru training schedule. He clarified that young men should not only be taught the value of cleanliness but also be instructed to embody hygienic practices: "We have to make the kids keep these rooms clean so that it becomes a habit. . . . We want them to see it as a regular activity. Having them do it very often makes them do it at home." Soldier Sa. later justified the enforcement of such practices by referring to a notion of good habits: "It's like trying to create small habits, what they call 'good habits.' When you are here in the camp, we create good habits. Once you have become used to doing good things, you will be on the good side. . . . They [the camp participants] will not like it and feel uncomfortable with it, and ask: 'Why do we have to do all these things?' But they don't know. We force them so that they get physically used to it."[54]

Soldier Sa.'s reasoning echoes imperial legitimations of colonial rule. He conceived of the young men as passive subjects, dependent on their military tutors for learning practices as basic as hygiene, and portrayed camp participants as inherently dirty, in line with constructions of southern Thailand as a less developed area inhabited by a racially darker populace. Young men raised in this environment, soldier Sa. seemed to suggest, embodied the dirty habits of the South and consequently required military hygiene. Sa.'s narrative here clearly resonates with the racialized ideas of hygiene that characterized the imperial civilizing mission of "washing and clothing the savage."[55]

Other Yalannanbaru instructors commonly expressed similar assumptions about the supposedly unclean habits of the southern population. One staff member, for instance, explained that young men in the South did not keep themselves and their environment clean and littered thoughtlessly. She referred to the central airport at Hat Yai, which in her eyes became especially dirty when families were seeing off relatives headed to Meccah. In a similar vein, one of the military instructors reasoned that young men in the southern provinces were unclean because "normally at home they never get up early, and other people clean up for them."[56]

In the disciplinary cure that soldier Sa. envisioned for this perceived lack of hygiene in southern young men, the body formed the primary target. What he called creating good habits is geared toward the embodiment of practices that accord with hygiene norms set by the military—body discipline is to effect a change of moral attitudes. In terms of the Yalannanbaru choreography, good habits would supposedly keep young men on the good path that led to the good side of the Thai state.

This focus on the body also depends on a typically imperial and integrally gendered division between rationality and irrationality that builds on the Cartesian divide between mind and body. Mirroring the construction of feminized and racialized Others "as enmeshed in [their] bodily existence in a way that makes attainment of rationality questionable," imperial discourses have often portrayed people of certain races and religions as incapable of abstraction and, consequently, more susceptible to embodied disciplinary regulation.[57] As discussed in chapter 2, Orientalists deduced from the grammatical structure of the Thai and Malay languages that the people of these races had a "defect in their logical powers." A similar racial logic still conceptualizes Muslims as governed by Islamic rituals of the body rather than their rational minds. Precisely this conception of Muslims as fundamentally embodied, and consequently racialized and feminized, subjects was implicit in the way soldier Sa. framed the hygiene training.

ENFORCING MUSLIM PRAYER

Muslim prayer played an important role in the camp curriculum. It was usually led by the camp's *ustadz* in the central meeting hall. Participants laid out long mats on the tiled floor of the hall, and the *ustadz* used a small prayer mat. Everyone had to wash themselves before praying, and some also changed into sarongs. Participants then stood in two or three rows during the prayer. On Fridays, soldiers drove the camp participants into the center of the town of Yala for the Friday prayer at the central mosque.[58]

Praying was not a voluntary activity at the camp. It was mandated at certain times of the day, enforced by military instructors, and framed as a necessary part of instructing participants to embody disciplinary practices. Thus, staff emphasized that they aspired to help participants properly practice Islam rather than just to provide them with access to correct Islamic teachings.[59] The staff handbook framed this everyday practice as a necessary part of a religious life and specifically referred to the notion of a Muslim way of life. As expressed in one of the strategy reports, teaching participants to live by the Muslim way of life was to enhance their faith (*sata*), which would also help young men to stay on the right path with confidence and determination.

The disciplinary element of the Muslim way of life was encapsulated in a timetable that hung in the center of the camp, entitled "Everyday Islamic Practices of Yalannanbaru Students." As Ustadz A. explained, the trainers attempted to adapt the camp curriculum to Islamic "religious tasks" as much as possible so that young Muslim men would "learn to live their religion on an everyday basis in the correct manner."[60] The schedule listed the precise timing of over twenty different activities that participants were obliged to follow throughout the day. Curiously, the program listed the five times for Muslim prayer at the exact same times every day—although prayer times alter with the changing position of the sun on an almost daily basis. This temporal regime followed secular timing instead of the continuously changing time of the Islamic tradition. The translation of traditional practices and their temporal regime into a secular disciplinary schedule not only enabled the surveillance and precise repetition of practices but also transformed their purpose and status. Praying was made equivalent to activities such as cleaning (scheduled at 7 a.m.), and similarly served the embodiment of good habits. Counterinsurgents sought to redirect submission to God, which practitioners embodied through the act of praying, to submission to military discipline and the accompanying counterinsurgency version of morality.

It was soldier Sa. who, again, was most outspoken about the obligation of Muslim participants to pray regularly. In line with other staff members, he emphasized that the religious activities at the camp did not cover any "high religious teachings." Rather, these activities instructed participants "to directly apply and exercise religion." He explained: "Even if they don't understand, we have to make them pray. You can compare this to a child who is sick and does not want to take medicine. The child does not want to have the medicine, because it's bitter and does not feel good, but we have to force him to have it, sometimes we have to put it in his mouth. . . . So in the seven days and six nights that we have at the camp, we have to force them to pray. If they pray every day at the camp and then go home after that they might be able to change."[61]

It is no coincidence that soldier Sa.'s depiction of praying at Yalannanbaru strongly resembled his elaboration on teaching hygiene cited in the previous section, although he expressed the notion of force here even more pointedly by justifying the coercion of prayer as a curative exercise. Even if the regular practice of prayer was resisted by participants, he seemed to suggest, the trainers were right to compel participants in their mission to improve and cultivate unreligious and metaphorically sick Muslim subjects. Whereas in monastic traditions self-submission to a disciplinary regime comes with a specific agency and potentiality, soldier Sa.'s statement revealed the near erasure of the agency of Muslim participants. He compared them to helpless and ignorant children who depended on benevolent military authority to direct them to the proper practice of their own religion. Such likening of participants to children, moreover, once again directly replicated imperial rhetoric that constructed colonized subjects as uneducated children requiring the paternal guidance guaranteed by colonial rule.[62]

Two issues are at play in this paternalistic relationship of Buddhist soldiers attempting to teach what they defined as significant Muslim practices to Muslim subjects. One is, again, the imperial practice of policing religious traditions in order to cultivate what colonial authorities construed as more civilized conduct. The other is the racialized and Orientalist assumptions mentioned above: that Muslims primarily define themselves through their religion and that their bodies are saturated with traditional practice. Ironically, however, not only is the Muslim landscape of southern Thailand diverse but southern Thai Muslims are also known for their moderate religious practice. Many villagers that I interacted with, for instance, did not follow a strict prayer schedule, a fact that advocates of different reformist movements regularly complain about.[63] At Yalannanbaru, it was thus the secular project of policing young Muslim men through mobilizing their religious practices that effectively increased the overall significance of the category of religion and strengthened certain practices that were defined as religious.

The notion of spirituality was key in this regard; as mentioned above, it functioned as the third factor necessary for the very conception of a human being on the core Yalannanbaru poster. Colonel S., in fact, held that practicing Islam properly could also teach young men to recognize their spiritual selves that existed beyond their material bodies.[64] Other trainers similarly highlighted that praying was a means to heighten the individual self-discipline of participants and support them in nurturing their own spirituality.

Framed in this way, the camp rules were also intended to train participants in gaining mindful control over their bodily cravings, and thus resonated with ascetic codes of conduct typical of the Buddhist monastic tradition. Allowing only a short period for sleep, for instance, required participants to remain awake and focused during the day despite their fatigue. In a similar manner, participants were regularly instructed to exercise patience before they were served food, and thus to overcome their physical feelings of hunger in order to practice proper virtuous conduct. In addition, participants had to sit in uncomfortable positions, closely resembling the typical seated *vipassana* meditation position, whenever they were seated in the central hall and listening to the instructions of the facilitator.

Crucially, this emphasis on the need for spiritual and physical self-government not only borrowed from Buddhist practices but also dovetailed with concerns raised by both Muslim reformists in the region and Muslim instructors at the camp. Ustadz A., for instance, referred to young men's lack of proper, disciplined prayer as a proof not only of their deficient religious practice but also of their confusion about their own religious identities. The southern Thai conflict, he reasoned, had damaged religious life in the southern provinces, and insurgents had profited from young men who were disoriented in their religious self-development. As he expressed it, young people no longer "knew themselves" properly and could therefore easily become objects of insurgent indoctrination. A local paramilitary at Yalannanbaru argued along similar lines; a key rationale for teaching Islamic practice, he explained, was the aspiration that young men could thereby learn to control both their minds and bodies, and thus resist being lured into the insurgency movement.[65]

Another way to teach self-discipline was the membership card that was given to each participant on the last day of the program. The membership number was printed on the front with the camp logo, and on the back the camp's schedule was printed with the title "Muslim religious schedule." As symbolized by the card, the training not only appealed to participants as members of the Yalannanbaru club but also aspired to prolong its disciplinary project beyond the one-week stay. Instructors wanted participants to keep practicing their religion properly on a disciplined daily basis after the program ended.

The enforcement of Muslim prayer at Yalannanbaru epitomized the military's mobilization of religious practices to police young Muslim men. Counterinsurgents claimed cultural sensitivity for not only respecting local religious practices but also effectively supporting the Muslim reformist agenda of strengthening their implementation. At the same time, they thereby significantly transformed praying into a practice of discipline within a counterinsurgency framework. In this militarized approach, which in some ways also appropriated Buddhist monastic codes of conduct, praying became a spiritual practice that was supposed to cure vulnerable subjects of their potential susceptibility to the insurgency movement. Far from constituting a practice that enhanced individual agency, praying was enforced on Muslim subjects to police their religiosity and make them fit with the counterinsurgency version of morality—one that reinforced the supposedly good order of the Thai imperial formation.

POLICING AFFECT

Policing the religiosity of Muslim participants often converged with policing their affective states, and gendered constructions of the family, especially the idea of the mother, were strategically deployed to this end at Yalannanbaru. As Ann Laura Stoler has shown for the Dutch East Indies, the policing of affect operated on two registers vital to colonial rule. On the one hand, policies sought to cultivate emotional dispositions in the children of colonizers to mark their membership in the white ruling elite; on the other, monitoring and managing the affect of colonized subjects, especially those deemed unruly or of mixed race, was central to the colonial state's "homage to reason."[66] What undergirded both efforts was an anxiety about the precariousness of the imperial formation. Through the policing of affective states, in other words, colonial governments sought to define the unstable boundaries of difference that formed the foundation of imperial rule.[67]

As exemplified in the counterinsurgency motto, the policing of southern Thailand similarly operates on a discourse that constructs the southern provinces as a distant country that Thailand has to understand, reach out to, and develop. The motto reveals a perception of southern Thailand that, in a manner typical of imperial settings, links geographical distance with a hierarchical set of differences that supposedly determine backward status (see introduction). In affective terms, however, this discursive distance of the deep south also produces an anxiety about the vulnerability of the imperial formation.

This worry undergirds a range of affective formulations evident even in official counterinsurgency policy. Prime Ministerial Order 206 (2006), for instance, describes the main objective of counterinsurgency as building a friendly "atmosphere" that would facilitate the creation of "love, unity, reconciliation, and peace in society." One of the regulations of the order directs counterinsurgents to eradicate those factors that foster people's disaffection. Counterinsurgents are to "reach out" to people and create both "proper feelings" and the "proper atmosphere" for "people to realize that everyone can live in Thailand with dignity and happiness in terms of their own way of life, society, religion, and culture."[68]

In these formulations, counterinsurgency is clearly configured as a project of altering the affective states of potentially unruly subjects so that they accept the order of the imperial formation. This emotional counterinsurgency discourse has depoliticizing effects. Emotions such as love and harmony, explicitly invoked by the order to bridge religious divides, obscure the inequalities that shape the ways different religious traditions can be lived in Thai society. At the same time, this affective discourse reconfigures political demands voiced by the insurgency movement as states of emotional confusion that a therapeutic counterinsurgency intervention can supposedly eradicate.

Psychological discourse has certainly fed into this emphasis on affect in counterinsurgency generally, and at Yalannanbaru more specifically. Not only have some counterinsurgency techniques developed in close alliance with different strands of psychology such as behavioral and social psychology but psychological interventions were also prevalent in the anticommunist counterinsurgency campaign in Thailand. At Yalannanbaru, military psychologists helped design the schedule, and one of them openly explained that the "creation of emotions" was integral to the whole program. Emotions, she clarified, were indispensable to the kind of "behavioral change" that the camp staff wanted to effect in young men at Yalannanbaru. In this regard, she highlighted the significance of the teachings on family and the role of mothers, borrowing from gendered stereotypes of women as both more emotional and more skilled in dealing with emotions than men.[69]

The orchestration of sentiment at Yalannanbaru also borrowed from Buddhist and Islamic traditions to emotionally discipline subjects to stay on the path of morality in the imperial order of the state. Although referencing moral emotions from the Buddhist tradition such as gratitude, the camp—in marked contrast to monastic practices in a Buddhist context—did not aim to enhance emotional self-control, but rather to intensify affects in specific, often highly symbolic, instances. And whereas for Muslims pious practice entails nurturing an affective relationship to the Prophet that allows them to emulate him, this "labor of love" at Yalannanbaru was redirected to serve the Thai state.[70] To this end, instructors also mobilized gendered images of the family, especially the tropes of the inherently good mother and her potentially bad sons who had fallen onto the wrong path, thus shaping, in affective terms, a familial model of authority that mirrored the imperial order.

PAIN AND GRATITUDE

Although gratitude (*katanyu*) already figured on the camp poster as a condition for the production of virtuous persons, it was further elaborated in camp lessons through the trope of the mother and depictions of her pain at childbirth. In the Theravada Buddhist tradition, gratitude is frequently figured in traditional stories about parental love, where the Buddha is, for instance, described as a "parent to all beings."[71]

In exercises on gratitude, Yalannanbaru trainers replicated patriarchal interpretations of the Theravada Buddhist order still rehearsed in Thai society, which contrast the mother and her natural attachment to the material world through childbirth with the notion of otherworldly spiritual detachment primarily attained by male monks. In Thailand, the ordination of women is still considered unusual because it departs from these gendered norms. The practice of ordaining young men in Buddhist monasteries reproduces this dichotomy and reinscribes a specific mother-son relationship marked by mutual moral responsibilities. In this stereotypical relationship, the mother gains moral merit through maternal sacrifice, which is symbolically represented in the pain of childbirth. In return, sons can repay their moral debt through practicing strict discipline and earning spiritual merit in monastic education. Against the backdrop of this orchestrated reciprocal relationship, male ordination in Thailand obtains an additional important function: to train male offspring as virtuous moral beings who show gratitude and respect to their mothers as nurturers and life givers. This relationship of mutual dependence and moral obligation between mother and son is also frequently used as part of moral education in Thai schools.[72] In the Thai context, gratitude is an emotional disposition that operates on a traditional Buddhist grammar, but it also has become centrally implicated in secular projects such as schooling, where it is used to emotionally discipline children to obey familial authority.

On the fourth night, instructors showed a video of a mother giving birth that displayed her extreme pain in great detail. The facilitator framed the video by playing two songs frequently used for moral education in Thai primary schools that concern the sacrifice mothers make and the pain they endure in giving birth to and bringing up their children. One, entitled "Tears of a Mother," tells the story of a poor mother who sells grilled bananas to support her family, and contrasts her suffering with an ungrateful son who spends his mother's money on drugs. The trainer explicitly connected the theme of the mother's pain to the young male participants at Yalannanbaru and pointed out that participants had caused their mothers great pain through the process of birth. Even worse, he added, they continued to inflict great pain on her through their ongoing bad behavior.

On the next day, instructors proceeded to address camp participants as bad sons in a group activity in which participants were asked to draw tables of comparison on large white sheets of paper. On the left side of the table, they had to write down keywords about the kinds of trouble they had already caused their parents. Points that participants mentioned included not listening to their parents, not attending school regularly, and even stealing money from family members. On the right side, participants were supposed to list the problems their parents had caused them. During the exercise I observed, this column remained blank in all of the groups. Happy about these results, the facilitator reiterated the basic lesson that participants' parents only wanted to do them good yet had been rewarded with a great amount of trouble.

One of the psychological meditations that formed part of the exercise subsequently accelerated the realization of this moral disequilibrium. Here, participants were ordered to stand together silently and were questioned by the facilitator while slow music played in the background. Questions he asked included: "Has your mother ever done anything bad to you?" "What would you be without her?" "Have you always treated her with respect?" "Has she not always responded with kindness and love despite your bad behavior?" These questions not only addressed young men as bad sons but were also clearly aimed at crafting feelings of guilt in relation to their mothers. During this meditation, many of the participants started to cry, a fact that some members of the camp team approved of and eagerly photographed.

It is instructive to read this lesson on gratitude through its successive sequences as generating a paternalistic relationship that structures the Thai imperial formation. The first exercise went back to the act of birth—that is, to the start of the path pictured on the poster about virtuous life explored above, where conception involves a third element in addition to the male sperm and the female ovum. The poster describes this third element as *chit winyan*, a term connected to Buddhist ideas of rebirth and the accumulation of merit. The lesson on birth worked by teaching participants that they were born with a certain level of merit, but it framed this negatively as a moral debt by highlighting that their birth caused excessive pain to their mothers. In this way, the exercise positioned young men in a relationship of moral indebtedness to their life giver.

The next exercise, where participants had to write down key points on a table of moral comparison, objectified this moral disequilibrium that constructed young men as troublemakers. The table implied not only that bad sons were born with a great moral deficit but also that they continued to inflict pain on their mothers through their ongoing immoral behavior, thus adding further to their moral debt. As a contrasting ideal, the notion of gratitude constituted the backdrop of this exercise. It undergirded a reciprocal relationship wherein the good son realized and repaid his moral debts by demonstrating good conduct such as gratitude and respect toward his mother.

The last exercise further individualized this moral debt through psychological meditation as the first step toward self-analysis. The questions that instructors posed in this exercise were normative; they evaluated the actions of participants according to a moral yardstick that operated through a military ideal of gratitude. In light of the inherently good mothers constructed by the military and the ideal reciprocal relation of mutual gratitude, the self-evaluation necessarily produced devastating results for the participants, and allowed military instructors to put young men in a vulnerable position from which a disciplinary project of molding could proceed most effectively. Rather than nurturing a more general ethic of dependency on other moral beings, gratitude in this secularized military version functioned to nurture negative emotions that served to underscore participants' dependency on military tutelage.

Practicing Repentance and Confession

Yalannanbaru strategy papers highlight religious instruction as central to teaching this military version of morality to participants.[73] They suggest that instructors deploy regulations inherent to the Islamic tradition to educate participants about how to properly differentiate between sin and merit, or good and bad behavior. As some Yalannanbaru staff members explained to me, they feared that insurgents would purposely confuse young men by indoctrinating them with a reversed version of sin and merit, teaching them that attacks against the Thai state were morally right.[74] The program consequently aspired to help participants practice what the military defined as the core principles of Islam while teaching them that following the path of the insurgency was a religious sin.

In a similar manner to the lesson on gratitude, the lesson on religious sins was intensified by adding an affective dimension and employing religious practices, this time appropriated from Islam. Thus, trainers mobilized the notion of repentance by referring to *tawba*, a term from Quranic Arabic that designates the practice of sincere repentance to God in the Islamic tradition.[75] As noted previously, on the core Yalannanbaru poster, *tawba* fulfils a key function as the barrier that hinders participants from walking farther down the wrong path and instigates turning back onto the new and correct path. A decisive military twist characterized the practice of *tawba* at the camp, however. Rather than constituting a self-initiated practice of Muslims in front of God, it was part of the schedule and organized as a form of confession to military instructors.

To provoke this specific form of repentance and confession, instructors deployed meditation techniques. In these exercises, meditation was not explicitly marked as

Buddhist but rather functioned as a psychoanalytical practice in accordance with some of its secular usages, which are designed to expose the unconscious to consciousness and liberate individuals from "repressed contents of mind."[76] Thus, after the morning prayer on the second day of a camp session, Yalannanbaru staff introduced meditation as a general technique to teach participants how to achieve concentration (*samathi*), and they underscored the compatibility of meditation with both Buddhism and Islam by outlining that it was also practiced in Saudi Arabia. They then asked participants to stand together in a group, close their eyes, and concentrate on their inner selves. At one of the meditations I observed, the instructor constantly enjoined his disciples to look at their inner brightness (*sawang*) emerging before their closed eyes, and to remain calm and concentrated. After this first introduction, meditation was performed as a regular feature of the schedule, usually two or three times a day.

Extending this practice of self-concentration, instructors employed meditation more directly in conjunction with repentance and confession on the last two days of the camp session. With relaxing music playing in the background, the trainer prompted young men to ask themselves questions about the bad deeds they had committed in the past. Further emphasizing the significance of repentance after such a meditation, facilitators lectured that participants would only have one chance to change their direction in life, and that this opportunity was here and now, provided by the new path camp. This lecturing involved another temporal element, in that instructors explained that there was no possibility of winding back time, and that sincere repentance of past misdeeds was key to opening the gateway to goodness. Again, this exercise ended with a number of participants starting to cry.[77]

On the fifth night, participants had to make their confessions by writing a letter to their mothers. To introduce the letter-writing exercise, the facilitator played yet another song on the topic of motherhood. This song, called "Essay about My Mother," tells the story of a young student who has lost his mother and is confronted with an assignment to write an essay about her. He first cries about his loss and the insurmountable task, but then decides to write the essay nevertheless and express how much he misses her. The song ends on the sentence "I promise that I will always remain a good child." The staff handbook elaborates in detail that facilitators should play this song, explain the main ideas, and read out each sentence of the lyrics to ensure everyone understands them and to motivate participants to write a letter from the very "inside of their hearts" to their mother or the ones they love. The song, moreover, continued to be played as background music during the writing exercise, which was not a private matter but conducted in the main camp hall.

The facilitator collected the letters and gave them to the camp administration before they eventually reached the participants' mothers. As advised in the handbook, staff were to check whether they could discern a change of attitude and to evaluate the training in terms of how much individuals had learned. In addition, these letters also gave direct access to information potentially valuable for counterinsurgency intelligence, which Colonel S. named as a positive side-effect of the camp.[78]

The psychological version of Buddhist meditation that was inserted into this exercise on *tawba* notably contrasts with the *vipassana* practice of meditation common in Theravada Buddhist contexts. Whereas *vipassana* aims at ascetic detachment from internal affective states, the psychomeditative technique at Yalannanbaru was used to provoke a negative affective state in participants. One staff member explained that this self-reflective exercise should help participants to get to know themselves better and see "where they stand."[79]

However, the fact that many participants were reduced to tears illustrates a key precondition for the operation of the exercise; it was constructed in a way that already marked participants as standing on the wrong path. The confessions written by participants to their mothers, after all, helped to create a discourse that positioned Muslim young men as failed subjects in the context of the imperial order of the national family. In this setting, the management of participants' affect also acquired a soteriological dimension, suggesting that psychological disclosure could provide for their future salvation. Repentance was staged as an exercise of purification that supposedly led to a strengthening of the participants, but it simultaneously effected their increased vulnerability in relation to military staff. Feeding into the lesson on gratitude, this affective orchestration of repentance at Yalannanbaru produced docile subjects who were willing to submit themselves to the military version of morality. Repentance, in this military framework, promoted participants' self-subjectification under moral norms that sustain the Thai imperial formation.

ORCHESTRATING MORAL REBIRTH

The choreography of the camp ended with a sentimental closing ceremony that constituted the climax of the whole week, combining elements of the lessons on gratitude and repentance. For this closing event, Yalannanbaru staff invited participants' parents to join and organized buses to the main camp in Yala for those without their own means of transportation. Once there, they were invited to have lunch together with the whole group and watch a presentation on the activities of the past week. Some of the Yalannanbaru assistants photographed and filmed the camp's activities, and they put together short clips that were screened in the central hall in a presentation that resembled a multimedia show. The facilitators explicitly framed the presentation as documenting the progress that participants had made during the week.

The most significant part of the closing ceremony, however, was the staging of confession and forgiveness. Participants' mothers were asked to sit on chairs in a row at the front of the main hall, with their sons kneeling in front of them—these physical positions literalized their respective places in the moral hierarchy (see fig. 8). The young men had to hand over their letters of confession, which they had received back from the Yalannanbaru team. The instructors guided the young men to remain kneeling while they confessed their misdeeds to their mothers. Once their confessions ended, they were allowed to stand up and ask for forgiveness. The enactment of this ceremony was highly emotional. Many of the young men began to weep as they knelt, and a number of the parents present also were in tears when they finally embraced their children.

As opposed to the lessons on gratitude and repentance, however, this closing ceremony had a positive ending, and it staged the possibility of a return to the good path as an act of moral rebirth. As a first step, the mothers were allowed to embrace their children, thus giving a benevolent response that contrasted with any kind of punishment. The act of embracing, furthermore, underscored the mothers' positive moral authority built on stereotypical maternal kindness along with their willingness to forgive.

In this setting, crying was imbued with a positive aspect of purification necessary for participants' return to the military's correct path. Here, the expression of pain of both mother and son centrally conditioned the moral rebirth of formerly bad sons, paving their way to starting a more hopeful new life. As the initial life givers who had endured great pain giving birth to their sons, the mothers were fashioned as instrumental agents

Figure 8. Closing ceremony involving participants' mothers at the Yalannanbaru camp, September 2011. Photograph by the author.

who now enabled the moral return of their offspring. Thus, through the presence of participants' mothers, Yalannanbaru leadership produced a positive reversal of the moralizing story performed in the exercises on gratitude and repentance.

The closing ceremony thereby situated participants' mothers on the good side of the Thai state and enlisted them in the project of policing young Muslim men, who were, by contrast, positioned as morally misled and consequently disloyal to the Thai state. In this framework, the enlistment of mothers thus became an instrumental means to strengthen the affective attachment of potentially unruly subjects to the Thai imperial formation. The celebration of a harmonic reconciliation between mothers and sons also clearly echoed the affective formulations of official counterinsurgency policy, which aims to create "love, unity, reconciliation and peace in society."[80] No wonder this orchestration of positive sentiments and family harmony formed the climax of the Yalannanbaru camp; it suggested military success in the mission of bringing potentially dangerous Muslim subjects back onto the right path of peace and reconciliation, and provided a confirmation of this success in affective terms. If affective counterinsurgency discourse framed political demands potentially voiced by unruly subjects as negative emotions, these were now dissolved through an overarching harmony that celebrated the Thai imperial formation as a family embracing Muslim sons despite their bad behavior.

CHAPTER FOUR

GUARDING THE DAUGHTER

Patriarchal Compromise and Military Sisterhood

In an interview with the southern Thai news service *Isara News* in 2010, General Anupong Paochinda explained that troops were not stationed in southern Thailand to "make war." Rather, he elaborated:

> The two million people [in the southern provinces] are like a daughter, and we are like the father to this daughter. Therefore we have to be on guard to impede any impudent young man who wants to seduce or deceive our daughter. The soldiers who are stationed here fulfill exactly this mission—that is, the mission of "guarding our daughter."[1]

General Anupong's conception of the southern population as being like the daughter of the imperial family epitomizes how the construction of the racialized and religious difference of the people of Patani is both gendered and sexualized. In a stereotypical framing of femininity through sexuality, Anupong implicitly casts the daughter as virgin, evoking a chain of colonial metaphors that have often depicted colonies as chaste women without sexual agency, "passively awaiting the thrusting, male insemination of history, language and reason."[2] This simultaneous feminization and sexualization of the South is, moreover, characteristic in the Thai context and reflects the long-standing sexual economy in the borderland as well as Orientalist ideas of the veiled Muslim virgin.[3] Most crucially, however, it attests to how family law regulations have privatized Islam, helped to conflate it with the feminized and sexualized realm of the family, and thus collapsed the difference of religion into a difference of gender and sex.[4] The South becomes in Anupong's rendering a precious but helpless sexualized object under constant threat from outside intrusion or seduction.

The fatherly protection promised by Anupong resonates with both a paternalism constitutive of modern Thai imperial discourse and imperial legitimations of military violence. Throughout Thailand's modern history, the Chakri dynasty, which has reigned since the late eighteenth century, and a number of military dictators have promoted the idea of the Thai ruler as the father to his Thai children, and contemporary counterinsurgents have associated themselves not only with the monarchy but also with a monarchical model of paternal benevolence.[5] The father, equated by Anupong with the collective "we" of the Thai military, thereby embodies the patriarchal code integral to modern modes of governance. The state's promise of protection from violence, predicated on the idea of male household authority, produces structures of vulnerability that render feminized subjects dependent and vulnerable.[6] In this imperial context, more importantly, the characterization of colonized subjects as feminine legitimizes military intervention in the South as "perhaps a regrettable but nonetheless a necessary component of 'enlightening' and 'civilizing' primitive, unruly (feminized) 'others.'"[7] Anupong's claim that the Thai Buddhist military safeguarded southern Muslim backwardness thus echoes racialized legitimations of violence that have frequently relied on constructions of white men as benevolently protecting brown women from brown men. The claim also reflects Western secular enlistment of Muslim women as objects in need of paternal salvation that resurfaced prominently during the war on terror (see chapter 2).[8]

The daughter in this setting has neither voice nor agency but constitutes the mere ground on which negotiations between men take place. Imperialism consequently emerges as an exclusively male enterprise based on a "traffic in women" between two different patriarch(ie)s that both seek to sexually possess women.[9] The daughter's primary purpose is to establish homosocial bonds between men (albeit ones that are clearly structured hierarchically) while also symbolizing the moral domestic realm of the private as separate from that of immoral public politics. This public-private split maps onto an inequality of rights. In the daughter's status as domestic property, she cannot protest her objectification. Accordingly, the military patriarch regulates her concerns. In effect, she stands for the part of the Muslim population that has been successfully domesticated under the guardianship of the Thai military head of household, a domestication conditioned by the secularization of the Islamic tradition and the racialization of the southern population. The outside intruder, by contrast, represents the untamed threat of insurgents seeking to lure her into political opposition.[10]

The intersectionality of power depicted in Anupong's gloss directly relates to the evolution of the public-private split in Siam/Thailand, which has helped to sustain gendered inequalities of the premodern empire while at the same time crosshatching them with modern categories such as race and religion. Thus the most important premodern legal code in Siam, the Three Seals Law, had through its system of social hierarchy called *sakdina* not only categorized people according to their status as royalty (*chao*), noblemen (*khunnang*), commoners (*phrai*), and slaves (*that*) but also privileged men in each category and controlled women's sexuality in order to uphold ethnic and religious distinctions.[11] Legal reforms at the beginning of the twentieth century replaced the *sakdina* with a division between the public and the private that relegated women to the private sphere; in the public realm, the Thai-Buddhist male became the normative legal standard. Rape, for instance, was excluded from the category of crimes against the public and instead defined as private and compoundable (for crimes in this category, charges can be dropped if the victim agrees). Subsequent laws on citizenship and surnames subordinated women to their husbands and fathers and fortified a patrilineal system.[12] The parallel installation of family law for the southern provinces relegated Islam to the realm of the private, additionally conflating religious difference with the public-private split (see introduction).

Yet no matter how different she is, the Muslim daughter—like other "Others within" Thailand—still belongs to a family that both includes and excludes her.[13] The focus of concern for the Thai military is thus not ultimately the daughter but the respectability of the family. The seduction of the daughter risks sullying the image of the imperial family and putting into question the father's masculine ability to protect; worse, the sexualized intrusion threatens the body politic because the undesired union might yield unwanted offspring. The "mission of 'guarding our daughter,'" as Anupong characterizes the counterinsurgency campaign, consequently aims at policing her sexuality in order to restore both the paternal authority of the Thai state over the southern provinces and the respectful order that regulates the rightful reproduction of the imperial formation. In fact, official terminology consistently invokes ideas of orderliness and propriety. The prime ministerial orders of 2004 and 2006, for instance, describe the insurgency as *panha khwam mai sangop*—literally, "the problematic lack of orderly peace and stability in the three southern border provinces." In military parlance, at the same time, insurgents were often called *phu ko het khwam mai sangop*—"the main actors causing this disreputable unrest."[14]

In the familial order that Anupong imagines, affective relations structure the organization of difference and help to legitimize military intervention. After all, Anupong's paternal love motivates and eventually naturalizes the violence of the counterinsurgency mission. As a point of contrast, Anupong denies the intruder any capacity to love, representing the latter's unsettling of the family union as malign impudence. Meanwhile, Anupong implicitly portrays the daughter as emotionally confused, potentially vulnerable, and unable to act rationally—silencing her actual feelings.

RAPE, RESISTANCE, AND THE SILENCING OF WOMEN

One topic, in particular, revealed the limits to my open and friendly reception by the military. Whenever I attempted to inquire about the official number of soldiers who had committed acts of sexual harassment toward local women, I would get no reply from military informants. Neither my written request to the southern military administration nor my efforts to use unofficial channels was successful. In an interview, the Internal Security Operations Command (ISOC) spokesperson admitted that the military had experienced problems with soldiers who had begun relationships with southern women—even a member of his own team had been sent back home after he had been caught with a woman in the Old Market of Yala. Yet the spokesperson denied that there had been any cases of harassment or rape, and he accused the insurgent movement and students at the Prince of Songkhla University in Pattani of spreading "rape rumors," which he described as "pure lies." Toward the end of the interview, he switched on the air conditioning, and I offered to close the door to increase the cooling effect. Yet he declined: "Why do you want to close the door? Leave it open so that people can see that there's nothing happening between you and me!"[15] The issue of sexual violation, which has haunted the counterinsurgency mission in southern Thailand, surfaced in this encounter in an objectifying and paternalistic joke.

Accusations of rape in the southern Thai conflict are so sensitive for counterinsurgents precisely because they threaten the hierarchy of masculinities that undergirds the imperial formation.[16] Besides the notion of the benevolent father invoked by General Anupong, the idea of the gentleman has significantly shaped the discourse of disciplined soldiering in the Thai context. Both of these models imply sexual restraint (as a mark of either fatherly protection or gentlemanly character, respectively). Both also markedly contrast with stereotypes of southern Muslim men as libidinous and abusive—the intruder in Anupong's gloss—that operate within a larger Orientalist framing of Islam as inherently misogynistic. The Islamic family law in the southern provinces has, moreover, helped to institutionalize this sexualized distinction. For many soldiers, the official licensing of polygynous marriages confirmed the inferiority of the Islamic tradition in the South and resulted in an ever-increasing number of children—too many to be educated properly.[17]

In this setting, the military attempted to strictly police the sexual behavior of its soldiers. Thus, although there were sixteen official rules of engagement for the military in the southern provinces, which were printed on a pocket-size laminated plastic card small enough for soldiers to carry around while on duty, most soldiers only highlighted military concerns about women and drugs.[18] Soldier P., for example, qualified his account of teasing women at checkpoints when asked about these guidelines: "Rules? Yes, there are two big issues. Two things that are really strictly prohibited. The first thing is this issue of affairs with women. To put it very simply, it's strictly forbidden to go and talk and meet them. I mean, you can talk to them just like that, but you are not allowed to talk to them and then get together and keep in contact. That's the first thing. The second thing is drugs. That's the two big things. That's the two big rules of being here."[19]

P., who had been in the army for a number of years, further expressed that he was especially worried about recruits who had affairs with local women. Many young conscripts, he explained, would not realize that by breaching this regulation they could get their team leader as well as the head of their unit into serious trouble. Employing the Thai term *chu sao*, which mostly refers to heterosexual love affairs by married men that are widely normalized in Thailand, he noted that any steps beyond a playful and momentary chat at a checkpoint were strictly prohibited because further contact could lead to a relationship.[20] The notion of sexual restraint implicit in P.'s account once again functioned to determine a hierarchy of masculinities—in this case, one within the military. Likewise, soldiers in higher positions would often deny that there had been any instances of sexual harassment, highlight the existing rules for soldiers, and admit that some younger, inexperienced conscripts from other rural areas of Thailand were sometimes caught having love affairs with local women.

Rape and Resistance

The army's overt emphasis on regulating soldiers' sexual behavior went hand-in-hand with an explosion of rumors in the southern Muslim community that Thai soldiers were not only having relationships with Muslim women but were sexually exploiting or even raping them. I had already heard some of these charges by the time I started to conduct research in the South, and I discovered how ubiquitous they were when I stayed there for several months. Students at the Prince of Songkhla University often mentioned video clips depicting instances of rape that friends had forwarded from their mobile phones. One of the clips that I received in 2011, which a number of nongovernmental organizations in the South later determined to be a fake likely produced and distributed by insurgents, shows a group of five men dressed in black uniforms assaulting a woman in a forest. Black uniforms in southern Thailand are mostly worn by paramilitary rangers—it is often these less educated, lower-class military personnel who are accused of violating women in the South.[21] In the clip, which is two and a half minutes long and saved in the small 3GP format to make it compatible with mobile phones, the camera largely focuses on the pain and distress of the victim, who appears without a headscarf and without a shirt while the rapists laugh in the background. The video ends on a still that foregrounds the woman's suffering face while a soldier in mid-assault smiles behind her. Viewed as insurgent propaganda, the scene is a metaphor for the suffering of the southern population at the hands of the military; here, as in Anupong's gloss, the woman stands in for the South. From this insurgent perspective, the message of the clip is clear. The pain of the southern population is produced for the pleasure of the Thai military; her victimization and complete degradation are the military's sexual satisfaction.

Pamphlets and stories also explicitly treated the topic of rape and were likely systematically spread by insurgents. In one cartoon, soldiers mentally undress three Muslim women crossing their checkpoint and anticipate sexual intercourse. Likewise, the title of another insurgent leaflet was "Mass Interaction or Mass Sexual Intercourse?"[22] In a story similar to that of the video, told by a local informant, two Thai soldiers talk about the beauty of a Muslim woman walking past them in a *niqab*. In order to find out whether she really is beautiful, the soldiers undress her and rape her. According to this informant, soldiers were deliberately stationed in southern villages to encourage sexual relations with local women and "mess up" communities.[23] Others likewise explained that these occurrences were part of an overarching counterinsurgency strategy that paralleled historical attempts by the Thai state to repopulate the area by relocating Buddhists from other Thai provinces to the South, implying that the Thai military was systematically encouraging the sexual exploitation of Muslim women to sexually conquer Patani.[24]

The trope of Thai state officials raping local women in the southern provinces has important precedents and forms a crucial part of the insurgency movement's historical narrative. In 1901, Tengku Abdul Kadir, one of the leaders of the resistance movement active shortly after the formal incorporation of Patani into Siam, appealed to British colonial authorities in Malaya on the grounds that Siamese officers had assaulted, seduced, and abducted local women.[25] Today, the Barisan Revolusi Nasional Coordinate (BRN-C) relays to prospective members that Siamese soldiers violated their great-grandmothers.[26] In insurgent discourse, the violation of women's bodies thus stands for a claim of historical continuity; the violent incorporation of Patani now manifests in the continuing victimization of Muslim women. At the same time, the rape rumors challenge the image of protective fatherhood that undergirded General Anupong's paternalistic vision of rule as well as the image of disciplined masculinity of soldiers that underlies the army's supposedly civilized force.

PATRIARCHAL COMPROMISE

One of the key conditions enabling and accompanying the explosion of rumors about rape was the silence of the victimized women. In most cases, men made political claims based on these silenced victims, and the perpetrators remained unaffected. In 2011, none of the cases that nongovernmental organizations had been trying to examine since 2004 had been investigated by government officials, and only in one highly publicized case were two soldiers who had raped a girl and forwarded a video of the abuse via mobile phone put on military trial in 2012.[27] This lack of official investigation did not only stem from the military's efforts to eliminate all charges against soldiers. Women's groups advocating for victimized women also reported that most were afraid to speak to investigators, and they cautioned that sexuality in general is not talked about openly in the southern provinces.[28]

In ensuring that women themselves had no say, the Thai security forces' policies dovetailed with an existing patriarchal system in the southern provinces that was upheld by, *inter alia*, the Islamic councils—official bodies established by the Thai state in 1947 to govern the Muslim community, which have been authorized to deal with matters of sexuality as a legacy of imperial family law. As Duncan McCargo has pointed out, cooptation has constituted "a central plank of the Islamic council system" since its inception as a top-down bureaucratic structure modeled on the modern Buddhist ecclesiastical system.[29] Currently, the Ministries of the Interior and Education supervise the councils, and since the renewed flare-up of the southern conflict in 2004, Islamic council members have been asked to cooperate even more closely with both government and military authorities.[30]

Interactions between students and lecturers at marriage preparation courses illustrate how sexuality was treated in the context of the southern Islamic councils. These one-day courses were mandatory for all Muslims in the South before marriage, and were aimed at clarifying the roles of women and men in matrimony, including sex education. Different members of the Islamic council, all of them men and of an older generation, were responsible for teaching the mostly young students (male and female). In the courses that I observed, sexuality often surfaced as a male privilege. When one participant asked about the regulation of polygynous marriage in the South, for example, the *ustadz* replied that polygyny was a solution to the problem of illicit relationships. Referring to common gender stereotypes, he elaborated that "men in their fifties experience their second youth" in terms of sexual desire, whereas women lose their sexual feelings at the same age. In this rendering, polygyny formed an outlet for a natural phallic necessity. A similar construction of naturalized male desire frequently emerged in the question and answer sessions at the end of each day. A question asked during another course, for instance, touched on the important issue of sexual consent: "If my husband wants to have sex, but I do not, can I decline?" The teacher's reply again established the man's sexual prerogative. "No," he said, "if there is no obvious reason such as menstruation or sickness, sexual intercourse cannot be rejected."[31] A member of the Islamic council sanctioning nonconsensual sexual intercourse on the grounds of a perpetual male entitlement to sex exemplified a patriarchal compromise at work in the southern provinces that is typical of colonial settings.[32] Male leaders in the councils and the military, regardless of their religious affiliation, were united by framing sexuality as a male prerogative.

It is obvious that in this setting it was hard for young women to talk openly not only about rape by Thai soldiers but about rape in general.[33] Although there are no statistics on sexual violence in the South available, women's groups reported that they sometimes encountered fierce resistance when they sought to raise the topics of sex education and domestic violence at workshops in villages. One group worked together with the Yala Provincial Hospital to secretly provide abortions to women with unwanted pregnancies—in 2009, twenty-nine women in Yala Province had taken this option. Although seeking to support women in these informal ways, activists also clarified that they would need to get the Islamic councils on board if they wanted to lobby for an official investigation of rape charges.[34]

MILITARY TACTICS

The patriarchal system of Islamic councils played into a military discourse that tried to erase any accusations of sexual violation from official record, which significantly hampered official investigations. More generally, practices of sexual exploitation have long been documented as integral to male-dominated military cultures, including peacekeeping and humanitarian operations, and impunity is an important factor in the perpetuation of such practices.[35] In my experience in southern Thailand, however, military commanders did not simply ensure that perpetrators went unpunished; rather, they actively sought to rebuff any accusations of sexual violation, and they deployed three tactics in particular to this end. First, they refused to give any information to outside observers. Second, they remunerated the families of alleged victims with large sums of money in exchange for the families dropping all charges. In one instance relayed to me by a relative of an alleged rape victim from the village of Rueso, the army compensated the family with THB 250,000 (approximately USD 7,500)—a sum that members of the family had hoped to increase to THB 1 million, arguing that it would be very difficult for the girl to find a husband. Nonetheless, the charges were withdrawn.[36]

Third, in one widely publicized case where protests had forced security forces to establish an investigative committee, military authorities worked toward having the committee dissolved. In a Pattani subdistrict in 2007, assailants dressed in black ranger uniforms had stormed a house and killed four members of a Muslim family; one of the survivors asserted that her sister had been raped before she was shot dead. The allegation was highly controversial—government and military officials claimed that the perpetrators were insurgents dressed in ranger uniforms, a claim supported by the fact that bombs were detonated when officials tried to examine the site. Nevertheless, the victim's sister played a central role in mobilizing a large student protest in the town of Pattani that also demanded official inquiry into twenty-one additional alleged cases of rape. A committee established by mediators between the protestors and the authorities to organize such official inquiry, however, never received its promised funding and was dissolved within weeks. According to a prominent women's activist and member of the committee, counterinsurgents had agreed to setting up the committee in order to stop the protests, but were unconcerned with determining the truth. The silence that followed the first and only committee meeting was all that they had wanted to achieve.[37]

Love as Imperial Privilege

In interviews with soldiers and in media representations, a frequent slippage between the notions of rape and romantic relationships between Muslim women and Buddhist soldiers contributed to muting discussions of sexual exploitation. A *Bangkok Post* article on the 2012 rape trial, for instance, is titled "Cross-Cultural Romances Raise Tensions in the South." It briefly mentions that two soldiers have been detained at a military camp pending trial on gang-rape charges, before continuing to discuss a larger problem of "forbidden love" in the "strife-torn region." It cites Col. Thakorn Niemrin of the Fourth Army, who states that the military's "iron rule" prohibiting relationships with local women is "impossible to enforce." Such relationships of "love," the colonel explains, are "natural" and a "matter of the heart." Given the long presence of the army in the South, he estimates the number of relationships to be as high as a thousand. "The best the military can do," the colonel adds, "is to ask commanders to strictly govern their soldiers and to ask those in a relationship to follow traditions, including converting to Islam and organizing a proper ceremony for the woman's family."[38]

The elision of violence through the focus on romance reveals an astounding disconnect in the military project of policing soldiers' sexual behavior. The iron rule forbidding relationships with women that soldiers dutifully repeated whenever I inquired about their regulations has become rather flexible in the colonel's telling. He paints himself as clearly defeated by natural powers of love that are impossible to govern. Even the carefully drawn imperial boundaries distinguishing civilized Buddhist soldiers from the southern Muslim population, which seemed to the military so important to uphold in discussions of rape, are apparently rendered irrelevant when the Buddhist colonel highlights the significance of lovelorn soldiers converting to Islam.

Rather than operating on a clear-cut delineation of racial and religious frontiers through controlling women's (and men's) sexuality, imperial power in the military support for cross-cultural romance rests on defining sexual access to women as a male privilege. It thus resembles a model of masculinity that Lora Wildenthal has called "imperial patriarchy," where patriarchal authority is expressed through rather than damaged by sexual relationships with colonized women and ideas of purity of blood do not figure as a precondition for a hierarchy of race.[39] The trope of cross-cultural romance, so central to both official and military representations of the southern Thai counterinsurgency, obscures this powerful sexual privilege of the imperial patriarch by couching it in a language of love, thus replicating the structures of affect that undergird the imperial formation.

The Privacy of Romance

The notion of romantic love also structured the way lower-rank soldiers talked about relationships between soldiers and local women. Soldier Sa., for instance, mapped out a typical romance in the southern conflict region; girls and soldiers would usually meet at checkpoints, exchange phone numbers, and then start to have phone conversations. Sa. ended his account on a romantic climax: "At last, the wall between the different cultures and traditions comes down [*laughs*] and the kids like each other [*laughs*]. You cannot build a wall between two hearts. . . . Yes, yes, there are many soldiers who have girlfriends here."

He further explained that such relationships were unproblematic as long as they were kept secret: "If they keep it on a personal level and take care of their love and are doing well, there's no problem. But if there is a problem, then it's a big problem. It's wrong in terms of the law, it's wrong in terms of religion, it's wrong in terms of culture, it's wrong in terms of everything! . . . If a third person knows about it, it becomes a big issue. If they don't want to make it a big issue, there's no problem. Because we cannot prohibit love." Sa., moreover, reasoned that it was the very prohibition of love affairs that made them so attractive.

The notion of romantic love performs important work both in Sa.'s account and Colonel Thakorn's reasoning cited in the *Bangkok Post*. It reinscribes the difference of the southern population as a precondition for romance; the metaphorical walls in Sa.'s rendering evoke the idea of a fixed border between the South and the rest of Thailand. At the same time, the power inequalities of the imperial encounters between soldiers and local women are erased by assuming a level playing field between the cultures and people that the walls divide. Also banished from the picture are the legal conditions structuring these encounters. Under martial law and the emergency decree in the southern provinces, local women were legally subordinated to male military personnel, and consequently rendered more dependent and vulnerable—impunity was the rule in cases of military misconduct.

The notion of romantic love, moreover, naturalizes flirtatious military practices as matters of the heart. The assumed power of nature replaces the power of politics and transforms military agents into apparently helpless victims of their emotions. Framing these relationships in terms of love thereby makes them a private issue irrelevant to public interest. Thus, in Sa.'s opinion, secrecy was key to the success of military romance because only public knowledge converted romantic love into a political error "wrong in terms of everything."

THE LOVE OF THE THAI RACE

This depoliticization of love in constructions of romance between soldiers and local women contrasted with a discourse in which love emerged as an explicit political strategy of the southern counterinsurgency, reflecting the imperial practice of nurturing positive emotional dispositions in those subjects recognized as racially and religiously distinct (see chapter 3). The nurturing of love consequently featured as one of the central goals of the military campaign in policy documents such as Prime Ministerial Order 206. Likewise, Vice-Marshal Nitaya Imanothai, a female officer responsible for civil affairs in the southern provinces, elaborated in a newspaper interview that "love and bonding can win over the hearts of young people [in southern Thailand]" and clarified that the people of Patani were "as Thai as anyone else." The Thais, rather than "tolerate any divisions. . ., should promote love among [them]selves."[40] Nitaya's comments exemplify how the political construction of love in the context of the modern imperial formation is centrally coupled with ideas of the Thai nation and race. For her, although the military promotion of love supports the classic counterinsurgency strategy of winning over the population, its main function is strengthening racial and national bonds. Love in this sense provides for a racial fusion of the imperial family and brushes aside past injuries with heartfelt emotion to reconcile political divides.

In historical terms, the political idea of love (*khwam rag*) has mostly been associated with King Vajiravudh (Rama VI, r. 1910–1925), who prominently mobilized the connection between love and the national family. Issuing a decree enforcing patrilineal surnames on the same day as promulgating the first Siamese citizenship law, which also privileged paternal lines of descent, Vajiravudh explicitly sought to secure respect for fathers within individual families while inculcating "love toward the head of government of the nation." In his literary works, he likewise compared the love for the Siamese nation and homeland to the familial love of a son for his father and mother.[41]

This discourse of national love came to replace the royal system of polygyny, which had been central to constructing and maintaining the Siamese empire and had flourished under both of Vajiravudh's predecessors despite harsh Western criticism of their royal harems.[42] Many of the women residing in the king's Inner Palace (also called Inner City because of its great size in the inner palace walls, housing at its height under King Chulalongkorn (Rama V, r. 1868–1910) 153 royal wives with their entourages) were members of ruling families from the capital, outer provinces or tributary states, and minority populations pledging their loyalty to the king. Consequently, the king's multiple marital ties served to establish "relationships of influence, obligation, and access between the monarch and other power centers in the kingdom."[43] The traffic in women cemented homosocial bonds that secured the stability of the imperial formation. It was the exclusive right of the king to access the Inner Palace—his sexual prerogative was ensured by strict regulations in the traditional legal code, conflating masculine virility with monarchical power. The male progeny of these women were typically assigned administrative posts in the kingdom's capital, so that the first administrative state apparatus of Vajiravudh's predecessor King Chulalongkorn functioned as an embodied extension of royal rule.[44]

Vajiravudh's dissolution of the system of polygyny into a discourse of national love was enabled by the racialization of the Thai vis-à-vis Others such as the Chinese or the Malays and by the construction of Buddhism as the religion common to the Thai. The love of the nation became the familial love of one racial and religious family, headed by the royal patriarch. In the pamphlet "The Jews of the Orient" (1914), for instance, Vajiravudh reasoned that the racial Otherness of Jews and their migrant status inhibited Gentiles from liking them, concluding that "this racial feeling also proves to be one of the principal drawbacks that go to make the Chinese somewhat undesirable." Likewise, in a lecture to the Wild Tigers, his scout soldiers, Vajiravudh asked: "How then can a real love of race be fostered, a love that makes a man willing to sacrifice his life?" Such love of race was for him inextricably bound to religion. Whereas "the white race must adhere to Christianity," he argued, the "yellow race" of the Thais was bound to be Buddhist (see chapter 2).[45]

Similar affective constructions of Thainess can be traced throughout the modern history of Thailand. In a famous speech to a foreign audience in 1927, for example, Prince Damrong Rajanubhab (1862–1943) elaborated that the "love of the nation" was one of the key characteristics of the "Thai race."[46] In 1940, Field Marshal Plaek Phibunsongkhram's political mastermind, Luang Wichit Wathakan, addressed his audience as "my loving Thais" and argued that the "racial feelings" he had when visiting the King of Cambodia proved that there were intimate "racial ties existing between the Thais and Cambodians."[47]

The invocation of love by military commanders and policymakers thus taps into a discourse key to the modern imperial formation. What replaced marital ties and the king's sexual prerogative to possess women of his realm was a state apparatus that deployed Thainess and Buddhism to discipline the whole population into willing submission to their royal father in the name of loving national intimacy. In this construction, however, the three southern provinces, marked as Malay and Muslim, could only feature as troublemakers characterizing the vulnerability of the family.

The Otherness of the southern provinces underlies both the promulgation of love in counterinsurgency policy and the narratives of cross-cultural romances. The military need to promote love in the South implies a lack of intimate racial feelings on the part of the southern population toward their Thai rulers while the imagined walls of difference in the romantic tales provide the foundation for sexual desire. Love in this setting becomes a modern tool of empire-making and political expansion with the potential to not only guarantee submission without force but also provide for a racial fusion that stabilizes the troubled family. "Love has no limits!" many soldiers would repeatedly explain when I inquired about the issue of relationships between local women and soldiers.[48] Of course, as in other colonial and imperial settings, this idea of boundless love also epitomizes the male privilege to disregard both military regulations and traditional practices concerning relationships and sexuality in the Muslim community. Thus it refurbishes with modern imperial terms the premodern empire's patriarchal traffic in women.

RELATIONSHIPS AND CONVERSIONS

Once I understood the ubiquity of relationships between soldiers and local women and inquired about them, I was provided with a wealth of examples. There were instances of girls "fleeing" (ni) the southern provinces to live with their boyfriends at the latter's original army stations in the Northeast and reports of unwanted pregnancies resulting from illicit relationships between girls and soldiers.[49] One of the video clips that students circulated during the period of my research shows a soldier and a girl in a headscarf embracing inside what appears to be a military camp. The clip is mostly likely authentic; when I asked an army officer at Wat Lak Mueang about it, he explained that it had gone viral after the soldier who filmed the kiss had his mobile phone repaired at a local shop.[50] In contrast to the likely fake rape video, the camera in this clip is unsteady. The scene is filmed from a hole in the wall, the two subjects are unaware of the hidden camera, and they sometimes look around anxiously as if they fear being observed. Nevertheless, the clip is highly sexualized, and it expresses the male military prerogative to sexually access the Muslim female without consent. By their styles of dress, the two subjects, who sit beside each other on plastic chairs, perform the difference between the Buddhist Thai soldier and southern Muslim woman. The soldier is older, has short black hair, and is dressed in khaki shorts and a T-shirt, exposing most of his legs and arms; the Muslim woman is younger, her body completely covered by a long green skirt, a black long-sleeved shirt, and a white headscarf, exposing only her face. He embraces her and is the one continually daring more obvious advances, while she resists steadily and laughingly, and smiles in relief when he eventually withdraws his hand from her body.

Perhaps the best official indications of the existence of such relationships are soldiers' conversions to Islam in order to marry local women, which the Islamic councils mostly viewed skeptically. In 2011, the scholar responsible for conversions to Islam at the Islamic Council in Yala estimated that around 70 percent of Thai-Buddhist men converting to Islam in the past five years had been soldiers or policemen.[51] At the marriage-preparation course in Pattani, for instance, one teacher tried to correct the notion of boundless love that the military promoted. "Love in Islam has limits," he highlighted, listing all kinds of rules for both women and men.[52] In Yala, council members attempted to implement means to ensure soldiers' wholehearted conversion to Islam. Would-be converts were invited for a personal interview with a member of the council, and if they answered the question about their reasons for conversion by citing their need to marry a local woman, their application was denied. If they successfully passed this test, the soldiers received a one-hour course on how to practice Islam, a handbook, and a certificate to change the religious classification registered on their identification cards. In response to the large number of security personnel converting to Islam, the councils produced another certificate; it was designed to ensure that Muslim converts were buried according to Muslim procedures even when they had hidden their conversion from their mostly Buddhist families in other Thai provinces.[53]

These findings suggest that soldiers often saw conversion as a temporary practical matter, relevant only while they were stationed in the South—a bureaucratic process necessary to license sexual access to the female part of the Muslim population. In accordance, the military often viewed proper Muslim marriages positively. It viewed the prospect of an increase in the number of Muslim soldiers as a consequence of cross-cultural unions not as a threat but rather as advantageous to a counterinsurgency mission aimed at conquering southern hearts and minds. In fact, there are historical precedents for counterinsurgency policies explicitly promoting mixed marriages. The French Bureaux Arabes in colonial Algeria, for instance, supported such unions as a way to strengthen the Franco-Arab association and eventually accomplish racial fusion. In many cases in southern Thailand, higher-ranking military commanders forced their subordinates to convert and officially marry a Muslim woman after their relationship had been discovered, and the army occasionally paid compensation to the family of the girl that clearly exceeded the conventional sum for a dowry.[54]

In many cases that I heard of, the Muslim women followed the converted soldiers back home to live in another Thai province.[55] The only converted soldier who agreed to talk to me was an exceptional case because he had arranged with the leader of his battalion not only to stay in the South permanently but also to live in an apartment outside the military camp in Pattani. Even he emphasized, however, that whenever the couple visited his family in the northeastern province of Udon, he made his wife take off her headscarf on the grounds that she would suffer from anti-Muslim discrimination otherwise. He also explained that he had asked her not to strictly abide by the rules to eat only *halal* food and admitted that he himself did not practice this rule. He joked, "I am afraid that I might have to only eat noodle soup for the rest of my life!"[56]

Although it is hard to generalize, this example nevertheless provides a glimpse into how the ordering of the imperial formation might structure cross-cultural relationships between Thai soldiers and local women. In this mixed marriage, although the male soldier had converted to Islam, he asked his Muslim wife to give up Muslim practices because he wanted her to adapt to his cultural norms. Conversion here meant nothing but a formal condition to marry a woman from a different religious community, and it became a functional means for the husband to define the rules of marriage, including those of her religious tradition. The fact that he made her take off her headscarf, moreover, recalls Orientalist framings of Islam as oppressive to women and invokes a liberal narrative of emancipation that has contributed to positive connotations of mixed marriages between white men and Muslim women in different (post-)colonial settings.[57]

CIVILIZED SOLDIERS

Perhaps reflecting love's entanglement with power, none of the women I met who were married to soldiers used the notion of love to describe their relationship. Many had gotten to know their future husbands in their home villages and had begun their relationships chatting on the phone. Most had also first hidden their affairs from parents, friends, and villagers; some continued to avoid spending too much time with their husbands in their home villages out of fear of insurgent attacks. In one case, the girl's father had discovered her, a fifteen-year-old schoolgirl, with a soldier and forced him to convert to Islam and arrange a marriage with a dowry of THB 300,000 (approximately USD 9,000).[58]

Instead of describing themselves as defeated by the powers of love, these women frequently listed a number of reasons why they liked being with their husbands and portrayed themselves as active partners in their relationships. Many said that they had "fun" together, that they "knew how to talk to each other," and that their husbands were able to take care of them. All of them denied that their relationships had anything to do with their husbands' military occupations. "I like him as a human being," one interviewee elaborated, "independent of what they call the 'environment' of the conflict." Although acknowledging that some girls in the South liked men in military uniform carrying weapons, she emphasized that she had learned to see beauty on the inside rather than the outside of a human being.[59]

Most southern women portrayed local men in a negative light in comparison to soldiers. A university student described how young men in the area were not enthusiastic about studying and always went out with their peers. "They often don't have a good character," she explained, "and like to behave like children rather than adults."[60] Another girl similarly drew a negative contrast between local men and soldiers: "Guys here like to be lazy. On some days, they don't do anything: they get up late, and so on. I don't like that. But soldiers, by contrast, have to have a good sense of duty, and they are able to also support us financially. And they don't smoke or anything like that." She further elaborated how one of her previous boyfriends from her home community had lacked money, so that she had to pay whenever they went out. Now, her husband even covered the monthly fees for her studies.[61]

The women's reflections on southern Thai men illustrate the still-powerful hold of a Western imperial imagery that painted the Malay character as essentially lazy, a stereotype equally central to contemporary Thai discourse about the southern provinces. Both historical and current stereotypes reflect the particular economic situation of the Malay peninsula. In the nineteenth century, residents had resisted the colonial system of plantation labor, prompting Thomas S. Raffles, the colonial founder of Singapore, to describe "the Malay as being so indolent that when he has rice nothing will induce him to work." Likewise, the British Resident of the Federated Malay States, Frank Swettenham, described "a disinclination to work" as "the leading characteristic of the Malay of every class."[62] Today, many southern Muslims are manual laborers, working as rubber farmers or fishermen, often finishing their daily tasks early in the morning and relaxing in coffee shops afterward. In contrast, many Chinese families own their own businesses in the city centers of the southern provincial towns, whereas Buddhist Thais are often employed in state institutions, which provide both a regular work schedule and a regular income. In this racialized economic context, ideas of the "lazy Malay-Muslim" as "sitting around doing nothing" still operate in Thai discourse about the South.[63]

The women's statements about young men in the southern provinces echo a number of these stereotypes. The complaint about southern men getting up late is reminiscent of the colonial preoccupation with colonized natives' lack of punctuality, and it registers the irregularity of the subsistence economy as a negative trait of locals. The deficient education, character, and sense of duty that girls diagnosed in native men starkly contrasts with pictures of the disciplined, gentlemanly Thai soldier. Last, the shortage of economic resources underscores the inability of Malay men to properly take care of their wives and families. These notions are structured by the hierarchical order of masculinities that operates alongside the racial and religious boundaries of the Thai imperial formation and centrally undergirds the military mission of policing the South. Even in the imaginary of many local women, the civilized Thai soldier trumps the lazy Malay man.

WOMEN'S PROTESTS AND FEMALE PARAMILITARIES

In late 2006, a new pattern of protest started to appear more regularly in the southern provinces, with groups of local women and children gathering to demonstrate against Thai state authorities. In some instances, the protestors accused authorities of being involved in incidents of violence and formed human shields or blocked roads to prevent security forces from accessing the scene of the violence. More frequently, they demanded the release of detainees, often their relatives or members of their community, some of whom had been arrested without evidence under martial law. In a number of cases, they successfully pressured police and the military to free suspects on bail.[64]

The success of these demonstrations directly related to the fears of the Thai military. If male Buddhist soldiers were to stop the Muslim women's demonstrations by force, images of fatherly protection and the military rescue of Muslim women would likely be destroyed. Worse, rumors about sexual harassment might spread even further and suggest that the army was violating rather than sheltering the most precious object of masculine military prowess: the conglomerate mass of "womenandchildren."[65]

Commanders, moreover, had orders to avoid the human-rights violations that coun-terinsurgents had committed in violently dispersing the protest at Tak Bai in 2005, where the mishandling and killing of civilians had contributed to delegitimizing the counterinsurgency mission and continued to be widely used in insurgent propaganda even years afterward.[66]

The response to these fears was the establishment of female paramilitary units (*thahan phran ying*) in 2006, marking the first time in Thai military history that women were employed in combat positions (see fig. 9).[67] In 2011, female paramilitaries were a small minority, numbering five hundred out of a total paramilitary force that had been increased to about thirteen thousand rangers. When the first groups were established in 2006, one of their main missions was to deal with the women's protests, labeled "mobs" in (para-)military parlance.[68] Although female rangers receive the same salary and training and have a similar work schedule (ten days of leave after thirty days of work) as male rangers, they are stationed at large military camps such as the Ingkha-yut Camp in Pattani Province, whereas male rangers are posted to strategic spots in areas of the South that the military coded as red (heavily infiltrated by insurgents).

Although the military claims that female rangers are recruited locally, only a small proportion of the female forces that I encountered in Pattani were local Muslims. The majority of recruits were Buddhists from the South and other parts of the country and Muslims from upper southern provinces outside Patani. Those Muslim women who had joined the paramilitary unit had often had one of their family members killed in the conflict. As one activist, whose father later became one of the first well-known cases of forced disappearance in the South, sharply observed: "I look at recruiting these women, who are—like me—daughters of fathers who have been killed or disap-peared, as a form of violence that the state uses against them, like they are revictim-izing these women. Turning them into perpetrators of violence does not help to solve the problem but makes the problem more serious."[69]

Neither male commanders nor female paramilitaries, however, framed their work in terms of perpetrating violence; rather, they referred to stereotypical notions of harmless femininity as a strategic asset of the female rangers. As a consequence of these gender stereotypes, the women were assigned tasks that differed significantly from those of their male counterparts. As one paramilitary commander put it, male rangers were deployed on the "front line," whereas women were better at talking to and gathering intelligence from villagers because they were gentler, had softer voices and were used to doing everything more carefully and slowly than men. Public rela-tions and psychological operations were also part of female rangers' portfolio, and they were sometimes called in to support male army units in order to search women at checkpoints.[70]

Likewise, the female rangers themselves highlighted that they were more polite, gentle, and trustworthy because of their gender: "It's like they trust in us being women," one of them reflected about her ability to build relationships with members of local communities.[71] Another described a concrete situation to explain female rang-ers' advantage over male paramilitaries: "Like if a male ranger enters a village, that looks scary, right? But if we go as a woman, we just go and smile. And the small kids, they like that! So that's different." In a similar vein, a paramilitary elaborated how vil-lagers would suddenly disappear when they saw a male ranger entering a village but would run to see and greet her instead.[72]

These ideas of essentialized femininity as a strategic military bonus are embedded in a larger international discourse that has styled counterinsurgency as a gentler form

Figure 9. Female paramilitaries training at the Ingkhayut Camp in Pattani, October 2011. Photograph by the author.

of war. Thus, feminist critics have highlighted a distinct notion of military masculinity in counterinsurgency, which has been represented as the gentlemanly alternative to a stereotypically aggressive form of war. Accordingly, contemporary advocates of counterinsurgency aim to foreground a softer form of masculinity that is explicitly distinguished from military hypermasculinity.[73] In this discursive framework, women have been assigned new roles in policymaking and combat operations. For instance, the US military recruited female engagement teams to support its mission in Afghanistan. These teams were explicitly designed to engage "with the Afghan female population in a culturally respectful manner."[74] Here, as in southern Thailand, women soldiers became key not only to representing counterinsurgency as an essentially humanitarian and culturally sensitive form of war but also to easing access and facilitating the policing of the traditional Muslim population. One female ranger in southern Thailand phrased a similar dynamic succinctly: "Our femininity is needed here as a way to successfully reach our goals."[75]

SISTERHOOD AND PROTESTS

Some paramilitaries who underscored the value of their womanhood for unconventional warfare also invoked ideas of an essential female solidarity. In these accounts, the sense of a shared gender facilitated building trust between conflict parties, generally seen as a basic precondition to successfully police the southern population. "We are all women, so we can talk together," one ranger elaborated. Another added that it was easier for women to "build understanding" as compared to their male counterparts: "If we talk between women, it is easier to understand each other."[76] In this counterinsurgent appropriation of the idea of global sisterhood, the category of woman functions simultaneously to erase the hierarchical differences between women and to eliminate the political conflict at stake. Repeating the official mantra encoded in documents like Prime Ministerial Order 206, most paramilitaries emphasized that at the root of the "problem" of the South were basic "misunderstandings"—for them, an appropriate solution lay in talking openly and on supposedly equal grounds "woman to woman."

Yet the Orientalizing imagery of the Other woman, which has historically shaped the imperial discourse of global sisterhood, became clear when the rangers discussed their handling of women's marches.[77] Here, ideas of religion and gender intersected to produce images of victimized women lured into political action against their will. The following conversation from a group interview with female paramilitaries about one of the larger demonstrations outside the Ingkhayut Camp provides an apt illustration:

B.: Well, there were women and children in the mob. And old people. But in the middle hidden in there, there were men who were wearing long-sleeved robes of women and who covered their faces and were wearing their *hijab*.
R: Oh, were there many of them?
B.: There was only one. He was the one ordering the mob of the women around. . . . Once we were able to get him, the whole mob dissolved.[78]

The paramilitary eventually collapsed her idea of evil forces behind the protests into a single male insurgent, veiled in disguise as a Muslim woman. He was responsible for the behavior of the crowd, and she construed the protesting women as objects without political agency, while at the same time the connotation of insurgent violence as

male remained intact. An understanding of these gatherings as peaceful demonstrations was thereby rendered impossible.[79]

A parallel victimization of female protestors operated through notions of Islam, as
in the following conversation about a large protest in Pattani:

B: That was the biggest mob. There were villagers from all subdistricts who gathered
together. It's been a long time, I cannot remember why they gathered. But I also
asked some villagers back then why they had come and they didn't know and just
said that they came to have *mao lid.*

R: What is that?

D: It's part of the Muslim religion, it's like you do sacrifice or something, during their
religious days, like Muhammad's birthday. So some people didn't have the slight-
est idea why they came. They just followed someone who said: "Come and eat
something; come, I will take you in my car!"[80]

In this account, which resounded with the military's accusations that religious leaders were indoctrinating southerners with false interpretations of Islam, the participants' blind belief in Islam and Muslim authorities rendered them objects of religious
manipulation and erased their political agency.

It is also notable that the paramilitary could not remember why people had gathered in Pattani in the first place; indeed, none of the interviewees recalled what had
sparked the protest. In fact, the demonstration that the rangers were talking about
was the 2007 student protest over the alleged rape of a young Muslim woman, which
was one of the largest political gatherings in the southern provinces, blocking the
inner city of Pattani for several days. Regardless of the impetus for this particular
protest, one paramilitary assured me, the most important thing for me to know was
that these rallies were based on "misunderstandings with state authorities" that had
been intentionally provoked.[81] The depoliticizing notion of "misunderstanding" once
again functioned as an erasure of sexual violence. Moreover, by completely eliding the
original cause, it even structured the military memory of the protests, thus echoing
longstanding state-led practices of truth management that have sought to remove
memories of political uprisings in the South from the records of official Thai history.[82]

Such erasure of women's politics is all the more conspicuous because women's
groups in southern Thailand became perhaps the most active and politically relevant
part of civil society in the course of the conflict, especially given that male protestors
were frequently arrested and thus more reluctant to take to the streets.[83] Women who
had participated in demonstrations, of course, strongly objected to the accusation that
they had been lured into demonstrating, and they gave reasons that ranged from simple frustration to the quest to help their male relatives and fight for justice.[84] In their
accounts, moreover, the decline in the number of women's marches after their peak in
2006 and 2007 had nothing to do with female paramilitary units. Rather, the security
forces had started to detain women without charge under martial law regulations.[85]

PARAMILITARY (UN)VEILING

In contrast to the framing of paramilitaries through the strategic assets of a stereotypical femininity, outside observers often labeled women rangers "masculine."
A military researcher who had conducted an in-depth study of the female forces, for
instance, described the manner of many rangers as *tom*, the Thai term for a masculine

woman attracted to the same sex.[86] Two military regulations contributed to this perception: female rangers were not allowed to be married (consequently, many were younger women likely to quit their jobs once they decided to have a family), and they were prohibited from wearing the *hijab* while on duty.

Southern Thailand has a long history of protests against similar bans on veil wearing at Thai state institutions. Most prominently, at the Teacher's College in Yala in the late 1980s, a number of Muslim girls started to oppose the school's dress regulations by wearing their *hijabs*. The ensuing conflict sparked large-scale protests; over ten thousand people fought for the girls' right to veil and eventually succeeded in convincing the Ministry of Education to change its school-uniform regulations. The involvement of the National Security Council in this decision illustrates that for Thai authorities, these marches also constituted matters of internal security in the politically sensitive southern provinces.[87]

Despite regulations that allow for religious diversity, debates about the compatibility of the veil with school uniforms continue to reappear in Thailand. One case in 2012, for example, involved a Muslim girl studying at a government high school in Bangkok that is located on the grounds of a Buddhist temple. The headmaster had prohibited wearing the *hijab*, explaining that the school uniform was secular, and that a school on a temple's property had to accept Thai and Buddhist traditions. "You've got to respect the host's rules," one monk told the Muslim girl who had started the protest. In a similar case in 2018 in Pattani, parents and human-rights groups eventually succeeded in pressuring the government to lift a ban on the *hijab* in a public primary school built inside a Buddhist temple compound.[88] These cases not only reveal the conflation of Buddhism with state power that characterizes the particular Buddhist-secular context of the Thai imperial formation but also demonstrate the perception of Muslims as a religious minority positioned as the unwanted guest of a generous host.

This imperial structure undergirds the prohibition against the *hijab* in female paramilitary units. Military uniform, after all, has historically functioned as a sartorial marker of Western civilization that Siam's modernizing monarchs appropriated even for their own dress code, and the attire of Thai male soldiers continues to connote good character and white skin in southern Thailand. In this hierarchical order of symbols, the veil—as the ultimate Other of Western civilization—would significantly alter the representational function of the military uniform.[89]

Paramilitaries themselves mostly cited reasons of practicality when asked about the headscarf ban; wearing the *hijab* would be uncomfortable, impractical, and unfitting for a member of the military. Yet they also admitted that they sometimes had difficulties explaining themselves to locals. M., for instance, elaborated:

> They would ask how come I decided to be a ranger, and what my political position is that led me to choose to be a ranger. And they do ask about the headscarf as well, and say something like: "It's a sin not to veil, isn't it?" . . . . What they don't understand is that I am a Muslim, and as a Muslim I have gone on the government side. . . . They are suspicious because if they see that I don't wear the headscarf, they think I am on the side of the government. . . . So I explain to them that I only work here because of the monthly salary, that's all.[90]

M.'s experience reflects the polarized discourse of the conflict, where the interior boundaries of racialized religion that structure the Thai state have become a question of sides. For the villagers, therefore, M.'s unveiling signaled that she had changed sides; her loyalty now clearly lay with the Thai-Buddhist military. Whereas in the discussion of women's protests, the paramilitaries had been suspicious of the veil as disguise, the villagers in this example were suspicious of M. for not wearing the veil.

This problematic position was also a dangerous one for female rangers. They constituted easy targets for insurgents, especially when they returned home for their ten-day leave. A member of one of the groups that I interviewed had been shot in her first year when visiting her family in a red area of Narathiwat.[91] Others admitted to being afraid:

B: When you go out to work, you are visible to everyone. Everyone can see my face all the time. Everyone can see: This person here, *na*, she is a ranger! Because I wear my ranger's uniform and the villagers know exactly and recognize who is a ranger.
D: It's like we are the target points and they can see us, but we cannot remember their faces.[92]

In this context, veiling for paramilitaries became a strategy of concealment for counterinsurgency rather than a bodily practice constitutive of the Islamic tradition. In 2016 a group of paramilitaries calling themselves the "Muslim Female Soldiers' Club" petitioned the prime minister, Prayut Chan-o-cha, to allow them to wear the *hijab* while on duty. The petition describes how militants are spreading rumors about the Thai military forcing paramilitaries to unveil in order to commit a sin and expose their hair. Consequently, it argues, permitting female soldiers to wear the headscarf might help them to eliminate such false accusations and make it easier for paramilitaries to enter the field. As one of the petitioners explained, "We hope the prime minister will understand our feeling and our difficulty when people see us as their enemy and look at us with hostility simply because we do not wear headscarves like they do—that we are different from them."[93] The veil, in this framing of a Muslim sisterhood, constitutes an advantage to counterinsurgency because it ostensibly allows for eliminating the power differentials that ground the conflict in southern Thailand.

Although the ISOC spokesman, who only heard about the petition from the press, promised to look into the issue, the *hijab* ban for paramilitaries has not, to my knowledge, been lifted. In addition, even though the police force officially allowed Muslim female officers to wear headscarves to work in 2013, Muslim women subsequently reported that they were forced to unveil when sitting the entrance examination. What is more, the military government that has ruled the country since 2014 has decided to generally reduce the number of women in the security forces. Women were banned from working as investigative officers in the police force at the beginning of 2018, and the major police academy in Bangkok no longer accepts female cadets.[94] In southern Thailand—the feminized, private part of the imperial family—however, female counterinsurgents are still allowed to operate.

WOMEN'S GROUPS AND THE POLICING OF THE PRIVATE SPHERE

The emergence of women's activism on the streets was paralleled by the emergence of women's groups (*klum phuying*). Because men were the main victims and suspects in the conflict, and many either fled over the border to Malaysia or no longer dared to go out to work, the widows and wives of suspects or detainees started to organize themselves. Most of the first grassroots women's groups were formed so that families relying on male breadwinners could "survive without having much money."[95] By 2010, supported by an increase of foreign aid flowing to the southern provinces as well as financial assistance from organizations in Bangkok, the range of groups had grown to be quite diverse.[96] There were groups campaigning for peace, working as human-rights defenders, and producing a community radio show for rural women affected by the conflict. The vast majority of them, however, continued to focus on women's economic self-support or small-scale employment. For example, they produced dishwashing liquid, grew vegetables, or made local snacks, and shared the profits of the sales among their members.

These economic self-support groups were of particular interest to the counterinsurgency campaign. In the town of Pattani, for instance, the army itself helped to found ten different women's groups and supported already existing ones; similarly, the civil-society unit of the task force in Yala tried to support one women's organization in every subdistrict. The budget for the civil-society work of the individual task forces was organized centrally under the ISOC Region 4 Forward Command. The head of the civil-society section at this level was a woman who would often join various meetings of women's groups in civilian clothes.[97]

The kind of help that counterinsurgents offered varied from group to group. In many cases, the women needed direct financial backing or equipment like sewing machines to get their small-scale business going. The military also invited these women to join them for workshops offered as part of its more general development work—for instance, women were taught marketing strategies to enhance their sales or were educated in gardening techniques to increase their harvest. The troops stationed in Pattani had, moreover, organized an exchange between women's groups in Pattani and the northeastern province of Udon.[98]

Military officers, when asked about their rationales for doing this kind of work, not only referred to general ideas of politics leading the military but also specifically highlighted the important role women were playing in quelling the insurgency. In this logic, both the women and the whole Thai nation were benefitting from these counterinsurgency initiatives, because the women would "not think about other things that are not good for the country" when engaged in a group. Additionally, military respondents often explained that women in southern Thailand were not properly looked after by their husbands and male terrorists were largely damaging rather than protecting civil society, so it was incumbent on the army to protect women and children.[99]

These assumptions are inserted into a larger discourse that continues to stress the strategic importance of approaching women in order to win over the population in unconventional warfare. As David Kilcullen, one of the current major advocates of counterinsurgency and coauthor of the US Army's *Counterinsurgency (Field Manual, FM 3–24)* (2006), writes, "[I]n traditional societies, women are hugely influential in forming the social networks that insurgents use for support. Co-opting neutral or friendly women, through targeted social and economic programs, builds networks of enlightened self-interest that eventually undermine the insurgents. . . . Win the women, and you own the family unit."[100]

Kilcullen's statement contrasts traditional societies with enlightened self-interest. On his imagined ladder of developmental progress, the military stands at the civilized pinnacle, whereas the women who support insurgents are positioned on the uncivilized lowest rungs. The civilizational mission of counterinsurgency (based on targeted social and economic programs) aims at not only coopting women into enlightenment but eventually possessing their families. Here, the liberation of women into a kind of self-interest that serves military means eventually culminates in their domination and ownership by male counterinsurgents.

In the Thai context, the rationales for supporting women's groups in counterinsurgency are enmeshed with an official discourse of women's advancement as essential to Thai civilization. For commanders in southern Thailand, supporting women's groups was directly tied to the good of the country. In fact, the historical roots of this discourse can be traced to the first feminist positions that mostly male advocates advanced in late nineteenth-century Siam, claiming that "if the country was to progress and join the world of modern civilized nations, females needed to be given greater social recognition and afforded the same educational opportunities as males."[101]

At the beginning of the twentieth century, King Vajiravudh, likely influenced by his studies of imperial anthropology, put forward similar arguments and linked them directly with ideas of race and religion. In an essay titled "The Status of Women: A Symbol of Civilization," he elaborated that the "jungle people"—such as the indigenous *Ngo* from southern Thailand, people from Borneo and other islands of the Pacific, or African tribes—were lowest on the scale of civilization and treated their women like animals. "For these kinds of jungle people," he noted, "horses are more valuable than women because in their logic women are easy to replace, but it is difficult to find good horses." At the same time, he equated authentic Thainess with the sexual equality supposedly practiced by Thai peasants, who in his eyes were more civilized than the Bangkok nobility, and he condemned the wearing of headscarves as a practice used by men to oppress women.[102]

Vajiravudh's arguments exemplify Orientalist discourses that connected women's advancement to civilizational progress and set white Christian nations as a general standard. At the World Fairs of the late nineteenth and early twentieth centuries, for example, the trope of the benighted woman was used to underscore the oppressive context of the colonies.[103] The sanctioning of polygyny in the southern provinces through family law regulations thus effectively legalized an imperial distinction that marked the South as the savage part of Siam, where women would continue to be oppressed because of their religion. Contemporary counterinsurgency continues to draw these distinctions in projects such as the exchange program between supposedly disadvantaged women from the South and their more progressive peers in the Northeast.

POLICING THE PRIVATE SPHERE

Commanders also stressed that supporting women's groups was important because Muslim women were the mothers of potential insurgents, thus framing Muslim women as the main points of access to the private realm of the family, otherwise inaccessible to counterinsurgents. If they could be "won over" to the "side" of the army, as one colonel put it, women could impede their children from "getting onto the wrong path."[104] In the context of southern Thailand, importantly, the collapse of Islam into the private realm through family law regulations means that women also symbolize the ultimate keys to Thailand's Other religion. They have thus featured centrally in military discourse as main actors potentially equipped to educate their sons to stay on the good path of the Thai state, with counterinsurgents attempting to involve mothers in flagship projects such as the drug-rehabilitation camp Yalannanbaru (see chapter 3).

The emphasis on women's roles in the social policing of the private sphere, moreover, relates back to historical discourses that emerged with Siam's transformation toward a modern imperial formation. Only with the emergence of a modern system of government was a relationship drawn between the management of the population and the internal strength of the state, and women were assigned an important role in shaping the newly configured realm of the private. This might be best illustrated by the writings of the intellectual Thianwan Wannapho (1842–1915), one of the first advocates for women's education in Siam. Thianwan explicitly highlighted that modern sciences might help women to better provide for their homes and husbands and to better educate their children, and he also argued that girls' schools should include lessons on child-rearing because women, in his eyes, played a key role in the moral guidance of their families. If women did not have the right knowledge to morally guide their husbands, he explained, they might drain their husbands' energy, which was needed for the public matters of the country. He therefore reasoned that a country with knowledgeable women had more strength and power than countries "full of stupid and ineffective women."[105]

In Thianwan's framing, women's education ultimately became important merely to support the public male leaders of the country. Likewise, current counterinsurgency strategies' support for women is aimed at furthering societal progress and strengthening the state. The military project of enlightening women thus not only reflects the gendered differences grounding the imperial formation but also accentuates such state-led advancement as a matter of political control and imperial domination.

CONCLUSION

Happiness and Military Rule

When I started to study the southern Thai conflict, much political commentary was concerned with the legacies of the coup of 2006, which had disrupted a comfortable narrative of political observers that had diagnosed Thailand's progressive democratization since the early 1990s. Now, as I close this book in 2020, it is clear that the 2006 coup was a precursor of the renewed military takeover in May 2014, when a junta under the leadership of Army Commander Prayut Chan-o-cha formed the National Council for Peace and Order (NCPO), ousted the Yingluck Shinawatra government, abrogated the constitution, and gave itself absolute powers to rule the country without any popular political participation. The NCPO remained in power for nearly five years, maintaining repressive laws, enforcing censorship, prosecuting activists on criminal charges, and "inviting" dissidents into military camps for what they called "attitude adjustment." In March 2019, the junta staged an election that allowed for the continuation of de facto military rule. Prayut has disbanded the NCPO but remains in power as Thailand's prime minister and defense minister.[1]

The continuities of the imperial formation are key to understanding how the current military regime operates. For one, the military centrally relies on counterinsurgency techniques. In this reading, the counterinsurgency campaign in the south has helped to revive important practices and institutions of policing that seemed to have vanished after the Cold War, and, as in other imperial laboratories—European colonies that served as sites for experimenting with modern practices of government—it has helped to develop innovations that the junta now deploys to govern the country.[2] What is more, the current military regime puts into play the axes of difference that undergird the Thai imperial formation, thus fortifying its structure to stabilize military rule.

In institutional terms, the Internal Security Operations Command (ISOC) provides an important case study demonstrating the continuity of imperial policing. The ISOC and its tactics germinated as a result of the US imperial project and Thailand's willing submission to it. In the 1960s, during the Cold War, the Central Intelligence Agency recommended the reorganization of the Thai anticommunist campaign on the grounds that any threat to Thai sovereignty constituted a threat to US forces—as a military report clarified, "strategically and tactically, the Kingdom of Thailand was crucial to US objectives in Southeast Asia." Following US advice, the Communist Suppression Operations Command—later renamed ISOC—adopted a classical counterinsurgency approach that emphasized passive and political measures, such as development and psychological and propaganda programs, over active suppression. US military tutors reported slow progress in their efforts of teaching Thai forces to adopt such a civic action approach.[3]

Although the ISOC's role had faded with the repeal of the Anti-Communist Law in 2001, the conflict in southern Thailand brought the agency back to life. The ISOC became the lead agency for policing the south, and the post-2006 military regime further provided it with vast powers on a national level to engage in acts of mitigation under a very broad definition of security.[4] Under the NCPO government, the ISOC gained even greater political relevance. As Puangthong Pawakapan notes, it became responsible for suppressing activities of "civilian resistance," for "mobilizing masses" in support of the junta, and for surveying activities of civilians. Moreover, military personnel occupy the highest positions in the ISOC, it operates without any kind of civilian oversight, and Prayut himself acts as its director. Consequently, the ISOC is likely to maintain its important political role under the current regime.[5] In this case, the insurgency in southern Thailand has not only facilitated the revival of institutional legacies of US imperial involvement but also allowed for strengthening military tactics that are now used to crush political dissent on a national scale.

The regime's current political discourse also borrows from depoliticizing terms coined in the southern Thai context. "Reconciliation" (*samannachan*), for instance, was first popularized by the National Reconciliation Commission tasked with working out peaceful solutions for the southern Thai conflict in 2005–2006, and was subsequently adopted into official language on the South. It now forms a central tenet of the military regime, which has established ISOC reconciliation centers in all Thai provinces.[6] The conflict the government seeks to resolve is often described in Thailand by the color codes used in mass protests, where supporters of business tycoon and ex–prime minister Thaksin Shinawatra ("red shirts") have clashed with opponents ("yellow shirts"). Yellow in this context represents the color of the old establishment that includes military and monarchical leaders and has successfully engineered the collapse of multiple elected governments—by, *inter alia*, supporting military coups. The parties of the red shirts, having won every election since 2001 under different names and political leaders, have been repeatedly forced out of office. People in favor of the red-shirt movement are the main target of the junta's current reconciliation efforts, which function similarly to the southern Thai counterinsurgency; they erase political contestation by positing the achievement of national harmony as a matter of individual virtue.[7] Moreover, reminiscent of imperial efforts to govern the emotional dispositions of potentially unruly subjects, the discourse of reconciliation transforms a political problem into a problem of individual subjectivity.

The imperial power structures at work in current military policing practices are perhaps best exemplified by the junta's main motto, "Returning Happiness to the People," which served as the title of Prayut's weekly television address to the Thai people during the five years of NCPO rule, and is also the title of a song penned by Prayut himself.[8] Happiness has constituted a central trope of policing populations in general, and imperial policing in particular. Following colonial concerns with affect as evidence of racial attachment, happiness in colonial warfare has long served to index people's loyalty and therefore indicate counterinsurgents' success at winning over the hearts and minds of local populations. With the rise of the science of social psychology after World War II, more professionalized means of engineering emotions for insurgency prophylaxis have been deployed.[9] Moreover, the fact that the chief of a military junta has taken to songwriting is itself telling in a counterinsurgency context. The composition and performance of songs continues to be a strategy deployed by the Royal Thai Army's Psychological Operations Unit, established under US tutelage during the Cold War, which has also regularly staged musical interventions during various street protests in the lead-up to the 2014 coup. Such use of music for purposes of policing is directly linked to imperial practices, where local songs were used to build relationships with the population of an "adversary culture."[10]

The lyrics of "Returning Happiness to the People" are even more significant in the context of Thailand's imperial past. The term "happiness" (*khwam suk*) directly invokes the glorious history of Siam's old royal empire and thus connotes paternal benevolence, the Thai race, and Buddhist religion. According to the teleological narrative of historiography that Prince Damrong Rajanubhab (1862–1943) helped to propagate at the turn of the twentieth century, the thirteenth-century Kingdom of Sukothai stands at the beginning of Thai history, and its ruler, King Ramkamhaeng (r. 1279–1298), represents the original "lord father," who reportedly governed his realm "not for the glory of himself or his family, but 'for the benefits and happiness' of the people in his trust."[11] The oath of accession pledged by kings of the Chakri dynasty directly references this historical prototype by including the line "We shall reign with righteousness, for the benefits and happiness of the Siamese people."[12] With the song's refrain, "Let us return happiness to you, the people," the military junta not only assumes this monarchical position but also reinstantiates Sukothai as the starting point of a continuous history of an imperial formation marked by the benevolence of patriarchal rule.

However, an unhappy moment of crisis, so says the song, has interrupted this long line of righteous rule and created the impetus for the military to intervene. There is danger and unrest everywhere—"the flames are rising." The flames in this line may refer to the violent confrontation between red-shirt protestors and Thai security forces in May 2010. Protestors had blocked central sites in the capital of Bangkok for three months, and when negotiations with the government failed, the army raided the protestors' main camp. Militant members of the red-shirt movement resorted to arson attacks, burning buildings such as the Stock Exchange, several banks, and a large shopping mall. Security forces, operating on the legal grounds of the Emergency Decree, a regulation imported from the southern Thai insurgency, deployed live ammunition to halt the attacks. Eighty-eight people died in these confrontations, and whereas many red shirts were charged with various offences, most of the military personnel implicated in abuses against civilians escaped punishment. Against this background, Prayut's song disassociates the junta from violence, constructs its members as heroic firefighters saving the country from political chaos, and legitimizes the temporal urgency of military interference: "Let us be the ones who step in, before it is too late." These lines also insinuate that military leaders have felt the need to intervene in order to straighten out Thailand's history and erase its unhappy episodes from public memory.[13]

This military version of history, of course, implies particular constructions of Thainess. It enshrines Sukothai as the quintessence of a happy polity, the first kingdom established by the people of the Thai race, who supposedly fled from southern Yunnan. What is more, together with returning happiness to the country, the rulers in the song aim "to bring back love," an ambition reminiscent both of official counterinsurgency policies in the South and a larger discourse that has constructed the love of the Thai race as integral to the Thai national character. A lack of love has consequently been identified as one of the affective causes of rebellion in the south. A revival of love, the song suggests, will recreate racial attachments and result in renewed national harmony.

The song also implicitly reflects the hegemony of Buddhism in Thailand's imperial formation in its references to moral principles that have been historically marked as Buddhist. In official historical accounts, the ruler of Sukothai mostly features as the ideal of a *dhammaraja*—a righteous Buddhist king ruling in accordance with the ten virtues of the *dhamma*: "almsgiving, morality, liberality, uprightness, gentleness, self-restriction, nonanger, noninjury, forbearance, and nonobstruction."[14] In fact, during the Cold War, Thai counterinsurgency even more explicitly involved efforts to revive *dhamma* virtues in order to fight communism through programs such as the missionary monk program, which was designed to strengthen "national and religious security" by providing for "public tranquillity and people's happiness."[15] In the southern Thai counterinsurgency, similar ideas appeared in a more medicalized language of psychology. For instance, at the Yalannanbaru camp, a lecture on *khwam suk* ("happiness") was an integral part of the third day's programming, instructing participants that practices such as praying or meditation could produce "happiness in the brain."[16] In a manner typical of Thailand's state formation, where the supremacy of Buddhism was fortified in secular state law, the song takes notions from the Buddhist tradition to secure the loyal attachment of the general populace.

Moreover, the song promises that military rulers will "guard and protect [the Thai people] with [their] hearts," thus citing the familiar trope of patriarchal protection, which works through a gendered binary that masculinizes the protectors while subordinating and feminizing those protected, and which has widely been used in imperial contexts to legitimize the paternalistic government of feminized colonized subjects.[17] The feminized subjects of the protecting patriarch in the song, however, are not merely the people in southern Thailand but the Thai population in general. The implication is clear: Thai citizens are ignorant, helpless, and have left the country in a state of chaos; Thai soldiers are morally upright saviors ready to risk their lives in order to fight for the good of the nation.

Commentators have highlighted that these hierarchical notions are part of Thailand's form of constitutional monarchy, which has codified a system currently known as "democracy with the king as head of state," also called "Thai-style democracy."[18] The first constitution of 1932, emerging out of a compromise between the palace and the revolutionary People's Party, was based on the British model of constitutional monarchy and clarified that people's sovereignty was to be "exercised by the king."[19] The latest constitutions (e.g., 1997, 2007, 2014, and 2017) have defined sovereignty in similarly ambiguous terms. They state that "the sovereign power belongs to the Thai people" but also assert that "the King as Head of State shall exercise such power." The NCPO, making use of this constitutional ambiguity, also exercise the sovereign power belonging to the Thai people, and Prayut likes to point out that he is exercising "Thai-style democracy."[20]

Although it is easy to see the basic principles of Southeast Asia's premodern empires represented in this discourse of Thai-style democracy (the king enshrined as the universal representative of the constituent parts of his realm), modern European imperialism and, by extension, Cold War counterinsurgency have also helped to sustain this ambiguous notion of sovereignty.[21] Thai-style democracy is characterized by what Partha Chatterjee has called the "rule of colonial difference," which marks "the colony as an exception in order to confirm the universality of the theory" and, in its postcolonial guise, erases "the violent intrusion of colonialism" by making "all of its features the innate property of an indigenous history."[22] Hence, the discourse of Thai-style democracy in its current form replicates the exemption that structured

Siam's relationship with European imperialism. Siam was denied full sovereignty until it had reformed its legal system under the tutelage of European advisers. Likewise, Thai-style democracy denies sovereignty to the Thai people on the grounds that Thais, in contrast to Westerners and by nature of their racialized indigeneity and linear history of monarchical rule, need strong paternal leadership.

US imperialism operated through the production of similar exceptions in Thailand during the anticommunist campaign. In fact, the term "Thai-style democracy" was coined under the regime of Gen. Sarit Thanarat (r. 1957–1973), whose dictatorship was also legitimized by the US counterinsurgency campaign generally and US researchers in particular.[23] In a 1964 report on the effects of culture and organization for the internal security of Thailand, for example, political scientists David Wilson and Herbert Phillips warned about the dangers of regime change. They claimed that Thais, because of their traditional cultural values, required a government with the "attributes of a strong, wise, but indulgent father." Benevolent paternalism rather than self-determination, they suggested, was conducive to the internal stability of Thailand.[24]

The last line of "Returning Happiness to the People" transforms the imperative of the refrain into a statement that predicts the future: "Happiness will return to Thailand." The 2019 elections and their aftermath have made abundantly clear that the NCPO has so profoundly changed the structures of Thailand's executive, legislative, and judiciary system that military power endures despite the alleged return to civilian rule.[25] Practices of military policing will likely remain pivotal to the functioning of the Thai state formation.

GLOSSARY

adat (Arabic)   A variety of local customary practices of Muslim communities in Southeast Asia and other regions.

bangsa (Malay)   Formerly "genealogy" or "lineage." Translated as "race" beginning in the eighteenth century.

borankhadi (Thai)   Archaeology (literally "antiquity studies"). Former term for history.

borisut (Thai)   Innocence or harmlessness. Connotes virginity or sexual purity.

chat (Thai)   Nation. Denoted race in from the nineteenth century through the early twentieth century. Derived from the Sanskrit term designating belonging to a certain caste in the Buddhist cycle of rebirth.

chit winyan (Thai)   Spirituality, originally derived from Buddhist ideas of rebirth.

chu sao (Thai)   Often referring to heterosexual love affairs by married men that are widely normalized in the Thai context.

chularajamontri (Thai)   Official head of the Islamic community in Thailand.

datoh (Malay) court   Court presided over by an Islamic judge dealing with civil cases pertaining to personal matters within Thailand's Muslim communities.

dawah (Arabic)   Invitation, usually connoting Muslim missionary activities.

dharma (Pali)   Common moral principles of the Buddhist tradition, derived from nature or the way things are.

farang (Thai)   White, Western foreigner.

halal (Arabic)   Permissible. Particularly associated with Islamic dietary traditions.

hijab (Arabic)   Islamic veil covering the hair but leaving face uncovered.

imam (Arabic)   Muslim community leader who leads prayers at a mosque.

Jalanan baru (Malay)   New path.

jihad (Arabic)   Literally means "struggling" but is mostly associated with warfare in connection with its use by Islamist terrorist groups in recent decades.

kanmueang nam kanthahan (Thai)   Approach to counterinsurgency directly invoking the anti-communist campaign in Thailand (literally "politics leading the military").

kapiyoh (Malay)   Muslim prayer cap.

katanyu (Pali)   Gratitude (literally "knowing what was done" and "acknowledging past services").

khaek (Thai)   Racialized term that connotes a guest or foreigner, long used to describe Muslims.

khunnang (Thai)   A nobleman in the premodern Siamese system of social categorization.

khwam suk (Thai)   Happiness.

klum phuying (Thai)   Women's organization.

kratom (Thai)   Extract or gum of the *mitragyna speciosa* tree native to Southeast Asia, which contains compounds that can have psychotropic (mind-altering) effects.

len (Thai)   To play. Connotes playful flirtation.

mao lid (Thai)   From the Arabic "mawlid," celebration commemorating the birthday of the Islamic prophet Muhammad.

monthon (Thai)   Administrative subdivisions of Thailand at the beginning of the twentieth century.

niqab (Arabic)   Islamic veil worn by women covering all but the eyes.

pai thiao (Thai)   Leisure travel popularized in the late nineteenth century.

Patani (Malay)   Former Islamic sultanate located in the northern part of the Malay peninsula.

phanung (Thai)   Traditional Thai garment consisting of a long strip of cloth wrapped around the waist and reaching below the knees.

phrai (Thai)   Premodern Siamese social category referring to commoners.

phut phro (Thai)   Talking in a pleasant or harmonious way.

pondok (Malay)   Used in southern Thailand for traditional Islamic boarding schools.

prawattisat (Thai)   History (literally "past-science").

riaproi (Thai)   Connotes propriety in terms of gender and sexuality.

roti (Malay)   Wheat flour–based pan-fried bread commonly served as a street food in southern Thailand.

sakdina (Thai)   Premodern Siamese system of social status categorization.

samathi (Thai)   Meditative absorption.

sangha (Pali)   Buddhist monkhood.

sarong (Malay)   Skirt that is usually also worn by men, especially in rural parts of southern Thailand.

sasana (Pali)   Living practice of teaching and learning in the Theravada Buddhist tradition.

sati (Sanskrit)   Originally chaste woman or good wife. Derived from the name of the Hindu goddess Sati, who died through self-immolation. Hindu practice of ritual self-sacrifice by widows on their husbands' funeral pyres.

sawang (Thai)   Inner brightness.

siwilai (Thai)   Civilized.

Tablighi Jamaat (Urdu)   South Asian missionary movement that has gained large numbers of followers in southern Thailand.

tae (Thai)   Smart, handsome, or trendy.

tak se dok (Malay)   Second step in the practice of sincere repentance (after *tawba*), entailing the obligation to never repeat a sin.

tambon (Thai)   Subdistrict-level administration unit in Thailand.

tawba (Arabic)   Islamic concept of repenting to God after committing sin.

thahan phran (Thai)   Paramilitary rangers.

thahan phran ying (Thai)   Female paramilitary unit.

thammathut (Thai)   Missionary monk program during Thailand's anti-communist campaign.

that (Thai)   Slaves in the premodern Siamese social order.

tom (Thai)   A masculine woman.

ustadz (Persian)   Islamic teacher.

yaentalimaen (Thai)   Translated from the English "gentleman" and associated with British military regulations on proper behavior.

vinaya (Sanskrit, Pali)   Collection of disciplinary rules for Buddhist monks and nuns.

vipassana (Pali)   Insight. Associated today with meditation practices of Theravada Buddhism.

yawi (Malay)   Arabic script for writing Malay (and several other languages in Southeast Asia). In Thai, the term is often used to designate the Malay dialect spoken in southern Thailand.

NOTES

INTRODUCTION

1 Monika Maier-Albang, "Thailand verliert sein Lächeln" [Thailand loses its smile], *Süddeutsche Zeitung*, August 12, 2016, http://www.sueddeutsche.de/reise/suedostasien-thailand-verliert-sein-laecheln-1.3118970; Kocha Olarn, Joshua Berlinger, and Lauren Said-Moorhouse, "Thailand Rocked by 11 Bombs in One Day," *CNN* (Cable News Network), August 12, 2016, http://edition.cnn.com/2016/08/12/asia/thailand-explosions/.

2 "South Insurgency Linked to Blasts," *Bangkok Post*, August 15, 2016, http://www.bangkok-post.com/news/politics/1061584/south-insurgency-linked-to-blasts; "First Suspect Arrested in Connection with Tourist-Town Bombs," *Bangkok Post*, September 5, 2016, http://www.bangkokpost.com/news/security/1078912/first-suspect-arrested-in-connection-with-tourist-town-bombs; Anders Engvall, "Bombs, Facts, and Myths in Southern Thailand," *New Mandala*, August 13, 2016, http://www.newmandala.org/bombs-facts-myths-southern-thailand/.

3 See the Prime Ministerial Order 206 "Nayobai Soem Sang Santisuk Nai Puenthi Changwat Chaidaen Phak Tai" [Policy to promote peace and happiness in the southern border provinces], October 30, 2006. Henceforth designated as PM Order 206.

4 "Patani" here refers to the former Islamic sultanate, whereas "Pattani" designates both one of the southernmost provinces and the name of its provincial capital.

5 PM Order 206.

6 "Can Thailand Really Hide a Rebellion?," International Crisis Group website, August 22, 2016, https://www.crisisgroup.org/asia/south-east-asia/thailand/can-thailand-really-hide-rebellion.

7 The term "imperial formation" has gained currency in postcolonial studies, but it has a longer genealogy in feminist Marxist debates and South Asian history. For postcolonial studies, see Ann Laura Stoler, "On Degrees of Imperial Sovereignty," *Public Culture* 18, no. 1 (2006): 125–46; Ann Laura Stoler, Carole McGranahn, and Peter C. Perdue, eds., *Imperial Formations* (Santa Fe, NM: School for Advanced Research Press, 2007). For feminist Marxist analysis, see Mrinalini Sinha, *Colonial Masculinity: The "Manly Englishman" and the "Effeminate Bengali" in the Late Nineteenth Century* (Manchester, UK: Manchester University Press, 1994); Mrinalini Sinha, "Mapping the Imperial Social Formation: A Modest Proposal for Feminist History," *Signs: Journal of Women in Culture and Society* 25, no. 4 (2000): 1077–82. For South Asian history, see Ronald Inden, *Imagining India* (Oxford: Basil Blackwell, 1990).

8 George Steinmetz, "The Sociology of Empires, Colonies, and Postcolonialism," *Annual Review of Sociology* 40 (2014): 79.

9 Michael W. Doyle, *Empires* (Ithaca, NY: Cornell University Press, 1986), 12; Stoler, "On Degrees of Imperial Sovereignty," 126.

10 Tamara Loos, *Subject Siam: Family, Law, and Colonial Modernity in Thailand* (Ithaca, NY: Cornell University Press, 2002). Following Thai studies conventions, I use the term Siam when referring to the period before the country's first name change in 1939 and Thailand for the period after.

11 Raymond Scupin, "Islam in Thailand before the Bangkok Period," *Journal of the Siam Society* 68, no. 1 (1980): 65.

12 Chris Baker and Pasuk Phongpaichit, *A History of Ayutthaya* (Cambridge: Cambridge University Press, 2017), 207; Loos, *Subject Siam*, 36.

13 Inden, *Imagining India*, 29. In Stanley Tambiah's influential account of traditional kingship in Siam, he describes this imperial form of rule as the cosmological structure of what he calls the "galactic polity," in which "the center ideologically represents the totality and embodies the unity of the whole." Stanley Tambiah, "The Galactic Polity: The Structure of Traditional Kingdoms in Southeast Asia," *Annals of the New York Academy of Science* (1976): 79.

14 Loos, *Subject Siam*, 36.
15 Baker and Pasuk, *A History of Ayutthaya*, 207.
16 Francis R. Bradley, *Forging Islamic Power and Place: The Legacy of Shaykh Dā'ūd bin 'Abd Allāh al-Faṭānī in Mecca and Southeast Asia* (Honolulu: University of Hawai'i Press, 2016).
17 Thai studies scholars have described these relationships as semi- or crypto-colonial. For a comprehensive discussion of the use of the term "semicolonialism" in critical Thai studies, see Peter A. Jackson, "The Ambiguities of Semicolonial Power in Thailand," in *The Ambiguous Allure of the West: Traces of the Colonial in Thailand*, ed. Rachel V. Harrison and Peter A. Jackson (Hong Kong: Hong Kong University Press, 2010), 43–47. For an overview of debates between Thai Marxists on semicolonialism, see Craig J. Reynolds and Hong Lysa, "Marxism in Thai Historical Studies," *Journal of Asian Studies* 43, no. 1 (1983): 77–104. For an elaboration of crypto-colonialism, see Michael Herzfeld, "The Conceptual Allure of the West: Dilemmas and Ambiguities of Crypto-Colonialism in Thailand," in Harrison and Jackson, *Ambiguous Allure of the West*.
18 Shane Strate, *The Lost Territories: Thailand's History of National Humiliation* (Honolulu: University of Hawai'i Press, 2015), 9.
19 Gerrit W. Gong, *The Standard of "Civilization" in International Society* (Oxford: Clarendon, 1984), 206.
20 Antony Anghie, *Imperialism, Sovereignty, and the Making of International Law*, vol. 37 (Cambridge: Cambridge University Press, 2007), 84. See also Hong Lysa, "'Stranger within the Gates': Knowing Semi-Colonial Siam as Extraterritorials," *Modern Asian Studies* 38, no. 2 (2004): 327–54; M. B. Hooker, "The 'Europeanization' of Siam's Law 1855–1908," in *Laws of South-East Asia*, vol. 2, *European Laws in South-East Asia*, ed. M. B. Hooker (Singapore: Butterworth, 1988), 531–77.
21 John Gallagher and Ronald Robinson, "The Imperialism of Free Trade," *Economic History Review* 6, no. 1 (1953): 11; Benedict Anderson, "Studies of the Thai State: The State of Thai Studies," in *The Study of Thailand: Analyses of Knowledge, Approaches, and Prospects in Anthropology, Art History, Economics, History, and Political Science*, ed. Eliezer B. Ayal (Athens: Ohio University Center for International Studies, 1978), 209.
22 Anderson, "Studies of the Thai State," 210.
23 Thongchai Winichakul, *Siam Mapped: A History of the Geo-Body of a Nation* (Honolulu: University of Hawai'i Press, 1994); Thongchai Winichakul, "The Quest for 'Siwilai': A Geographical Discourse of Civilizational Thinking in the Late Nineteenth and Early Twentieth-Century Siam," *Journal of Asian Studies* 59, no. 3 (August 2000): 528–49.
24 Tomoko Masuzawa, *The Invention of World Religions: Or, How European Universalism Was Preserved in the Language of Pluralism* (Chicago: University of Chicago Press, 2005).
25 Loos, *Subject Siam*, 81; Damrong Rajanubhab, *Chaophaya Yommarat* (Bangkok: Samnakphim Praphat Ton, 1948).
26 Thanet Aphornsuvan, "History and Politics of the Muslims in Thailand" (working paper, Thammasat University, 2003).
27 The term "counterinsurgency" was coined by the John F. Kennedy administration in the United States as a strategy for anticommunist campaigns during the Cold War. Douglas Blaufarb, *The Counterinsurgency Era: US Doctrine and Performance 1950 to the Present* (New York: Free Press, 1977). For a concise overview of contemporary counterinsurgency doctrine, see Karsten Friis, "Peacekeeping and Counter-Insurgency—Two of a Kind?," *International Peacekeeping* 17, no. 1 (2010): 50–55.
28 Noel Alfred Battye, "The Military, Government, and Society in Siam, 1868–1910" (PhD diss., Cornell University, 1974), 419.
29 A. Cecil Carter, *The Kingdom of Siam* (New York: Knickerbocker, 1904), 73.
30 Battye, "Military, Government, and Society in Siam," 448.
31 Battye, "Military, Government, and Society in Siam," 119–21; Anderson, "Studies of the Thai State."
32 See, for instance, Mark Neocleous, "Theoretical Foundations of the 'New Police Science,'" in *The New Police Science: The Police Power in Domestic and International Governance*, ed. Mariana Valverde and Markus D. Dubber (Stanford, CA: Stanford University Press, 2006), 17–41; Colleen Bell, "The Police Power in Counterinsurgencies: Discretion, Patrolling, and Evidence," in *War, Police, and Assemblages of Intervention*, ed. Jan Bachmann, Colleen Bell, and Caroline Holmqvist (London: Routledge, 2015), 17–35.

33 Franz-Ludwig Knemeyer, "Polizei," *Economy and Society* 9, no. 2 (1980): 172–96; Michel Foucault, *Security, Territory, Population: Lectures at the Collège de France, 1977–78*, ed. Michel Senellart, trans. Graham Burchell (London: Palgrave Macmillan, 2007), lectures 11–13. Mark Neocleous, *War Power, Police Power* (Edinburgh: Edinburgh University Press, 2014), 8.

34 Laleh Khalili, "Gendered Practices of Counterinsurgency," *Review of International Studies* 37 (2011): 1472.

35 Manuals on unconventional warfare were produced during the first wave of colonization of the Americas in the sixteenth century. Laleh Khalili, *Time in the Shadows: Confinement in Counterinsurgencies* (Stanford, CA: Stanford University Press, 2013), 12. The colonial wars in French Algeria and British Malaya in the nineteenth and twentieth centuries are even more prominent models of counterinsurgency, often cited by contemporary military advocates. See, for example, John A. Nagl, *Counterinsurgency Lessons from Malaya and Vietnam: Learning to Eat Soup with a Knife* (Westport, CT: Praeger, 2002). See also Ruth Mas, "On the Apocalyptic Tones of Islam in Secular Time," in *Secularism and Religion-Making*, ed. Markus Dressler and Arvind-Pal S. Mandair (Oxford: Oxford University Press, 2011), 96; Ann Laura Stoler, " 'The Rot Remains': From Ruins to Ruination," in *Imperial Debris: On Ruins and Ruination*, ed. Ann Laura Stoler (Durham, NC: Duke University Press, 2013), 1–58.

36 See especially Ann Laura Stoler, "Rethinking Colonial Categories: European Communities and the Boundaries of Rule," *Society for Comparative Study of Society and History* 31, no. 1 (1989): 134–61; Ann Laura Stoler, *Race and the Education of Desire: Foucault's History of Sexuality and the Colonial Order of Things* (Durham, NC: Duke University Press, 1995); Ann Laura Stoler, *Carnal Knowledge and Imperial Power* (Berkeley: University of California Press, 2002), chap. 6.

37 Chris Baker and Pasuk Phongpaichit, *A History of Thailand* (Cambridge: Cambridge University Press, 2005), 68.

38 Loos, *Subject Siam*, 87.

39 For a good overview of the 1932 events and the subsequent instability, see Scott Barmé, *Luang Wichit Wathakan and the Creation of Thai Identity* (Singapore: ISEAS Publishing, 1993), 62–103. The military coup was planned together with government officials, illustrating the often cooperative ties between the civilian bureaucracy and military leaders. James Ockey, "Thailand: The Struggle to Redefine Civil-Military Relations," in *Coercion and Governance: The Declining Political Role of the Military in Asia*, ed. Muthiah Alagappa (Stanford, CA: Stanford University Press, 2001), 192.

40 Chai-Anan Samudavanija, *The Thai Young Turks* (Singapore: ISEAS Publishing, 1982), 1; Suchit Bunbongkarn, *The Military in Thai Politics* (Singapore: ISEAS Publishing, 1987), 2.

41 Human Rights Watch, "Thailand: Structural Flaws Subvert Election," March 19, 2019, https://www.hrw.org/news/2019/03/19/thailand-structural-flaws-subvert-election.

42 Carl E. Pletsch "The Three Worlds, or the Division of Social Scientific Labor, circa 1950–1975," *Comparative Studies in Society and History* 23, no. 4 (1981): 565–90; Blaufarb, *Counterinsurgency Era*.

43 Jefferson P. Marquis, "The Other Warriors: American Social Science and Nation Building in Vietnam," *Diplomatic History* 24, no. 1 (2000): 79–105.

44 E. H. Ashby and D. G. Francis, "COIN in Thailand Jan 1967–Dec 1968," Contemporary Historical Evaluation of Combat Operations (CHECO) (Washington, DC: US Air Force, 1969); Thomas A. Marks, "The Thai Approach to Peacemaking since World War II," *Journal of East and West Studies: Perspectives on East Asian Economies and Industries* 7, no. 1 (1978): 138.

45 Hans Heymann, *Seminar on Development and Security in Thailand—Part II: Development-Security Interactions* (Santa Monica, CA: RAND Corporation, 1969), 90. According to Thak, the United States granted USD 111.2 million to the Thai military in the period between 1946 and 1952. Thak Chaloemtiarana, *Thailand: The Politics of Despotic Paternalism* (Chiang Mai: Silkworm, 2007), 58. On the strengthening of the police in this era, see Eric J. Hanstaad, "Constructing Order through Chaos: A State Ethnography of the Thai Police" (PhD diss., University of Wisconsin–Madison, 2008), 62–75.

46 The Thai military assigned 37,644 staff to the allied forces in South Vietnam from 1965 to 1972. All deployment costs were covered by the United States. Richard A. Ruth, *In Buddha's Company: Thai Soldiers in the Vietnam War* (Honolulu: University of Hawai'i, 2011), 1.

47 Ashby and Francis, "COIN in Thailand," 35.

48 Sarit staged a coup in 1957 and a second one in 1958 to strengthen his hold on power, after which he "declared martial law, annulled parliament, discarded the constitution, banned political parties, and arrested hundreds of politicians, journalists, intellectuals, and activists." Although Sarit died in 1963, his paternalistic government was continued by his close allies, Field Marshals Thanom and Praphat. Baker and Pasuk, *History of Thailand*, 148. See also Thak, *Thailand*.

49 Thak, *Thailand*, 138n111; Eugene Ford, *Cold War Monks: Buddhism and America's Secret Strategy in Southeast Asia* (New Haven, CT: Yale University Press, 2017).

50 *Thammathut* training programs covered a variety of topics such as proper "self-government, the application of national traditions and customs to everyday life, public health and hygiene" as well as the need for "loyalty to the government and the king." Somboon Suksamran, *Political Buddhism in Southeast Asia: The Role of the Sangha in the Modernization of Thailand* (London: Hurst, 1977), 100.

51 Sinae Hyun, "Building a Human Border: The Thai Border Patrol Police School Project in the Post–Cold War Era," *SOJOURN: Journal of Social Issues in Southeast Asia* 29, no. 2 (2014): 332–63.

52 United States Operations Mission (USOM), *Briefing Book on Southern Thailand* (Bangkok, 1962), 54, accessed at the Thailand Information Center, Chulalongkorn University, Bangkok; Ashby and Francis, "COIN in Thailand," 5.

53 Surin Pitsuwan, "Islam and Malay Nationalism: A Case Study of the Malay-Muslims of Southern Thailand" (PhD diss., Harvard University, 1982), 231–32.

54 In Thai: *"Khao-chai, khao-thueng, phatthana."* See PM Order 206 (2006) and PM Order 68, "Nayobai Sang Santisuk Puenthi Sam Changwat Chaidaen Tai" [Peacebuilding policy for the area of the three southern border provinces] (2004) and International Crisis Group (ICG), *Southern Thailand: Dialogue in Doubt*, Asia Report no. 270 (Bangkok/Brussels, 2015), 13n73.

55 E.g., Duncan McCargo, "Thaksin and the Resurgence of Violence in the Thai South: Network Monarchy Strikes Back?" *Critical Asian Studies* 38, no. 1 (2006): 39–71; Ukrist Pathmanand, "Thaksin's Achilles' Heel: The Failure of Hawkish Approaches in the Thai South," *Critical Asian Studies* 38, no. 1 (2006): 73–93.

56 The full title of the decree is "Emergency Decree on Public Administration in Emergency Situations." It replaced martial law for a period of fourteen months in 2005 and 2006 and was again applied in combination with martial law after the military coup of 2006.

57 See Amnesty International, "Thailand: Torture in the Southern Counter-Insurgency" (London: Amnesty International, 2009), 23, https://www.amnesty.org/download/Documents/48000/asa390012009eng.pdf.

58 Despite these serious human rights violations by security forces, the official investigation concluded without sentencing any of the officials involved, asserting that most of the victims had died of asphyxiation. See Human Rights Watch, "No One Is Safe: Insurgent Attacks on Civilians in Thailand's Southern Border Provinces," *Human Rights Watch Report* 19, no. 13 (March 2007); International Crisis Group, *Southern Thailand: Insurgency, Not Jihad*, Asia Report no. 98 (Bangkok/Brussels, 2005).

59 After the Tak Bai tragedy, Thaksin first declared that the deaths had been caused by the fasting of the Muslim victims during Ramadan. He had to concede the truth a few days later and then forced the commander of the Fourth Army Region out of office. See ICG, *Insurgency, Not Jihad*; James Ockey, "Thailand in 2006: Retreat to Military Rule," *Asian Survey* 47, no. 1 (2007): 133–40; Duncan McCargo, "The Coup and the South," *NIAS nytt—Asia Insights* 3 (2007): 12–14.

60 See, for example, McCargo, "Thaksin and the Resurgence of Violence in the Thai South"; Ukrist, "Thaksin's Achilles' Heel: The Failure of Hawkish Approaches in the Thai South."

61 Chaiwat Satha-Anand, "The Silence of the Bullet Monument: Violence and 'Truth' Management, Dusun-Nyor 1948, and Kru-Ze 2004," *Critical Asian Studies* 38, no. 1 (2006): 11–37.

62 In 2011, security officials believed that around two hundred of the roughly fifteen hundred villages in the three southern provinces were supporting insurgents (personal communication with ISOC official, October 7, 2011). See also ICG, *Dialogue in Doubt*, 2; ICG, *Southern Thailand's Peace Dialogue: No Traction*, Asia Briefing no. 148 (Bangkok/Brussels, 2016).

63 For more background on the BRN-C, see Marc Askew and Sascha Helbardt, "Becoming Patani Warriors: Individuals and the Insurgent Collective in Southern Thailand," *Studies in Conflict & Terrorism* 35 (2012): 779–80; Sascha Helbardt, "Deciphering Southern Thailand's Violence: Organisation and Insurgent Practices of BRN-Coordinate" (PhD diss., University of Passau, 2011); Don Pathan and Joseph Liow, *Confronting Ghosts: Thailand's Shapeless Southern Insurgency* (Sydney: Lowy Institute for International Policy, 2010).

64 See PM Orders 206 (2006) and 68 (2004).

65 The ISOC was authorized to engage in actions of suppression in situations severe enough to threaten internal security but not yet meeting the threshold for declaring a state of emergency. Although the ISOC is officially commanded by the prime minister, Paul Chambers contends that it is "essentially a military-controlled agency." See Paul Chambers, "In the Shadow of the Soldier's Boot: Assessing Civil-Military Relations in Thailand," in *Legitimacy Crisis in Thailand*, ed. Marc Askew (Chiang Mai, Thailand: Silkworm, 2010), 206. See also International Commission of Jurists (ICJ), *Thailand's Internal Security Act: Risking the Rule of Law?* (Bangkok, 2010).

66 See Marc Askew, "The Spectre of the South: Regional Instability as National Crisis," in Askew, *Legitimacy Crisis*, 246; Matt Wheeler, "People's Patron or Patronizing the People? The Southern Border Provinces Administrative Centre in Perspective," *Contemporary Southeast Asia* 32, no. 2 (2010): 222.

67 The four army regions are central Thailand (First Army), northeastern Thailand (Second Army), northern Thailand (Third Army) and southern Thailand (Fourth Army). See also Srisompob Jitpiromsri, "The New Challenge of Thailand's Security Forces in the Southern Frontiers," in *Knights of the Realm: Thailand's Military and Police, Then and Now*, ed. Paul Chambers (Bangkok: White Lotus, 2013), 553.

68 ICG, *Southern Thailand: The Problem with Paramilitaries*, Asia Report no. 140 (Bangkok/Brussels, 2007).

69 Field notes, October 13, 2010.

70 ICG, *Dialogue in Doubt*, 16.

71 See Srisompob, "The New Challenge of Thailand's Security Forces"; Diana Sarosi and Janjira Sombutpoonsiri, "Arming Civilians for Self-Defense: The Impact of Firearms Proliferation on the Conflict Dynamics in Southern Thailand," *Global Change, Peace & Security* 23, no. 3 (2011): 387–403; Rungrawee Chaloemsripinyorat, "The Security Forces and Human Rights Violations in Thailand's Insurgency-Wrecked South," in *Imagined Land? The State and Southern Violence in Thailand*, ed. Chaiwat Satha-Anand (Tokyo: Research Institute for Languages and Cultures of Asia and Africa, 2009).

72 Interview with Paul Chambers, Chiang Mai, March 21, 2016.

73 "Thailand Unsettled #4: The Deep South (with Deep South Watch)," interview with Romadon Panjor, *New Mandala*, March 20, 2019, https://www.newmandala.org/thailand-unsettled-4-the-deep-south-with-deep-south-watch/.

74 The use of color codes is a well-known counterinsurgency method not unique to southern Thailand. For instance, David Galula, whose writings have significantly influenced current US counterinsurgency policy, suggests mapping the area of counterinsurgency operations in the colors white, pink, and red. David Galula, *Counterinsurgency Warfare: Theory and Practice* (New York: Greewood, 1964), 52.

75 See Michael Jerryson, *Buddhist Fury: Religion and Violence in Southern Thailand* (Oxford: Oxford University Press, 2011).

76 Interview with conscript N., Wat Lak Mueang, Pattani, December 30, 2010.

77 Pattana Kitiarsa, "An Ambiguous Intimacy: Farang as Siamese Occidentalism," in Harrison and Jackson, *Ambiguous Allure of the West*, 57–74.

78 David Szanton, ed., *The Politics of Knowledge: Area Studies and the Disciplines* (Berkley: University of California Press, 2003); Christopher Simpson, "Universities, Empire, and the Production of Knowledge: An Introduction," in *Universities and Empire: Money and Politics in the Social Sciences during the Cold War*, ed. Christopher Simpson (New York: New Press, 1998), xi–xxxiv; Peter F. Bell, "Western Conceptions of Thai Society: The Politics of American Scholarship," *Journal of Contemporary Asia* 12, no. 1 (1982): 61–74; Eric Wakin, *Anthropology Goes to War: Professional Ethics and Counterinsurgency in Thailand* (Madison: University of Wisconsin Press, 1992).

79 Field notes, December 31, 2010.

80 Field notes, October 12, 2010.

81 Field notes, March 7, 2016.

82 Donna Haraway, "Situated Knowledges: The Science Question in Feminism and the Privilege of Partial Perspective," *Feminist Studies* 14, no. 3 (1988): 575–99; Lisa Wedeen, "Scientific Knowledge, Liberalism, and Empire: American Political Science in the Modern Middle East," in *Middle East Studies for the New Millennium: Infrastructures of Knowledge*, ed. Seteney Shami and Cynthia Miller-Idress (New York: Social Science Research Council and New York University Press, 2016), 31.

83 Barak Kalir, "The Field of Work and the Work of the Field: Conceptualising an Anthropological Research Engagement," *Social Anthropology* 14, no. 2 (2006): 235–46. For a detailed self-reflective discussion of my fieldwork experiences in southern Thailand, see Ruth Streicher, "Die Macht des Feldes: Für Selbstreflexivität als methodologische Strategie feministischer Feldforschung in Konfliktgebieten" [The power of the field: self-reflexivity as a methodological strategy of feminist research in areas of conflict] in *Geschlechterverhältnisse, Frieden und Konflikt: Feministische Denkanstöße für die Friedens- und Konfliktforschung* [*Gender relations, peace and conflict: Feminist food for thought for peace and conflict studies*], ed. Bettina Engels and Corinna Gayer (Baden-Baden: Nomos, 2011).

84 All translations from Thai are my own unless stated otherwise.

85 Genealogy calls for a critical history of the present that challenges the authoritative truth-claims of seemingly universal concepts. Instead of searching for timeless historical origins, genealogy tracks the contingent reconstitution of conceptual grammars through discursive practices in specific historical contexts and hence unfolds conceptual closures as products of discursive power-knowledge formations. Michel Foucault, "Nietzsche, Genealogy, History," in *Language, Counter-Memory, Practice: Selected Essays and Interviews*, ed. Donald Bouchard (Ithaca, NY: Cornell University Press, 1977), 139–64; Michel Foucault, *"Society Must Be Defended": Lectures at the Collège De France, 1975–1976*, ed. Mauro Bertani et al., vol. 1 (New York: Picador, [1976] 2003), lecture 1. See also Edward Schatz, "Introduction: Ethnographic Immersion and the Study of Politics," in *Political Ethnography: What Immersion Contributes to the Study of Power*, ed. Edward Schatz (London: University of Chicago Press, 2009), 1–22; Ruth Streicher and Schirin Amir-Moazami, "Reflections on Hegemonies of Knowledge Production and the Politics of Disciplinary Divisions," *TRAFO—Blog for Transregional Research*, August 4, 2016, https://trafo.hypotheses.org/3439.

1. POLICING HISTORY

1 Field notes, September 18, 2010.

2 Helbardt, "Deciphering Southern Thailand's Violence," 91. See also Duncan McCargo, "Patani Militant Leaflets and the Uses of History," in *Ghosts of the Past in Southern Thailand*, ed. Patrick Jory (Singapore: NUS Press, 2013), 277–97; Askew and Helbardt, "Becoming Patani Warriors";

3 National Reconciliation Commission, "Overcoming Violence through the Power of Reconcilitation," report (Bangkok: National Reconciliation Commission, 2006), 36; Davisakd Puaksom, "Of a Lesser Brilliance: Patani Historiography in Contention," in *Thai South and Malay North: Ethnic Interactions on a Plural Peninsula*, ed. Michael J. Montesano and Patrick Jory (Singapore: NUS Press, 2008), 72.

4 Dipesh Chakrabarty, *Provincializing Europe* (Princeton, NJ: Princeton University Press, 2000), 9.

5 Fernando Coronil, "After Empire: Reflections on Imperialism from the Americas," in Stoler, McGranahn, and Perdue, *Imperial Formations*, 245.

6 Mas, "On the Apocalyptic Tones of Islam in Secular Time," 88.

7 Thongchai Winichakul, "Siam's Colonial Conditions and the Birth of Thai History," in *Southeast Asian Historiograph: Unraveling the Myths*, ed. Volker Grabowsky (Bangkok: River Books, 2011), 22.

8 Patrick Jory, "Books and the Nation: The Making of Thailand's National Library," *Journal of Southeast Asian Studies* 31, no. 2 (2000): 367; Maurizio Peleggi, "From Buddhist Icons to National Antiquities: Cultural Nationalism and Colonial Knowledge in the Making of Thailand's History of Art," *Modern Asian Studies* 47, no. 5 (2013): 1522.

9 See Loos, *Subject Siam*.

10 See also Maurizio Peleggi, *Lords of Things: The Fashioning of the Siamese Monarchy's Modern Image* (Honolulu: University of Hawai'i Press, 2002), 131–32; Thongchai, "Siam's Colonial Conditions."

11 Chris Baker, trans., "The Antiquarian Society of Siam Speech of King Chulalongkorn," *Journal of the Siam Society* 89, nos. 1–2 (2001): 96, 97–98.

12 Steven Feierman, "Africa in History: The End of Universal Narratives," in *After Colonialism: Imperial Histories and Postcolonial Displacements*, ed. Gyan Prakash (Princeton, NJ: Princeton University Press, 1995).

13 Baker, "Antiquarian Society," 95.

14 Mas, "On the Apocalyptic Tones of Islam in Secular Time," 90.

15 Field notes, June 4, 2019.

16 Internal Security Operations Command (ISOC) 5th Operational Cooperation Centre, "Khumue chut ong khwamru prakopkan damnoenkan khong chao nathi phu patibat ngan nai phuen thi changwat chaidaen phak tai" [Handbook of operational knowledge for officers working in the southern border provinces] (Bangkok, 2010). Hereafter "ISOC Handbook."

17 "ISOC Handbook," n.p.

18 On the view from nowhere, see Haraway, "Situated Knowledges."

19 US Army, *Counterinsurgency (Field Manual, FM 3–24)* (Washington, DC: US Army, 2006). For a critique of the use of anthropological approaches in the manual, see David Price, "Faking Scholarship," in *The Counter-Counterinsurgency Manual: Or, Notes on Demilitarizing American Society*, ed. Network of Concerned Anthropologists (Chicago: Prickly Paradigm, 2009), 59–76. See also Derek Gregory, "'The Rush to the Intimate': Counterinsurgency and the Cultural Turn," *Radical Philosophy*, no. 150 (2008): 8–23; Markus Kienscherf, "Plugging Cultural Knowledge into the U.S. Military Machine: The Neo-Orientalist Logic of Counterinsurgency," *Topia: Canadian Journal of Cultural Studies* 23–24 (2010): 121–43; Maximilian C. Forte, "The Human Terrain System and Anthropology: A Review of Ongoing Public Debates," *American Anthropologist* 113, no. 1 (2011): 149–53; Roberto González, "Indirect Rule and Embedded Anthropology: Practical, Theoretical, and Ethical Concerns," in *Anthropology and Global Counterinsurgency*, ed. John D. Kelly et al. (Chicago: University of Chicago Press, 2010), 231–44.

20 Paul Chambers, "US-Thai Relations after 9/11: A New Era of Cooperation?," *Contemporary Southeast Asia: A Journal of International and Strategic Affairs* 26, no. 3 (2004): 460–79; Royal Thai Embassy, *The Eagle and the Elephant: Thai-American Relations since 1833; Part 3: Current Cooperation* (Washington DC: Royal Thai Embassy, 2009), 106–107.

21 Royal Thai Embassy, *The Eagle and the Elephant*, 107.

22 Conversation with Colonel W., Bangkok, February 11, 2011.

23 Thomas Rid, "The Nineteenth Century Origins of Counterinsurgency Doctrine," *Journal of Strategic Studies* 33, no. 5 (2010): 727–58; Roberto González, "Towards Mercenary Anthropology? The New UU Army Counterinsurgency Manual FM 3–24 and the Military-Anthropology Complex," *Anthropology Today* 23, no. 3 (2007): 14–19.

24 Montgomery McFate, "Anthropology and Counterinsurgency: The Strange Story of Their Curious Relationship," *Military Review* 85, no. 2 (2005): 28.

25 Thongchai Winichakul, "The Others Within: Travel and Ethno-Spatial Differentiation of Siamese Subjects 1885–1910," in *Civility and Savagery: Social Identity in Tai States*, ed. Andrew Turton (Richmond, UK: Psychology Press, 2000), 46–47.

26 Wakin, *Anthropology Goes to War*; Peter F. Bell, "Thailand's Northeast: Regional Underdevelopment, 'Insurgency,' and Official Response," *Pacific Affairs* 42, no. 1 (1969): 47–54; Military Research and Development Center, "Rai ngan khrongkan wichai khang san nai changwat chaidaen phak tai (khumue si changwat chaidaen phak tai)" [Report on the research project concerning the southern border provinces (handbook for the four southern border provinces)] (Bangkok, 1974).

27 For more on the general importance of handbooks for "organizing, preserving, retrieving, transmitting and consuming . . . knowledge throughout the Southeast Asian region," see Nicholas Farrelly, Craig J. Reynolds, and Andrew Walker, "Practical and Auspicious: Thai Handbook Knowledge for Agriculture and the Environment," *Asian Studies Review* 35, no. 2 (2011): 235–51. On the historical significance of handbooks in Thailand, see Craig J. Reynolds, *Seditious Histories: Contesting Thai and Southeast Asian Pasts* (Seattle: NUS Press, 2006), chap. 10; field notes, October 31, 2011.

28 Pimonpan Ukoskit, "The Internal Culture of Military Units and Its Impact on the Conflict Resolution in Thailand's Far South," in Chaiwat, *Imagined Land*, 98, 103.

29 Walter F. Vella, *Chaiyo! King Vajiravudh and the Development of Thai Nationalism* (Honolulu: University of Hawai'i Press, 1978), 198–99; Lak than prasa nayobai samrap monthon Patani [Policy principles for the monthon Patani], B.E. 2466 [1923], reprinted in *Naeo Thang Patibat Ratchakan. Samrap Kha Ratchakan Nai Phuen Thi Changwat Chai Daen Pak Tai* [Methods for the performance of officers: For officers in the area of the southern border provinces] (Bangkok, Thailand: Ministry of the Interior, 2004), 5–9.

30 A *monthon* was the major administrative unit before the territory of Siam was divided into provinces. For a discussion of this and other handbooks, see also Decha Tangseefa, "Reading 'Bureaucrat Manuals,' Writing Cultural Space: The Thai State's Cultural Discourses and the Thai-Malay in-between Spaces," in Chaiwat, *Imagined Land*, 121–44.

31 Archival research in Thai National Archives, Library of the Ministry of the Interior, Thai National Library, Bangkok, October/November 2014. See also Decha, "Reading 'Bureaucrat Manuals.'"

32 The *chularajamontri* is a government official tasked with protecting Islam on the king's behalf. He heads the Central Committee for Thai Islam with provincial Islamic Committees as local branches. Yoneo Ishii, *Sangha, State, and Society: Thai Buddhism in History* (Honolulu: University of Hawai'i Press, 1986), 127.

33 The 1923 handbook, for instance, solely deals with different aspects of Islam.

34 See also Decha, "Reading 'Bureaucrat Manuals.'"

35 "ISOC Handbook," 44–45, 78.

36 See especially Thongchai, *Siam Mapped*.

37 Reynolds, *Seditious Histories*, 52; Tambiah, "The Galactic Polity."

38 Davisakd, "Of a Lesser Brilliance."

39 Bradley, *Forging Islamic Power and Place*, 44–45.

40 Tej Bunnag, *The Provincial Administration of Siam 1892–1915: The Ministry of Interior under Prince Damrong Rajanubhab* (Kuala Lumpur: Oxford University Press, 1977), 5.

41 Tamara Loos, "Competitive Colonialisms: Siam and the Malay Muslim South," in Harrison and Jackson, *Ambiguous Allure of the West*, 75–92.

42 Loos, *Subject Siam*, 82.

43 Patani's last sultan was denied any control over political, fiscal, and legal matters and was replaced by a Siamese appointee after his death. His son, Prince Abdul Kadir, led the first major rebellion against the government of King Chulalongkorn in 1902. Thanet Aphornsuvan, "History and Politics of the Muslims in Thailand" (working paper, Thammasat University, 2003), 15.

44 Kennon Breazeale, "A Transition in Historical Writing: The Works of Prince Damrong Rachanuphap," *Journal of the Siam Society* 59, no. 2 (1971): 25–49.

45 Damrong Rajanubhab, "Laksana kanpokkhrong prathet sayam tae boran" [The nature of government in Siam since antiquity], in *Prawatisat lae kanmuang: nangsu an prakop wicha phunthan arayatham thai* [History and politics: Reading book for a course on Thai civilization] (Bangkok: Thammasat University Press, [1927] 1975).

46 Jory, "Books and the Nation," 363; Winai Pongsripian, "Traditional Thai Historiography and Its Nineteenth-Century Decline" (PhD diss., University of Bristol, 1983).

47 Jory, "Books and the Nation"; Lorraine M. Gesick, *In the Land of Lady White Blood: Southern Thailand and the Meaning of History* (Ithaca, NY: Cornell University Press, 1995), 15.

48 Damrong emphasized that history must be based on written sources that he considered trustworthy, and he consulted histories of Siam written by Westerners to correct errors in the chronicles. He also highlighted the need to write rational histories that explained the circumstances of an event, its causes, and its consequences. See Winai, "Traditional Thai Historiography," 432.

49 Winai, "Traditional Thai Historiography," 434.

50 Damrong, "Laksana kanpokkhrong," 7; Winai, "Traditional Thai Historiography," 434.

51 Davisakd, "Of a Lesser Brilliance," 72.

52 "ISOC Handbook," 141.

53 "ISOC Handbook," 118.

54 Gil Anidjar, *Semites: Race, Religion, Literature* (Stanford, CA: Stanford University Press, 2008), 20.

55 Christopher M. Joll, "Thailand's Muslim Kaleidoscope between Central Plains and Far-South: Fresh Perspectives from the Sufi Margins," in *Ethnic and Religious Identities and Integration in Southeast Asia*, ed. Volker Grabowsky and Oi Keat Jin (Chiang Mai, Thailand: Silkworm, 2016), 319–58; Christopher M. Joll, *Muslim Merit-Making in Thailand's Far-South* (Heidelberg, Germany: Springer, 2012); Muhammad Arafat Bin Mohamad, "Be-Longing: Fatanis in Makkah and Jawi" (PhD diss., Harvard University, 2013); Joseph Chinyong Liow, *Islam, Education, and Reform in Southern Thailand: Tradition and Transformation* (Singapore: ISEAS Press, 2009).

56 Piyada Chonlaworn, "Contesting Law and Order: Legal and Judicial Reform in Southern Thailand in the Late Nineteenth to Early Twentieth Century," *Southeast Asian Studies* 3, no. 3 (2014): 538; Loos, *Subject Siam*, chap. 3.

57 Talal Asad, *Formations of the Secular: Christianity, Islam, Modernity* (Stanford, CA: Stanford University Press, 2003), 227; Janet Halley and Kerry Rittich, "Critical Directions in Comparative Family Law: Genealogies and Contemporary Studies of Family Law Exceptionalism," *American Journal of Comparative Law* 58 (2010): 751, 757.

58 For the case of the Dutch East Indies, see M. B. Hooker, "Introduction: European Laws in South-East Asia," in Hooker, *Laws of South-East Asia*, vol. 2, 11. See also Ulrike Schaper, "Universalizing the Province Europe in Early German Legal Anthropology," *TRAFO—Blog for Transregional Research*, April 27, 2016, https://trafo.hypotheses.org/3982.

59 Schaper, "Universalizing the Province Europe."

60 Thomas S. Raffles, the colonial founder of Singapore, for instance, held that "it was the absence of a well-defined and generally accepted system of law which . . . was the greatest influence in the deterioration of the Malay character." Syed Hussein Alatas, *The Myth of the Lazy Native* (London: Frank Cass, 1977), 38.

61 Cited in Michael G. Peletz, *Islamic Modern: Religious Courts and Cultural Politics in Malaysia* (Princeton, NJ: Princeton University Press, 2002), 42.

62 Cited in Peletz, *Islamic Modern*, 41.

63 Max Weber, *Wirtschaft und Gesellschaft: Die Wirtschaft und die gesellschaftlichen Ordnungen und Mächte* [Economy and society: The economy and the arena of normative and de facto powers] (Tübingen, Germany: Mohr Siebeck, [1922] 2005), 188.

64 Asad, *Formations of the Secular*, 228.

65 Thongchai, "The Others Within."

66 Loos, *Subject Siam*, 81, 91.

67 Patrick Jory, "Thai and Western Buddhist Scholarship in the Age of Colonialism: King Chulalongkorn Redefines the Jatakas," *Journal of Asian Studies* 61, no. 3 (2002): 891–918; Erick White, "Fraudulent and Dangerous Popular Religiosity in the Public Sphere: Moral Campaigns to Prohibit, Reform, and Demystify Thai Spirit Mediums," in *Spirited Politics: Religion and Public Life in Contemporary Southeast Asia*, ed. Andrew C. Wilford and Kenneth M. George (Ithaca, NY: Southeast Asia Program Publications, Cornell University, 2005), 69–91.

68 "ISOC Handbook," 78.

69 Joll, *Muslim Merit-Making*; Bradley, *Forging Islamic Power and Place*, 22, 30–31. For a good overview of ethnographic literature on the cohabitation of Buddhists and Muslims in southern Thailand, see Alexander Horstmann, "Ethnohistorical Perspectives on Buddhist-Muslim Relations and Coexistence in Southern Thailand," *SOJOURN: Journal of Social Issues in Southeast Asia* 19, no. 1 (2004): 76–92.

70 Loos, *Subject Siam*, 95–97.

71 Thongchai, "The Others Within," 42–43; Thanet Aphornsuvan, "The West and Siam's Quest for Modernity: Siamese Responses to Nineteenth Century American Missionaries," *South East Asia Research* 17, no. 3 (2009): 412.

72 Charnvit Kasetsiri, "Message," in *Through the Eyes of the King: The Travels of King Chulalongkorn to Malaya*, ed. Patricia Lim Pui Huen (Singapore: ISEAS Press, 2009): x–xi; Peleggi, "From Buddhist Icons to National Antiquities"; Thongchai, "The Quest for 'Siwilai,'" 543.

73 Peleggi, "From Buddhist Icons to National Antiquities," 1533–34; Strate, *Lost Territories*, 160.

74 Jerryson, *Buddhist Fury*, 198n62; Thongchai, "Siam's Colonial Conditions."

75 Penny Edwards, *Cambodge: The Cultivation of a Nation* (Honolulu: University of Hawai'i Press, 2007), 36.

76 Marieke Bloembergen and Martijn Eickhoff, "Exchange and the Protection of Java's Antiquities: A Transnational Approach to the Problem of Heritage in Colonial Java," *Journal of Asian Studies* 72, no. 4 (2013): 1–24.

77 Laurie J. Sears, "Intellectuals, Theosophy, and Failed Narratives of the Nation in Late Colonial Java," in *A Companion to Postcolonial Studies*, ed. Henry Schwarz and Sangeeta Ray (Malden, MA: Blackwell, 2000), 338; Chao Phraya Thiphakorawong, *Nangsue Sadaeng Kitchanukit* [Elaboration on major and minor matters] (Bangkok: [1872] 1971), 145.

78 Strate, *Lost Territories*.

79 Field notes, March 8, 2016; Duncan McCargo, *Tearing Apart the Land: Islam and Legitimacy in Southern Thailand* (Ithaca, NY: Cornell University Press, 2008).

80 See Jerryson, *Buddhist Fury*.

81 Field notes, December 8, 2010.

82 Johannes Fabian, *Time and the Other: How Anthropology Makes Its Objects* (New York: Columbia University Press, 1983); Haraway, "Situated Knowledges."

83 Julia Clancy-Smith and Frances Gouda, "Introduction," in *Domesticating the Empire: Race, Gender, and Family Life in French and Dutch Colonialism*, ed. Julia Clancy-Smith and Frances Gouda (Charlottesville: University of Virginia Press, 1998), 7.

84 Frances Gouda, "The Gendered Rhetoric of Colonialism and Anti-Colonialism in Twentieth-Century Indonesia," *Indonesia* 55 (1993): 5.

85 Tony Day, *Fluid Iron: State Formation in Southeast Asia* (Honolulu: University of Hawai'i Press, 2002), 71; B. J. Terwiel, *The Ram Kamhaeng Inscription: The Fake That Did Not Come True* (Gossenberg, Germany: Ostasien Verlag, 2010), 21; Damrong, "Laksana kanpokkhrong," 6.

86 Thongchai, "Siam's Colonial Conditions," 34; Paul M. Handley, *The King Never Smiles: A Biography of Thailand's Bhumibol Adulyadej* (New Haven; CT: Yale University Press, 2006); Christine E. Gray, "Hegemonic Images: Language and Silence in the Royal Thai Polity," *Man, New Series* 26, no. 1 (1991): 43–65.

87 Vella, *Chaiyo!*, xvi.

88 Anthony V. N. Diller, "Islam and Southern Thai Ethnic Reference," in *Politics of the Malay-Speaking South*, vol. 1, *Historical and Cultural Studies*, ed. Andrew D. W. Forbes (Gaya, India: Centre for South East Asian Studies, 1989).

89 See Lak than prasa nayobai samrap monthon Patani [Policy principles for the monthon Patani].

90 Pavin Chachavalpongpun, "Thaksin, the Military, and Thailand's Protracted Political Crisis," in *The Political Resurgence of the Military in Southeast Asia: Conflict and Leadership*, ed. Marcus Mietzner (London: Routledge, 2011), 45–62.

91 PM Order 206.

92 ISOC, "Vision of the ISOC Region 4," my translation, http://www.southpeace.go.th/th/About/Vision-Mission.html.

93 Interviews with Conscript T., Pattani, January 9, 2011; Conscript S., Pattani, December 31, 2010; Conscript Ch., Pattani, January 9, 2011.

94 Field notes, November 22, 2010.

95 Field notes, December 8, 2010.

96 "Report of the Seminar on Village Defence and Development, Bangkok, March 15–21, 1970," Thailand Information Center, Bangkok, SVDD/70/REP.

97 According to Thak, Sarit's initial idea of development was largely paternalistic; he wanted to increase welfare, especially in rural areas, to strengthen the legitimacy of his regime. Therefore, he invited the first World Bank mission to Thailand immediately after his coup. The World Bank report resulted in the codification in Thailand's first five-year development plan of 1961. Thak Chaloemtiarana, *Thailand: The Politics of Despotic Paternalism* (Chiang Mai, Thailand: Silkworm, 2007), 167–68. See also Baker and Pasuk, *A History of Thailand*, 151.

98 Heymann, *Seminar on Development and Security in Thailand*, 8; Duncan McCargo, "Security, Development, and Political Participation in Thailand: Alternative Currencies of Legitimacy," *Contemporary Southeast Asia* 24, no. 1 (2002): 50–67.

99 Kanok Wongtrangan, *Change and Persistence in Thai Counter-Insurgency Policy*, Institute of Security and International Studies (ISIS) Occasional Paper no. 1 (Bangkok: Chulalongkorn University, 1983).

100 E.g., Khalili, *Time in the Shadows*, 34–39; Rid, "The Nineteenth Century Origins of Counterinsurgency Doctrine," 728.

101 Galula, *Counterinsurgency Warfare*, 7.

102 Michel Foucault, *"Society Must Be Defended": Lectures at the Collège De France, 1975–1976*, ed. Mauro Bertani et al., vol. 1 (New York: Picador, [1976] 2003), 15.

2. Checkpoints

1 Permanent checkpoints involved immovable elements like concrete blocks and normally remained in the same place for long periods of time. Flexible checkpoints, by contrast, were set up only temporarily by individual army units after military intelligence warning of attacks or after an attack had occurred; they often consisted of removable elements. One army unit at a permanent checkpoint could install up to three flexible checkpoints on demand. Therefore, it was hard to estimate their total number. Interview with chief of Public Relations Centre, ISOC 4 Forward Command, Yala, October 21, 2010; and interview with Head of Yala 11 Task Force, Yala, September 30, 2011.

2 Field notes on visit to Ban Puro, November 24, 2010.

3 When I visited the region again in 2016, the setup of some of the permanent checkpoints had changed; watchtowers and video cameras had been added. Moreover, many of the checkpoints were no longer manned by soldiers but by paramilitaries and policemen. In this chapter, I analyze material collected in 2010 and 2011.

4 Jan Robyn Weisman, *Tropes and Traces: Hybridity, Race, Sex and Responses to Modernity in Thailand* (PhD diss., University of Washington, 2000), 128.

5 Juliana Ochs in her study of Israel talks about "everyday practices of suspicion" to show how "in daily life Israelis embodied government classifications of the affect, dress and gestures of 'suspicious people.'" Ochs, *Security and Suspicion: An Ethnography of Everyday Life in Israel* (Philadelphia: University of Pennsylvania Press, 2011), 92. Although similarly inquiring into the materialization of racialized discursive categories, I am interested, by contrast, in practices enacted by the military in the name of policing.

6 Pradeep Jeganathan, "Checkpoint: Anthropology, Identity, and the State," in *Anthropology in the Margins of the State*, ed. Veena Das and Deborah Poole (Santa Fe, NM: School for Advanced Research Press, 2004), 67–81.

7 Interview with journalist D., Pattani, October 7, 2010.

8 Neelawat Ngoensongsee and Nootara Saengsooreet, "The Military Operations of Task Force 23 at the Checkpoint of Yan Pana, Pattani Province" (master's thesis, Prince of Songkhla University, 2010).

9 See Jerryson, *Buddhist Fury*, chap. 5. For a discussion of Thainess, see Saichol Sattayanurak, "The Construction of Mainstream Thought on 'Thainess' and the 'Truth' Constructed by 'Thainess,'" trans. Sarinee Achavanuntakul (paper presented at Conference on Thai Humanities II, 2005, Chiang Mai: Chiang Mai University), https://pdfs.semanticscholar.org/9a10/5c84daaca1b2d41b93aaa5885acd18de7b28.pdf.

10 Victor B. Lieberman, "Ethnic Politics in Eighteenth-Century Burma," *Modern Asian Studies* 12, no. 3 (1978): 455–82; Anderson, "Studies of the Thai State," 213.

11 Statistics was one of the most prominent fields of knowledge that helped to fortify and verify racial taxonomies to measure populations. For the inner functioning of states, it provided supposedly scientific evidence to improve the government of the population. In an imperial context, statistics allowed for dividing the world into barbarous and civilized races. See Linda Supik, *Statistik und Rassismus: Das Dilemma der Erfassung von Ethnizität* [Statistics and racism: The dilemma of recording ethnicity] (Frankfurt, Germany: Campus, 2014), 55–60.

12 David Streckfuss, "The Mixed Colonial Legacy in Siam: Origins of Thai Racialist Thought, 1890–1910," in *Autonomous Histories, Particular Truths: Essays in Honor of John R. W. Smail*, ed. Laurie J. Sears (Madison: University of Wisconsin Center for Southeast Asian Studies, 1993), 123–53; Soren Ivarsson, "Making Laos 'Our' Space: Thai Discourses on History and Race, 1900–1941," in *Contesting Visions of the Lao Past: Lao Historiography at the Crossroads*, ed. Soren Ivarsson and Christopher E. Goscha (Copenhagen: NIAS Press, 2003), 239–64.

13 Volker Grabowsky, "The Thai Census of 1904: Translation and Analysis," *Journal of the Siam Society* 84, no. 1 (1996): 49–85.

14 Stuart Hall, "Conclusion: The Multi-Cultural Question," in *Un/Settled Multiculturalisms: Diasporas, Entanglements, "Transruptions,"* ed. Barnor Hesse (London: Zed, 2000), 223.

15 Bangkok Times. *Directory for Bangkok and Siam* (Bangkok: Bangkok Times Press, 1914), 189.

16 Hall, "Conclusion," 223.

17 Carter, *Kingdom of Siam*, 58.

18 Charles Lemire, *La France et Le Siam* (Paris: A. Challamel, 1903); "Ethnographische Karte: Verbreitung der Menschenrassen" [Ethnographic map: Distribution of human races], in

Meyers Konversationslexikon: Eine Encyklopädie des allgemeinen Wissens [Meyers encyclopedia of general knowledge], 4th edition (Leipzig: Meyers und Verlag des Bibliographischen Institut Autorenkollektiv, 1885–1892), https://commons.wikimedia.org/wiki/File:Meyers_b11_s0476a.jpg.

19 Anthony Milner, *The Malays* (Malden, MA: Wiley, 2008), 124.

20 Anthony Milner, *The Invention of Politics in Colonial Malaya* (Cambridge: Cambridge University Press, 1994), 51.

21 Helbardt, "Deciphering Southern Thailand's Violence," 120.

22 Clive J. Christie, *A Modern History of Southeast Asia: Decolonization, Nationalism, and Separatism* (London: I. B. Tauris, 1996), 173.

23 Surin, "Islam and Malay Nationalism," 223.

24 Jerryson, *Buddhist Fury*, 157. *Chat* connotes common blood ties and lineage as well as a community of shared tradition, and can also refer to the concept of an extended family. See Loos, *Subject Siam*, 133; Eiji Murashima, "The Origin of Modern Official State Ideology in Thailand," *Journal of Southeast Asian Studies* 19, no. 1 (1988): 82; Craig J. Reynolds, "Introduction: National Identity and Its Defenders," in *National Identity and Its Defenders: Thailand, 1939–1989*, ed. Craig J. Reynolds, Monash Papers on Southeast Asia no. 25 (Clayton, Australia: Centre of Southeast Asian Studies, Monash University, 1991), 20.

25 Vajiravudh, *Lectures on Religious Topics* (1914), lectures 1, 7, 8, https://archive.org/details/cu31924022930204/page/n18.

26 This was not the only time the name of the country was changed. For a concise discussion of the name changes, see Reynolds, "Introduction"; Preecha Juntanamalaga, "Thai or Siam?," *Names: Journal of the American Name Society* 36, nos. 1–2 (1988): 69–84.

27 Vichitr Vadakarn, *Thailand's Case* (Bangkok: Thai Commercial Press, 1941), 121. Wichit Wathakan (sometimes spelled Vichit or Vichitr Vadakarn) referred to a philological discourse of race promoted by a number of scientists and missionaries who had become interested in the evolution of the Thai race (variously called "Tai," "Taï," "Shan" or "Ai-Lao"). He cited extensively, for instance, from late-nineteenth-century works by the Oxford University philologist Terrien de Lacouperie, who argued that Chinese civilization derived from numerous "pre-Chinese tribes" of the "Taï-shan race" that had migrated southward and eventually settled on the Indo-Chinese peninsula. Likewise, Wichit relied on the work of the missionary William Clifton Dodd. Terrien de Lacouperie, *The Languages of China before the Chinese* (London: David Nutt, 1887), 68; William Clifton Dodd, *The Tai Race: Elder Brother of the Chinese* (Cedar Rapids, Iowa: Torch, 1923). Translated into Thai in 1926. See also Scott Barmé, *Luang Wichit Wathakan and the Creation of Thai Identity* (Singapore: ISEAS Publishing, 1993), 49.

28 Veena Das, "Violence, Gender, and Subjectivity," *Annual Review of Anthropology*, no. 37 (2008): 287; Tracey Banivanua Mar, "Stabilizing Violence in Colonial Rule: Settlement and the Indentured Labour Trade in Queensland in the 1870s," in *Writing Colonial Histories: Comparative Perspectives*, ed. Tracey Banivanua Mar and Julie Evans (Melbourne, Australia: University of Melbourne conference and seminar series, 2002), 146; Reynolds, "Introduction," 24.

29 US Marine Corps, *Small Wars Manual (NAVMC 2890)* (Washington DC: US Marine Corps, 1940), 22. This connection is epitomized in the notion of martial races, which still influences contemporary recruitment strategies of private militarized security firms such as Blackwater. See Pradeep Barua, "Inventing Race: The British and India's Martial Races," *Historian* 58, no. 1 (1995): 107–16; Paul Higate, "Martial Races and Enforcement Masculinities of the Global South: Weaponising Fijian, Chilean, and Salvadoran Postcoloniality in the Mercenary Sector," *Globalizations* 9, no. 1 (2012): 35–52.

30 Patrick Porter, *Military Orientalism: Eastern War through Western Eyes* (London: Oxford University Press, 2009). I also discuss this in the last chapter.

31 Kasian Tejapira, *Commodifying Marxism: The Formation of Modern Thai Radical Culture, 1927–1958* (Kyoto: Kyoto University Press, 2001); Sinae Hyun, "Building a Human Border: The Thai Border Patrol Police School Project in the Post–Cold War Era," *SOJOURN: Journal of Social Issues in Southeast Asia* 29, no. 2 (2014): 335. On the Buddhist missionary programs, see Somboon Suksamran, *Political Buddhism in Southeast Asia: The Role of the Sangha in the Modernization of Thailand* (London: Hurst, 1977); Charles F. Keyes, "Political Crisis and Militant Buddhism in Contemporary Thailand," in *Religion and Legitimation of Power in Thailand, Laos, and Burma*, ed. Bardwell L. Smith (Chambersburg, PA: ANIMA, 1978), 147–64.

32 Markus Kienscherf, "A Programme of Global Pacification: US Counterinsurgency Doctrine and the Biopolitics of Human (In)Security," *Security Dialogue* 42, no. 6 (2011): 528–30. The US Army's counterinsurgency manual FM 3-24 explains the core function of "population and resource control" measures as "determining who lives in an area and what they do," which includes "determining societal relationships—family, clan, tribe, interpersonal, and professional." The manual also names conducting a census and issuing identification cards as the first steps in this direction. These measures are, moreover, mentioned by the counterinsurgency theorist David Galula, whose writings on the 1950s anti-guerrilla warfare in Algeria have been central to the formulation of US counterinsurgency doctrine. The measures should be employed, Galula clarifies, "to cut off, or at least reduce significantly, the contacts between the population and the guerrillas." US Army, *Counterinsurgency (Field Manual, FM 3-24)*, 5–21; Galula, *Counterinsurgency Warfare*, 118.

33 Derek Gregory, "The Biopolitics of Baghdad: Counterinsurgency and the Counter-City," *Human Geography* 1, no. 1 (2008): 6–27; Laleh Khalili, "The Location of Palestine in Global Counterinsurgencies," *International Journal of Middle East Studies* 42, no. 3 (2010): 413–33; United Nations Office for the Coordination of Humanitarian Affairs, "The Monthly Humanitarian Bulletin" (East Jerusalem: United Nations Office for the Coordination of Humanitarian Affairs, September 2018), https://www.ochaopt.org/content/monthly-humanitarian-bulletin-september-2018; Sherene Razack, "A Hole in the Wall; a Rose at a Checkpoint: The Spatiality of Colonial Encounters in Occupied Palestine," *Journal of Critical Race Inquiry* 1, no. 1 (2010): 90–108; Hagar Kotef and Merav Amir, "(En)Gendering Checkpoints: Checkpoint Watch and the Repercussions of Intervention," *Signs: Journal of Women in Culture and Society* 32, no. 4 (2007): 973–96; Gil Z. Hochberg, "'Check Me Out': Queer Encounters in Sharif Waked's *Chic Point: Fashion for Israeli Checkpoints*," *GLQ* 16, no. 4 (2010): 577–97.

34 Some senior colonels underlined the function of checkpoints as a population- and resource-control measure in accordance with the US manual. The head of the Yala Task Force, for instance, outlined three main functions of checkpoints: they could hinder insurgents from passing through before attacks, they could enable insurgents to be arrested at after attacks, and they made it possible for soldiers to warn the local population passing through against entering an area in danger of an attack. See notes on interview with head of Yala 11 Task Force, Yala, September 30, 2011. See also Jacob Abadi, *Israel's Quest for Recognition and Acceptance in Asia: Garrison State Diplomacy* (London: Routledge, 2004), 223.

35 Embassy of Israel to Thailand, "Bilateral Treaties and Agreements" (Bangkok: Embassy of Israel to Thailand, n.d.), https://embassies.gov.il/bangkok-en/Relations/Pages/Relations.aspx, accessed June 26, 2019; Ahron Shapiro, "Thailand, Israel Defence Ties Highlight Jerusalem's Increasing Focus on Asia," Australia/Israel & Jewish Affairs Council website, June 20, 2012, https://aijac.org.au/update/thailand-israel-defence-ties-highlight-jerusalem/.

36 For details on Israeli arms exports to Thailand, see Boycott, Divestment and Sanctions Thailand, *Israel-Thailand Relations: Complicity of Thailand over Israel's Occupation, Colonialism, and Apartheid in Palestine* (Bangkok: Boycott, Divestment and Sanctions Thailand, 2014); Southeast Asia–Israel Security Summit, Homeland Security Track, February 21, 2017, Bangkok, http://securitysummit.asia/homeland.html, accessed June 26, 2019.

37 Extract from group interview with soldiers at Wat Lak Mueang, Pattani, December 28, 2010.

38 The issue of cooperation with the police was controversial in army circles and Thai academia. It was argued, for instance, that if soldiers had to implement tasks that were usually police activities, they should also get proper training for these kinds of activities. Neelawat and Nootarat, "The Military Operations of Task Force 23."

39 Interview with conscript S., Checkpoint Bang Bla Mo, Pattani, December 31, 2010.

40 Field notes, December 31, 2010.

41 Carlo Bonura, "Indeterminate Geographies of Political Violence in Southern Thailand," *Alternatives* 33, no. 4 (2008): 383–412.

42 See Human Rights Watch, "'It Was Like Suddenly My Son No Longer Existed': Enforced Disappearances in Thailand's Southern Border Provinces," *Human Rights Watch Report* 19, no. 5 (2007), 47–49; field notes, March 15, 2010; interview with volunteer at the Muslim Attorney Centre, Pattani, October 18, 2010.

43 An independent fact-finding committee later concluded that the rangers were guilty of shooting innocent civilians, and relatives of the dead villagers were given financial compensation. See "Rangers at Fault in Fatal Shooting," *Bangkok Post*, March 21, 2012.

44 See "Police Go on Hunt for Defence Volunteer Killers," *Bangkok Post*, May 3, 2012; interview with Sergeant U., Pattani, January 2, 2011.

45 Field notes, March 24, 2010; field notes, October 19, 2010.

46 Group interview with third-year political science students, Prince of Songkhla University, Pattani, October 19, 2010.

47 Field notes, November 24, 2010.

48 Interview with conscript S., Checkpoint Bang Bla Mo, December 31, 2010.

49 Notes from interview with head of unit at Laem Nog, Pattani, December 8, 2010. He emphasized that soldiers were provided with pictures of the alleged perpetrators in addition to the poster that was put up at the checkpoint. On the poster that was distributed in the province of Pattani, police photographs of the faces of around eighty exclusively male suspects were reproduced under an announcement that these were persons sought on national security charges. The names of the suspects were written below the photographs. Different phone numbers were provided for people to call should they have any knowledge of the suspects' whereabouts.

50 Interview with conscript Aw., Checkpoint Bang Bla Mo, December 31, 2010.

51 As a consequence, the examination of weapons at checkpoints sometimes triggered conflicts between members of certain paramilitary organizations and soldiers who asked for official documentation. Notes from conversation with the head of the Pattani Battalion of Village Protection Volunteers (Or Ror Bor), January 13, 2011.

52 I observed one of these training sessions at Camp Naresuan, Pattani, January 5, 2011. Here, the commanding military officer explicitly asked me not to take photographs of villagers training to shoot because he feared this would paint a bad image. On the distribution of firearms in the southern provinces, see Sarosi and Janjira, "Arming Civilians for Self-Defense."

53 Interview with soldier P., Checkpoint Bang Bla Mo, January 9, 2011; group interview at Wat Lak Mueang, December 28, 2010.

54 Judith Butler, *Bodies That Matter: On the Discursive Limits of "Sex"* (London: Routledge, 1993), 2.

55 Ian Hacking, *Historical Ontology* (Cambridge, MA: Harvard University Press, 2002), chap. 6.

56 Diller, "Islam and Southern Thai Ethnic Reference."

57 Jean-Baptiste Pallegoix, *Siamese, French, English Dictionary* (Bangkok: Imprimerie de la Mission Catholique, 1896); Dan Beach Bradley, *Dictionary of the Siamese language* (Bangkok, 1873), 77, my translation.

58 Chao Phraya Thiphakorawong, *Nangsue Sadaeng Kitchanukit*, 144–45.

59 Charles Keyes, "Muslim 'Others' in Buddhist Thailand," *Thammasat Review* 13, no. 1 (2009): 21, 22

60 My translation. See http://www.royin.go.th/dictionary/.

61 Keyes, "Muslim 'Others' in Buddhist Thailand," 27.

62 Jasbir K. Puar and Amit S. Rai, "Monster, Terrorist, Fag: The War on Terrorism and the Production of Docile Patriots," *Social Text* 20, no. 3 (2002): 117–48; V. Spike Peterson, "Gendered Identities, Ideologies, and Practices in the Context of War and Militarism," in *Gender, War, and Militarism: Feminist Perspectives*, ed. Laura Sjoberg and Sandra Via (Santa Barbara, CA: Praeger, 2010), 21.

63 "Kan kae khai panha khwam man khong nai phuen thi changwat chaidaen pak tai" [Strategy of the Internal Security Operations Command], ISOC 4, http://www.southpeace.go.th.

64 Field notes, January 5, 2011; interviews with conscripts: S., T., and Ch. at Checkpoint Bang Bla Mo, December 31, 2010; interviews with conscripts Pai. and An., at Checkpoint Pattani Concrete Company, Pattani, January 7, 2011.

65 Interview with conscript Aw., Checkpoint Bang Bla Mo, December 31, 2010; field notes from observations at a checkpoint in Yala, December 9, 2010; field notes from observations at Checkpoint Dalad Muang Mai, Yala, September 20, 2011.

66 Interview with conscript C., Checkpoint Bang Bla Mo, January 9, 2011; interview with soldier N., at Wat Lak Mueang, December 30, 2010.

67 Field notes on observations at a checkpoint in Yala, September 30, 2011.

68 Masuzawa, *The Invention of World Religions*, chap. 5; Maurice Olender, *The Languages of Paradise: Race, Religion, and Philology in the Nineteenth Century* (Cambridge, MA: Harvard University Press, 2008).

69 Friedrich Max Müller, *Letter to Chevalier Bunsen on the Classification of the Turanian Languages* (London: A. & G. A. Spottiswoode, 1854), 8.
70 Müller, *Letter to Chevalier Bunsen*, 149, 152. The common racial origins of Malay and Indo-Chinese people was a point of contention for Oriental scholars at the time. Another writer who argued for the commonality of the Malay and the Indo-Chinese was J. G. D. Campbell, a British adviser to the Siamese government: "Till not long ago it was customary to regard the Malays as a distinct branch of the human race; but though at first sight their speech, which has quite lost its tonic character, seemed to bear little or no resemblance to that of the other inhabitants of Indo-China, recent research has shown a certain affinity between the Malay and Mon languages. Moreover, it is impossible to resist the strong physiological evidence of their kinship. The short stature, the broad features, and flat noses all point to a common ancestry." J. G. D. Campbell, *Siam in the Twentieth Century: Being the Experiences and Impressions of a British Official* (London: Edward Arnold, 1904), 61.
71 Rachel Leow, *Taming Babel: Language in the Making of Malaysia* (Cambridge: Cambridge University Press, 2016), chap. 2.
72 Anthony Diller, "What Makes Central Thai a National Language?," in Reynolds, *National Identity and Its Defenders*, 75. Preecha states that a British administrator in Malaya was the first to suggest the English spelling "Thai" in the title of his work on the grammar of Th'ai or Siamese language. See Preecha, "Thai or Siam?"
73 Bangkok Times, *Directory for Bangkok and Siam*, 189.
74 Carter, *Kingdom of Siam*, 90.
75 Diller, "What Makes Central Thai a National Language?," 95; Vella, *Chaiyo!*, 234n1; Joseph Chinyong Liow, *Islam, Education, and Reform in Southern Thailand: Tradition and Transformation* (Singapore: ISEAS Publishing, 2009), 57.
76 Christopher M. Joll, "Why Monolingual Mind-Sets, Linguistic Justice, and Language Policy Are All Central to a Peaceful, Political Resolution to Thailand's Southern Impasse" (paper presented at the International Conference on Political Transition, Non-Violence, and Communication in Conflict Transformation, Pattani, January 26–27, 2017).
77 Interview with Ahmad Somboon Bualuang, one of the members of the National Reconciliation Commission, Pattani, October 14, 2010.
78 For remarks on the official taxonomy of language, see Reynolds, "Introduction," 8.
79 Adding to these complications, the insurgency movement has similarly sought to exploit the distinction between Thai and the Malay dialect spoken in Patani as an essential difference that also overwrites the category of religion. Muslim friends from other regions who had moved to the South frequently reported that people in the southern provinces had doubted their religious affiliation because they did not speak Malay. A Muslim professor who had researched the predecessors of the insurgency movement similarly attested to his exclusion from certain discussions in Malay on the grounds that he did not understand the Malay dialect and therefore could not share the Patani Malay history. Interview with Chaiwat Satha-Anand, February 10, 2011, Bangkok.
80 Statement by C., group interview with soldiers at Wat Lak Mueang, Pattani, December 28, 2010; group interview with students at Azizstan Foundation School, Khok Pho, Pattani, November 29, 2010.
81 For a description of sumptuary regulations at the royal court in premodern Siam, see Leslie Ann Woodhouse, "A 'Foreign' Princess in the Siamese Court: Princess Dara Rasami, the Politics of Gender, and Ethnic Difference in Nineteenth-Century Siam" (PhD diss., University of California, 2009), 159. See also Bernard S. Cohn, *Colonialism and Its Forms of Knowledge: The British in India* (Princeton, NJ: Princeton University Press, 1996), 109–10.
82 Campbell, *Siam in the Twentieth Century*.
83 Grabowsky, "Thai Census of 1904," 53, 61.
84 E.g. Jean-Baptiste Pallegoix, *Description du Royaume de Siam* (Bangkok: DK Book House, [1854] 1976), 56; Étienne Aymonier, *Le Cambodge* (Paris: Leroux, 1900), 11; Peleggi, *Lords of Things*, chap. 2. Peleggi reports a royal decree issued on the occasion of the visit of Prince Henri of Prussia in 1899 that ordered, for instance, that all women should have "their breasts covered in public." Peleggi, *Lords of Things*, 62.
85 Thak Chaloemtiarana, *Thai Politics: Extracts and Documents, 1932–1957* (Bangkok: Thammasat University Printing Office, 1978), 257.

86 Nantawan Haemindra, "The Problem of the Thai-Muslims in the Four Southern Provinces of Thailand (Part Two)," *Journal of Southeast Asian Studies* 8, no. 1 (1977): 92.

87 Christie, *Modern History of Southeast Asia,* 228.

88 Judith Butler, "Endangered/Endangering," in *The Body: A Reader,* ed. Mariam Fraser and Monica Greco (London: Routledge, 2005), 141.

89 Sudarat Musikawong, "Art for October: Thai Cold War State Violence in Trauma Art," *Positions: East Asia Cultures Critique* 18, no. 1 (2010): 32.

90 Arnika Fuhrmann, *Ghostly Desires: Queer Sexuality and Vernacular Buddhism in Contemporary Thai Cinema* (Durham, NC: Duke University Press, 2016), 112.

91 On practices of praying in southern Thailand, see also Joll, *Muslim Merit-Making.*

92 Conversation with student A., Tanyong Luloh, September 29, 2010; interview with students at Triam Suksa Wittaya School, Pattani, January 11, 2011.

93 Interview with Ahmad Somboon Bualuang, October 14, 2010, Pattani.

94 Alexander Horstmann, "The Inculturation of a Transnational Islamic Missionary Movement: Tablighi Jamaat al-Dawa and Muslim Society in Southern Thailand," *SOJOURN: Journal of Social Issues in Southeast Asia* 22, no. 1 (2007): 107–30; conversation with soldier at Wat Lak Mueang, October 29, 2010; group interview with soldiers at Wat Lak Mueang, Pattani, December 28, 2010. For more on ideas about religious indoctrination, see chap. 3.

95 Kate Crosby, *Theravada Buddhism: Continuity, Diversity, and Identity* (Malden, MA: Wiley-Blackwell, 2014), 198.

96 See, for instance, the sign for priority seating on Bangkok's metro trains, https://commons.wikimedia.org/wiki/File:Priority_seats,_Bangkok_-_2016-06-17_(001).jpg, June 17, 2017.

97 Jerryson, *Buddhist Fury.*

98 "Monk, Soldiers Hurt by Patani Bomb," *Bangkok Post,* January 28, 2011.

99 Field notes, December 8, 2010 and December 23, 2010.

100 Field notes, October 13, 2010; Michael Jerryson, "Appropriating a Space for Violence: State Buddhism in Southern Thailand," *Journal of Southeast Asian Studies* 40, no. 1 (2009): 33–57.

101 Interview with private Ak. at Wat Lak Mueang, December 30, 2010; interview with conscript Ch., Checkpoint Bang Bla Mo, January 9, 2011; group interview with soldiers at Wat Lak Mueang, December 28, 2010.

102 Guidelines for soldiers working in the southern border provinces, obtained in 2010; group interview, Islamnitivit School, Pattani, December 6, 2010.

103 Interview with Private Ch., Checkpoint Bang Bla Mo, January 9, 2011; interview with Sergeant J., Pattani, December 31, 2010; field notes on observations at checkpoint in Yala, September 30, 2011.

104 Thak, *Thai Politics,* 256, 258.

105 Barmé, *Luang Wichit Wathakan and the Creation of Thai Identity,* 151; Stoler, *Race and the Education of Desire.*

106 Thongchai, "The Quest for 'Siwilai'"; Campbell, *Siam in the Twentieth Century,* 94–95, 105.

107 Patrick Jory, "Thailand's Politics of Politeness: Qualities of a Gentleman and the Making of 'Thai Manners,'" *South East Asia Research* 23, no. 3 (2015): 362.

108 Elahe Haschemi Yekani, "Enlightened Imperialism"—Der englische Gentleman-Hero als Erlös(t)er" ["Enlightened imperialism"—the English gentleman-hero as savior] in *Erlöser: Figurationen männlicher Hegemonie* [Saviors: Figurations of male hegemony], ed. Sven Glawion, Elahe Haschemi Yekani, and Jana Husmann-Kastein (Bielefeld, Germany: Transcript Verlag, 2007); Battye, "Military, Government, and Society in Siam," 128n32; For the case of the German military, see Ute Frevert, "Das Militär als Schule der Männlichkeiten" [The military as a school of masculinities], in *Männlichkeiten und Moderne: Geschlecht in den Wissenskulturen um 1900* [Masculinities and modernity: Gender in cultures of knowledge around 1900], ed. Ulrike Brunotte and Rainer Herrn (Bielefeld, Germany: Transcript Verlag, 2008).

109 Sukunya Bumroongsook, "Chulachomklao Royal Military Academy: The Modernization of Military Education in Thailand, 1887–1948" (PhD diss., Northern Illinois University, 1991), 80.

110 Hanstaad reports his difficulties in arranging observations at a police checkpoint in Bangkok and even suspected that a special police unit set up a fake checkpoint to display to him as a foreign researcher. Hanstaad, "Constructing Order through Chaos," 29.

111 PM Order 206, 3.11.

112 The need to cooperate with the Organization of Islamic Cooperation is explicitly mentioned in the ISOC strategy. See "Kan kae khai panha khwam man khong nai phuen thi changwat chaidaen pak tai."

113 Quote from interview reprinted in "General Anupong Opens His Heart on the Southern Situation," *Isara News*, August 24, 2010.

114 See, for instance, the definition provided by the Oxford English Dictionary, which glosses the etymological origin of Thai as "free." *Oxford English Dictionaries* online, https://www.oed.com/view/Entry/200056?redirectedFrom=Thai#eid, accessed August 13, 2019.

115 Thanet Aphornsuvan, "Slavery and Modernity: Freedom in the Making of Modern Siam," in *Asian Freedoms: The Idea of Freedom in East and Southeast Asia*, ed. David Kelly and Anthony Reid (Cambridge: Cambridge University Press, 1998), 180; Pallegoix, *Déscription du Royaume de Siam*: 90; Campbell, *Siam in the Twentieth Century*.

116 Thanet, "Slavery and Modernity," 178.

117 These are Damrong's own words; he translates his Thai definition into English. Damrong, "The Nature of Government," 6; Sunait Chutintaranond, "The Image of the Burmese Enemy in Thai Perceptions and Historical Writing," *Journal of the Siam Society* 80, no. 1 (1992): 89–98.

118 W. A. R. Wood, who wrote one of the first history books on Siam in the English language, worked closely with Prince Damrong and reproduced his narrative of the freedom-loving Thai race: "It will, I think, be frankly admitted that the Siamese have some right to feel a pride in the history of their country. It is the story of a collection of more or less uncultivated immigrants from Southern China, who settled in the country now known as Siam, overcoming a mighty Empire, and establishing a number of free States, which became finally fused into the Siam of to-day. We see them humbled to the dust again and again by a more powerful neighbour, yet always rising up and regaining their freedom. A hundred years ago there were dozens of independent States in South-Eastern Asia. To-day there remains but one—Siam." W. A. R. Wood, *A History of Siam* (London: T. Fisher Unwin, 1926), 7–8.

119 Preecha, "Thai or Siam?," 75.

120 Interviews with students at the Prince of Songkla University, Pattani, October 19, 2010.

121 Interview with soldier P., Checkpoint Bang Bla Mo, January 9, 2011; see Laura Sjoberg, "Women Fighters and the 'Beautiful Soul' Narrative," *International Review of the Red Cross* 92, no. 877 (2010): 53–68.

122 Interview with soldier S., October 9, 2010; field notes, September 28, 2011.

123 Gayatri Chakravorti Spivak, "Can the Subaltern Speak?," in *The Post-Colonial Studies Reader*, ed. Bill Ashcroft, Gareth Griffiths, and Helen Tiffin (London: Routledge, 1996); Miriam Cooke, "Saving Brown Women," *Signs: Journal of Women in Culture and Society* 28, no. 1 (2002): 468–70.

124 Carter, *Kingdom of Siam*, 45.

125 John H. Freeman, *An Oriental Land of the Free* (Philadelphia: Westminster, 1910), 23.

126 Campbell, *Siam in the Twentieth Century*, 112.

127 Interview with soldier N., at Wat Lak Mueang, December 30, 2010; interview with soldier Y., at checkpoint Bang Bla Mo, December 31, 2010.

128 Penny van Esterik, *Materializing Thailand* (New York: Berg, 2000), 36; interviews with soldiers An. and Pai., Checkpoint Pattani Concrete Company, January 2, 2011; notes from conversation with soldier at a checkpoint in Tanyong Luloh, October 4, 2010; notes from conversation with soldier Sa. (employee at Yalannanbaru), October 10, 2010.

129 Interview with soldier P., Checkpoint Bang Bla Mo, January 9, 2011; group interview at Wat Lak Mueang, December 28, 2010; group interviews with Satri Pattana Saksa Groups 2 and 3, December 2, 2010.

130 Interview with female student W., Tanyong Luloh, Pattani, October 2, 2010 (see transcript lines 163–169).

131 Saroja Dorairajoo, "All My Men Are Dead: Women, the Real Victims of Violence in Southern Thailand" (paper presented at International Symposium: Gender and Islam in Southeast Asia, University of Passau, Germany, 2005), 11, http://www.susanne-schroeter.de/pdf/all_my_men_are_dead.pdf; Leila Ahmed, *Women and Gender in Islam: Historical Roots of a Modern Debate* (New Haven, CT: Yale University Press, 1992), chap. 8; Frantz Fanon, *A Dying Colonialism* (New York: Grove, 1965), 43–44.

132 Group interview, Satri Patana Suksa School, December 2, 2010.

133 Group interview, Islamnitivit School, Pattani, December 6, 2010; field notes, January 8, 2011; group interview, Yala Islamic University, Yala, October 6, 2010.

134 Group interviews, Azistan and Triam Suksa Wittaya Schools, November 29, 2010 and January 11, 2011; field notes, September 30, 2011.

135 Group interviews, Islamnitivit School, December 6, 2010; field notes, October 6, 2011.

136 Peleggi, *Lords of Things*, 2; Sukunya, "Chulachomklao Royal Military Academy," 80.

137 Battye, "The Military, Government, and Society in Siam," 128.

138 Kitiarsa, "Ambiguous Intimacy."

3. The New Path to Peace

1 Field notes, March 19, 2010. This origin was obscured in the Thai pronunciation used by the military. Instead of the Malay *jalan*, for instance, the military used *yalan*, and the emphasis was put on the last syllable (*barú*) instead of the Malay-style emphasis on the penultimate syllable (*báru*).

2 My fieldwork material does not allow me to make claims concerning the present operation of Yalannanbaru.

3 Interview with Colonel S., Pattani, October 20, 2010.

4 ISOC and Office of Narcotics Control Board, "Sarup phon kan kae khai panha ya sep tit nai phuen thi changwat chaidaen pak tai" [Summary of strategies to solve the problem of drug abuse in the southern provinces]. Internal document obtained by Colonel S. in October 2010.

5 For more general Orientalist notions, see Naomi Davidson, *Only Muslim: Embodying Islam in Twentieth-Century France* (Ithaca, NY: Cornell University Press, 2012). On Thailand specifically, see Loos, *Subject Siam*.

6 Jerryson, "Appropriating a Space for Violence," 57. Duncan McCargo, "The Politics of Buddhist Identity in Thailand's Deep South: The Demise of Civil Religion?," *Journal of Southeast Asian Studies* 40, no. 1 (2009): 11–32.

7 See Masuzawa, *Invention of World Religions*.

8 Talal Asad, *Genealogies of Religion: Discipline and Reasons of Power in Christianity and Islam* (Baltimore: Johns Hopkins University Press, 1993), 1; and Asad, *Formations of the Secular*.

9 Michel Foucault, *Discipline and Punish: The Birth of the Prison* (New York: Vintage, [1975] 1995); Asad, *Genealogies of Religion*, 165.

10 Thongchai Winichakul, "Buddhist Apologetics and a Genealogy of Comparative Religion in Siam," *Numen* 62, no. 1 (2015): 76–99; Craig J. Reynolds, "Buddhist Cosmography in Thai History, with Special Reference to Nineteenth-Century Culture Change," *Journal of Asian Studies* 35, no. 2 (1976): 203–20; Thanet, "The West and Siam's Quest for Modernity"; Jory, "Thai and Western Buddhist Scholarship."

11 I discuss these issues more extensively in Ruth Streicher, "Imperialism, Buddhism, and the Secular in 19th-Century Siam—Notes on Provincializing Secularism," *TRAFO—Blog for Transregional Research*, April 25, 2016, https://trafo.hypotheses.org/3941.

12 White, "Fraudulent and Dangerous Popular Religiosity in the Public Sphere"; Thongchai, *Siam Mapped*.

13 For an exploration of this policy with regards to Burma/Myanmar, see Alicia Turner, *Saving Buddhism: The Impermanence of Religion in Colonial Burma* (Honolulu: University of Hawai'i Press, 2014).

14 See articles 1.4 and 2.13 of the 1932 Constitution (in Thai). See also Yoneo Ishii, "Thai Muslims and the Royal Patronage of Religion," *Law & Society Review* 28, no. 3 (1994): 453–60.

15 Charles F. Keyes, "Buddhism and National Integration in Thailand," *Journal of Asian Studies* 30, no. 3 (1971): 551–67.

16 Interview with Colonel S., Pattani, October 20, 2010.

17 The *kratom* tree belongs to the family of coffee plants. It is indigenous to Southeast Asia and is widespread in southern Thailand. Chewing *kratom* leaves has a long tradition in the region and is also part of certain traditional ceremonies. The boiling of leaves and mixing them with different substances is a trend that developed in the early twenty-first century.

Depending on the concentration of the tea, it can have stimulating or depressing effects on the nervous system. According to a 2011 report by the International Drug Policy Consortium, however, *kratom* leaves as such are relatively harmless—the researchers therefore recommended decriminalizing their use. See Pascal Tanguay, "Kratom in Thailand: Decriminalisation and Community Control?," Series on Legislative Reform of Drug Policies, no. 13 (Transnational Institute, April 2011), https://www.tni.org/en/page/introduction.

18 "Drugs and Disaffection in Southern Thailand," *Asia Times*, February 18, 2010.
19 Conversation with Abae, young man in the village of Tanyong Luloh, September 30, 2010; interview with Rohseeda Busu, women's activist and journalist, Pattani, December 27, 2010.
20 Interview with Muhammed Ayub Pathan, journalist and editor of *Deep South Watch*, Pattani, September 29, 2010.
21 See Mrinalini Sinha, "Colonial and Imperial Masculinities," in *International Encyclopedia of Men and Masculinities*, ed. Michael Flood et al. (London: Routledge, 2007), 73–76.
22 Field notes, October 3, 2011.
23 Interview with soldier Sa., military assistant at Yalannanbaru, October 9, 2010.
24 For a critical assessment of this official discourse on the insurgency and drug abuse, see International Crisis Group, *Recruiting Militants in Southern Thailand*, Asia Report No. 170 (Bangkok/Brussels, 2009), 6; Srisompob Jitpiromsri and Duncan McCargo, "The Southern Thai Conflict Six Years On: Insurgency, Not Just Crime," *Contemporary Southeast Asia* 32, no. 2 (2010): 167.
25 Saroja Dorairajoo, "Peaceful Thai, Violent Malay (Muslim): A Case Study of the 'Problematic' Muslim Citizens of Southern Thailand," *Copenhagen Journal of Asian Studies* 27, no. 2 (2009): 61–83.
26 Field notes, October 20, 2010.
27 *Chularajamontri* is the Thai translation of the Arabic *Shaikh al-Islam*, designating the official with the function of providing Islamic advice to the government. The *chularajamontri* is royally appointed for a lifetime and also has to act as an adviser to the king on Islamic matters. Imtiyaz Yusuf, "Islam and Democracy in Thailand: Reforming the Office of *Chularajamontri/Shaikh al-Islam*," *Journal of Islamic Studies* 9, no. 2 (1998): 277.
28 "Chularajamontri Helps to Build Up Project against Drugs in the South," *Chularajamontri* 1, issue 2 (September 2011) (in Thai): 34–35; field notes, October 2, 2011.
29 Field notes, September 24, 2010 and October 2, 2011.
30 Notes on informal conversation with Ustadz A., Yala, October 2, 2011.
31 Ellen Herman, "Project Camelot and the Career of Cold War Psychology," in Simpson, *Universities and Empire*, 121. See also Vanessa Pupavac, "War on the Couch: The Emotionology of the New International Security Paradigm," *European Journal of Social Theory* 7, no. 2 (2004): 149–70.
32 Interview with conscript Ao. at Wat Lak Mueang, Pattani, December 28, 2010. This notion was often voiced in conjunction with the anxiety that soldiers themselves were clearly visible because of their uniform. See field notes, October 6, 2011. A common related metaphor depicted insurgents as ghosts. Marc Askew, "Fighting with Ghosts: Querying Thailand's 'Southern Fire,'" *Contemporary Southeast Asia* 32, no. 2 (2010): 118.
33 See William Chu, "Path," in *Encyclopedia of Buddhism*, ed. Robert E. Buswell (New York: Macmillan Reference USA, 2004), 635–40.
34 The principle of the middle path between sensual indulgence and self-mortification is part of the first sermon Buddha taught to his disciples, and practicing the principles of the middle path also forms the last of the four noble truths leading ultimately to the cessation of suffering. Craig J. Reynolds, "Chumchon/Community," in *Words in Motion: Toward a Global Lexicon*, ed. Carol Gluck and Anna Lowenhaupt Tsing (Durham, NC: Duke University Press, 2009), 209; Soren Ivarsson and Lotte Isager, "Strengthening the Moral Fibre of the Nation: The King's Sufficiency Economy as Etho-Politics," in *Saying the Unsayable: Monarchy and Democracy in Thailand*, ed. Soren Ivarsson and Lotte Isager (Copenhagen: NIAS Press, 2010), 223–40.
35 PM Order 68, paragraph 4.1.
36 Stephen C. Berkwitz, "History and Gratitude in Theravāda Buddhism," *Journal of the American Academy of Religion* 71, no. 3 (2003): 583.
37 Vichitr, *Thailand's Case*, 136.
38 Notes from conversation with ranger I., working at Yalannanbaru, October 4, 2011.

39 Conversation with soldier Sa., Yala, field notes, September 15, 2010.

40 ISOC and Office of Narcotics Control Board, "Sarup phon kan kae khai panha ya sep tit nai phuen thi changwat chaidaen pak tai."

41 *Yawi* (or *Jawi*) is more correctly a script (Malay written in Arabic), but the term was often used by soldiers to describe the Malay dialect spoken in southern Thailand.

42 Field notes, March 19, 2010 and September 15, 2010.

43 One of the Muslim teachers interviewed referred to the notion of correct Muslim subjects. See field notes, October 2, 2011.

44 Interview with Si., Office of Narcotics Control Board officer responsible for Yalannanbaru, Yala, October 9, 2010.

45 Field notes, October 9, 2010 and October 23, 2010.

46 Foucault, *Discipline and Punish*, 160.

47 Chris Lyttleton, "Magic Lipstick and Verbal Caress: Doubling Standards in Isan Villages," in *Coming of Age in South and Southeast Asia: Youth, Courtship, and Sexuality*, ed. Lenore Manderson and Pranee Liamputtong (Richmond, UK: Psychology Press, 2002), 165–87; Michael Chladek, "'They Will Be Like Diamonds': Novice Summer Camps, Being Riaproi, and Adjusting Selves" (unpublished paper, Theravada Civilizations Workshop, Seattle, 2016); John Powers, *A Bull of a Man: Images of Masculinity, Sex, and the Body in Indian Buddhism* (Cambridge, MA: Harvard University Press, 2009); Joanna Cook, *Meditation in Modern Buddhism: Renunciation and Change in Thai Monastic Life* (Cambridge: Cambridge University Press, 2010); Craig J. Reynolds, "Power," in *Critical Terms for the Study of Buddhism*, ed. Donald S. Lopez (Chicago: University of Chicago Press, 2005), 211–28.

48 *Krabuan kan fuek oprom khai "yalannanbaru—thang sai mai"* [Procedure of practice for the camp "Yalannanbaru—the New Path"], staff handbook, September 2011. Obtained by Yalannanbaru staff. Hereafter referred to as "staff handbook."

49 Katherine A. Bowie, *Rituals of National Loyalty: An Anthropology of the State and the Village Scout Movement in Thailand* (New York: Columbia University Press, 1997), 20–21.

50 Staff handbook, explanations of the fourth day; field notes, October 6, 2011.

51 Foucault, *Discipline and Punish*, 138.

52 Asad, *Genealogies of Religion*, chap. 4; Saba Mahmood, *Politics of Piety: The Islamic Revival and the Feminist Subject* (Princeton, NJ: Princeton University Press, 2005), 128; Cook, *Meditation in Modern Buddhism*, chap. 1; Asad, *Formations of the Secular*.

53 Field notes, October 3, 2011.

54 Interview with soldier Sa., October 9, 2010.

55 Anne McClintock, *Imperial Leather: Race, Gender and Sexuality in the Colonial Contest* (London: Routledge, 1995), 208.

56 Field notes, October 9, 2010.

57 Kathleen Lennon, "Feminist Perspectives on the Body," *Stanford Encyclopedia of Philosophy* online, fall 2010 edition, https://plato.stanford.edu/entries/feminist-body/; Davidson, *Only Muslim*, 3–4.

58 Field notes, October 7, 2011.

59 Notes from conversation with Colonel S., Pattani, March 19, 2010; notes from conversation with soldier N., Yala, September 15, 2010; notes from interview with officer Si., Yala, October 9, 2010.

60 Field notes, October 2, 2011.

61 Interview with soldier Sa., October 9, 2010.

62 Clancy-Smith and Gouda, "Introduction," 1–20.

63 Nicholas B. Dirks, "The Policing of Tradition: Colonialism and Anthropology in Southern India," *Society for Comparative Study of Society and History* 39, no. 1 (1997): 182–212; Joll, *Muslim Merit-Making*; notes from conversation with Aj. Sole Tadik, dean of the Faculty of Science and Technology, Islamic College, Yala, March 20, 2010.

64 Notes from conversation with Colonel S., March 19, 2010.

65 Field notes, October 2, 2011; notes from conversation with soldier N., September 15, 2010.

66 Ann Laura Stoler, "Affective States," in *A Companion to the Anthropology of Politics*, ed. David Nugent (Oxford: Blackwell, 2004), 4.

67 See Stoler, *Race and the Education of Desire*; Stoler, "Affective States"; Ann Laura Stoler, "Intimidations of Empire: Predicaments of the Tactile and Unseen," in *Haunted by Empire: Geographies of Intimacy in North American History*, ed. Ann Laura Stoler (Durham, NC: Duke University Press, 2006).

68 PM Order 206, 3.3.

69 Field notes, October 23, 2010.

70 Saba Mahmood, "Religious Reason and Secular Affect: An Incommensurable Divide?," *Critical Inquiry* 35, no. 4 (2009): 848.

71 Berkwitz, "History and Gratitude," 592.

72 Van Esterik, *Materializing Thailand*, 211; Charles F. Keyes, "Mother or Mistress but Never a Monk: Buddhist Notions of Female Gender in Rural Thailand," *American Ethnologist* 11, no. 2 (1984): 229; Lyttleton, "Magic Lipstick and Verbal Caress," 171; Andrea Whittaker, *Abortion, Sin, and the State in Thailand* (New York: Routledge, 2004), 67.

73 Internal ISOC document on Yalannanbaru.

74 Field notes, October 2, 2011.

75 F. M. Denny, "Tawba," in *Encyclopaedia of Islam*, second edition, ed. Th. Bianquis P. Bearman et al. (Leiden, The Netherlands: Brill, 2012), doi: http://dx.doi.org/10.1163/1573-3912_islam_SIM_7450.

76 David L. McMahan, "Buddhist Modernism," in *Buddhism in the Modern World*, ed. David L. McMahan (New York: Routledge, 2012), 168.

77 Field notes, October 7–8, 2011. See also staff handbook, explanations of day five.

78 Field notes, October 8, 2011.

79 Field notes, October 2, 2011.

80 PM Order 206.

4. Guarding the Daughter

1 Modified quotation from "General Anupong Opens His Heart on the Southern Situation," *Isara News*, August 24, 2010.

2 McClintock, *Imperial Leather*, 30.

3 Because prostitution and gambling are prohibited in Malaysia and Singapore, the southern borderland caters in particular to male tourists from these countries. Marc Askew, "Sex and the Sacred: Sojourners and Vistors in the Making of the Southern Thai Borderland," in *Centering the Margin: Agency and Narrative in Southeast Asian Borderlands*, ed. Alexander Horstmann and Reed L. Wadley (Oxford: Berghahn, 2006), 177–206. For more on Orientalist ideas of the *khaek* woman, see chapter 2

4 The gendered implications of family law regulations are elaborated by Saba Mahmood. See Mahmood, *Religious Difference in a Secular Age: A Minority Report* (Princeton, NJ: Princeton University Press, 2015), chap. 3.

5 I provide a detailed discussion of the notion of paternal benevolence in chapter 1.

6 Wendy Brown, "Finding the Man in the State," in *The Anthropology of the State: A Reader*, ed. Aradhane Sharma and Akhil Gupta (Malden, MA: Blackwell, 2006); Iris Marion Young, "The Logic of Masculinist Protection: Reflections on the Current Security State," *Signs: Journal of Women in Culture and Society* 29, no. 1 (2003): 1–25.

7 Peterson, "Gendered Identities," 21.

8 Spivak, "Can the Subaltern Speak?"; Lila Abu-Lughod, "Do Muslim Women Really Need Saving? Anthropological Reflections on Cultural Relativism and Its Others," *American Anthropologist* 104, no. 3 (2002): 783–90.

9 Gayle Rubin, "The Traffic in Women: Notes on the Political Economy of Sex," in *The Second Wave: A Reader in Feminist Theory*, ed. Linda Nicholson (London: Routledge, [1975] 1997), 27–62.

10 For classical texts on the public-private split and the mechanism of the traffic in women, see Jean Bethke Elshtain, "Moral Woman and Immoral Man: A Consideration of the Public-Private Split and Its Political Ramifications," *Politics & Society* 4, no. 4 (1974): 453–73; Rubin, "Traffic in Women." Eve Kosofsky Sedgwick extends the idea of the traffic in women with regards to the establishment of homosocial male bonds. Sedgwick, *Between Men: English Literature and Male Homosocial Desire* (New York: Columbia University Press, 2015). For postcolonial interpretations of domesticity and the public-private split, see Lisa Lowe, *The Intimacies of Four Continents* (Durham, NC: Duke University Press, 2015), 29–30; Amy Kaplan, "Manifest Domesticity," *American Literature* 70, no. 3 (1998): 581–606.

11 Most conspicuously, until the late 1860s commoners (who formed the majority of the population) were allowed to pledge their wives and children as security for a loan and to sell them into slavery without consent. Moreover, in the patrilineal order of the *sakdina* system, a father passed his rank on to his children, so that the *sakdina* centrally turned on

policing women's sexuality while encouraging relationships between men of higher status and women of lower status. For a woman, the act of "marrying down" constituted a form of adultery and was considered "one of the most reprehensible sex crimes." Loos, *Subject Siam*, 36, 37; Tamara Loos, "Gender Adjudicated: Translating Modern Legal Subjects in Siam" (PhD diss., University of Michigan, 1999), 32.

12   Loos, "Gender Adjudicated," 126, 241.

13   Thongchai, "The Others Within."

14   PM Orders 206 and 68; interview with Rohanee Juenara, Pattani, November 25, 2010.

15   Field notes, October 18, 2010 and January 13, 2011; interview with Col. Banphot, Yala, October 21, 2010.

16   The notion of a hierarchy of masculinities is key to attempts to explain male hegemony in masculinity studies. See, for example, R. W. Connell and James W. Messerschmidt, "Hegemonic Masculinity: Rethinking the Concept," *Gender & Society* 19, no. 6 (2005): 829–59. For a postcolonial interpretation, see Sinha, "Colonial and Imperial Masculinities."

17   Notes from conversation with Captain W., Saiburi, November 22, 2010; notes from conversation with Col. U., Yala, September 28, 2011.

18   Interview with soldier Aw., Checkpoint Bang Bla Mo, Pattani December 31, 2010.

19   Interview with soldier P., Checkpoint Bang Bla Mo, Pattani, January 9, 2011.

20   John Knodel et al., "Sexuality, Sexual Experience, and the Good Spouse: Views of Married Thai Men and Women," in *Genders & Sexualities in Modern Thailand*, ed. Peter A. Jackson and Nerida M. Cook (Chiang Mai, Thailand: Silkworm, 1999), 93–113; interview with soldier P., January 9, 2011.

21   Interview with Rungrawee Chaloemsripinyorat, former analyst for the International Crisis Group, Bangkok, February 17, 2011; notes from conversation with girls at coffee shop, October 7, 2010; group interview, Satri Pattana Saksa School, December 2, 2010; International Crisis Group, *Problem with Paramilitaries*.

22   Duncan McCargo, *Tearing Apart the Land: Islam and Legitimacy in Southern Thailand* (Ithaca, NY: Cornell University Press, 2008), 104.

23   Notes from conversation with A., Pattani, September 18, 2010.

24   Surin Pitsuwan cites a joint communique issued by separatist organizations in the 1980s, according to which, "since 1960, some 100,000 Thai people from North-East Thailand . . . have been relocated to Pattani, Yala and Narathiwat. The Thai target is to shift at least another 650,000 Thai-Buddhists into the Muslim areas." Surin, "Islam and Malay Nationalism," 229. See also interview with Ahmad Bualuang, Pattani, October 14, 2010; notes from conversation with Fateeha, January 19, 2011.

25   Loos, *Subject Siam*, 84.

26   Helbardt, "Deciphering Southern Thailand's Violence."

27   At the beginning of 2011, the Working Group for Peace and Justice was investigating three alleged cases of rape stretching back to 2004. The National Human Rights Commission had not received any complaints on which to base an investigation in any of these cases (personal communication with Amara Pongsapich, May 11, 2011). The only documentation of a case of rape by a soldier in the South that I have found is the one reported by Amporn Marddent and mentioned by Saroja Dorairajoo. Cf. Amporn Marddent, "From Adek to Mo'ji: Identities of Southern Thai People and Social Realities," in *Knowledge and Conflict Resolution: The Crisis of the Border Region of Southern Thailand*, ed. Utai Dulyakasem and Lertchai Sirichai (Nakhon Si Thammarat, Thailand: Walailak University, 2005), 269–338; Dorairajoo, "All My Men Are Dead." See also "Forbidden Love Stirs Up Resentment in Deep South," *Bangkok Post*, September 3, 2012, https://www.bangkokpost.com/print/283525/.

28   Interview with Pateemoh Poh-itaeda-oh, Yala, October 6, 2010; interview with Lamai Managarn, Pattani, January 7, 2011. An officer at the local branch of the International Committee of the Red Cross similarly reported that Red Cross staff had tried to examine an alleged case of rape, but the woman did not want to talk to them. Field notes, January 8, 2011.

29   For more background on Islamic Councils, see Yusuf, "Islam and Democracy in Thailand"; Duncan McCargo, "Co-Optation and Resistance in Thailand's Muslim South: The Changing Role of Islamic Council Elections," *Government and Opposition* 45, no. 1 (2010): 97.

30   Ishii, "Thai Muslims and the Royal Patronage of Religion"; "Royal Decree Concerning the Administration of Islamic Organization, B.E. 2540 (1997)," www.ThaiLaws.com, accessed July 4, 2019; interview with Aj. Zakee, Bangkok, October 24, 2014.

31 Field notes from marriage preparation courses at the Islamic Councils of Pattani and Yala, December 11, 2010 and October 10, 2011.

32 Sinha, "Colonial and Imperial Masculinities," 74.

33 Unreported rape in southern Thailand is part of a more general problem in the country. For all of Thailand, a UN study of 2017 estimated, only 13 percent of rape cases were reported to the police. See Eileen Skinnider, Ruth Montgomery, and Stephanie Garrett, *The Trial of Rape: Understanding the Criminal Justice System Response to Sexual Violence in Thailand and Viet Nam* (Bangkok: United Nations Women, United Nations Development Program, United Nations Office of Drugs and Crime, 2017), 11.

34 See, for example, interview with Rohseeda Busu, Pattani, December 27, 2010; interview with Rungrawee, Bangkok, February 17, 2011; field notes, January 24, 2011; interview with Lamai Managarn, Pattani, January 7, 2011.

35 Paul Higate, "Peacekeepers, Masculinities, and Sexual Exploitation," *Men and Masculinities* 10, no. 1 (2007): 99–119.

36 Field notes, January 26, 2011.

37 International Crisis Group, *Problem with Paramilitaries*; interview with Soraya Jamjuree, September 15, 2010.

38 See "Cross-Cultural Romances Raise Tensions in South," *Bangkok Post*, September 3, 2012, https://www.bangkokpost.com/print/283622/ and https://www.bangkokpost.com/print/283525/.

39 Lora Wildenthal, *German Women for Empire, 1884–1945* (Durham, NC: Duke University Press, 2001), chap. 3.

40 *Bangkok Post*, November 29, 2009, https://www.bangkokpost.com.

41 Vella, *Chaiyo!*, 130; Loos, *Subject Siam*, 134; Thamora V. Fishel, "Romances of the Sixth Reign: Gender, Sexuality, and Siamese Nationalism," in Jackson and Cook, *Genders & Sexualities in Modern Thailand*, 163. There has so far been no thorough examination of this notion of love and its connection to modernity in Siam. Authors like Scott Barmé, unfortunately, do not provide an in-depth discussion of the concept despite its centrality to early twentieth-century popular debates about gender relations. Cf. Barmé, *Woman, Man, Bangkok: Love, Sex, and Popular Culture in Thailand* (Chiang Mai, Thailand: Silkworm, 2002). The word *khwam rag* had been translated as "love" in Pallegoix's nineteenth-century dictionary. See Pallegoix, *Siamese, French, English Dictionary*. Nevertheless, there seems to have been an important conceptual shift with Vajiravudh's popularization of the love of nation. Whereas in the Buddhist tradition, the loving bonds between parents and children would have been characterized as bonds of compassion and gratitude under the term *karuna*, Vajiravudh reconceptualized familial love in a secular manner as *khwam rag*, thus hinting at the centrality of love for the biopolitics of the modern state. Cf. Berkwitz, "History and Gratitude in Theravāda Buddhism"; John Ross Carter, "Love and Compassion as Given," *Eastern Buddhist*, New Series 22, no. 1 (1989): 37–53; Barbara Watson Andaya, "Localizing the Universal: Women, Motherhood, and the Appeal of Early Theravada Buddhism," *Journal of Southeast Asian Studies* 33, no. 1 (2002): 1–30.

42 Tamara Loos, "Sex in the Inner City: The Fidelity between Sex and Politics in Siam," *Journal of Asian Studies* 64, no. 4 (2005): 881–909.

43 Reynolds, *Seditious Histories*, 195.

44 Hong Lysa, "Palace Women at the Margins of Social Change: An Aspect of the Politics of Social History in the Reign of King Chulalongkorn," *Journal of Southeast Asian Studies* 30, no. 2 (1999): 310–24; Loos, "Sex in the Inner City."

45 Vajiravudh [Asvabahu, pseud.], *The Jews of the Orient* (Bangkok: Siam Observer Press, 1914), 34; Vajiravudh, *Lectures on Religious Topics*, lectures 1, 7, 8.

46 Baker and Pasuk, *A History of Thailand*, 78.

47 Vichitr Vadakarn, *Thailand: Thai-Khmer Racial Relations* (Bangkok: Department of Publicity, 1940), 6.

48 In a global framework, similar ideas of love are related to Christian ideas of *agape* as elaborated in the New Testament. The Thai military discourse regarding love may possibly relate to missionary encounters and their propagation of love in nineteenth-century Siam. On missionaries in Siam, see Thanet, "The West and Siam's Quest for Modernity."

49 Interview with Pratubjit Neelapaijit, Bangkok, February 14, 2011; notes from conversation with Ga, Tanyong Luloh, September 21, 2010.

50 Notes from conversation with Capt. Sukhit, Pattani, January 17, 2011.
51 Notes from conversation with Khun Ramree at Yala Islamic Council, Yala, October 19, 2011. In Yala Province, the number of people converting to Islam each year from 2008 to 2011 ranged from 81 to 106.
52 Field notes, December 11, 2010.
53 Notes from conversation with Khun Ramree at Yala Islamic Council, Yala, October 19, 2011.
54 Jean-Loup Amselle, *Affirmative Exclusion: Cultural Pluralism and the Rule of Custom in France* (Ithaca, NY: Cornell University Press, 2003), 60–61; notes from conversation with Col. S., Yala, September 17, 2010; notes from conversation with P'Moo, Pattani, January 13, 2011.
55 Interview with Pratubjit Neelapaijit, Bangkok, February 14, 2011; notes from conversation with P'Moo, Pattani, January 13, 2011; notes from conversation with Ga, Tanyong Luloh, September 21, 2010.
56 Field notes, January 5, 2011.
57 Ruth Mas, "Secular Couplings: An Intergenerational Affair with Islam," in *New Dangerous Liaisons: Discourses on Europe and Love in the Twentieth Century*, ed. Luisa Passerini, Liliana Ellena, and Alexander Greppert (Oxford: Berghahn, 2010), 269–88.
58 Interview with Nayeemah, Yala, October 13, 2011.
59 Interview with Norisa, Yala, October 13, 2011.
60 Interview with Arina, Yala, October 13, 2011.
61 Interview with Nayeemah, Yala, October 13, 2011.
62 Cited in Alatas, *The Myth of the Lazy Native*, 39, 44.
63 Duncan McCargo, "Thai Buddhism, Thai Buddhists, and the Southern Conflict," *Journal of Southeast Asian Studies* 40, no. 1 (2009): 1–10; Saroja, "Peaceful Thai, Violent Malay (Muslim)."
64 Wiphusana Klaimanee, "The Need to Improve Population and Resource Control in Thailand's Counterinsurgency" (master's thesis, Naval Postgraduate School, 2008), 42–44; International Crisis Group, *Southern Thailand: The Impact of the Coup*, Asia Report No. 129 (Bangkok/Brussels, 2007), 10–12.
65 Cynthia Enloe coined this term to describe the gendered construction of armed conflict, where, historically, the category of the civilian was feminized and marked as vulnerable and innocent. Cynthia Enloe, *Bananas, Beaches, and Bases: Making Feminist Sense of International Politics* (Berkeley: University of California Press, 2014).
66 Janjira Sombutpoonsiri, "Policing Protest in Ethnic Minority Conflict: A Case of Thai State Agents' Policing of the 2007 Pattani Protest" (master's thesis, University of Queensland, 2008), 26.
67 Suwadee Tanaprasitpatana writes that the term *thahan ying* already appeared in the Three Seals Law of 1805 and suggests that women were probably employed "in some work concerning the army"; this might, however, have excluded combat positions. Moreover, Field Marshal Phibun during World War II decided to allow women to attend the cadet school, where they were "trained to serve in the fighting units like their male counterparts." The program was, however, discontinued after two years with Phibun's resignation in 1944, and former female cadets were moved to noncombat positions. Suwadee, "Thai Society's Expectations of Women, 1851–1935" (PhD diss., Sydney University, 1989), 31; Sukunya, "Chulachomklao Royal Military Academy," 247–52.
68 Interview with Master Serg. Wichai, Ingkhayut Camp, Pattani, October 14, 2011; group interview with female rangers, Ingkhayut Camp, Pattani, January 22, 2011 (group 1).
69 Interview with Pratubjit Neelapaijit, Bangkok, February 14, 2011.
70 Interview with Master Serg. Wichai, Ingkhayut Camp, Pattani, October 14, 2011; Naphang Kongsetthagul and Pimonpan Ukoskit, *The Study of Female Ranger Operation in 3 Southern Border Provinces Through the Thought of Technology of the Self* (in Thai with an English abstract) (Bangkok: Chulachomklao Royal Military Academy, 2007).
71 Group interview with female rangers, Ingkhayut Camp, Pattani, December 28, 2010.
72 Cited in Naphang and Pimonpan, *Study of Female Ranger Operation*, 45.
73 Laleh Khalili, "Gendered Practices of Counterinsurgency," *Review of International Studies* 37 (2011): 1471–91; Keally McBride and Annick T. R. Wibben, "The Gendering of Counterinsurgency in Afghanistan," *Humanity: An International Journal of Human Rights, Humanitarianism, and Development* 3, no. 2 (2012): 199–215.
74 Synne Laastad Dyvik, "Women as 'Practitioners' and 'Targets': Gender and Counterinsurgency in Afghanistan," *International Feminist Journal of Politics* 16, no. 3 (2013): 2, 7.

75 Group interview with female rangers, December 28, 2010.

76 Group interview with female rangers, January 22, 2011 (group 2); group interview with female rangers, December 28, 2010.

77 Antoinette M. Burton, "The Feminist Quest for Identity: British Imperial Suffragism and 'Global Sisterhood' 1900–1915," *Journal of Women's History* 3, no. 2 (1991): 46–81; Chandra Talpade Mohanty, "Under Western Eyes: Feminist Scholarship and Colonial Discourses," *Feminist Review*, no. 30 (1988): 61–88.

78 Group interview with female rangers, Ingkhayut Camp, Pattani, January 22, 2011 (group 1).

79 See also interview with Chaiwat Satha-Anand, Bangkok, February 10, 2011.

80 Group interview with female rangers, January 22, 2011 (group 1). *Mao lid* derives from the Arabic "mawlid," an event commemorating the birthday of the Islamic Prophet Muhammad.

81 Group interview with female rangers, January 22, 2011 (group 1).

82 Chaiwat, "Silence of the Bullet Monument."

83 Interview with Soraya Jamjuree, September 15, 2010.

84 See also Angkhana Neelapaijit, *Roles and Challenges for Muslim Women in the Restive Southern Border Provinces of Thailand* (Bangkok: Working Group on Justice for Peace, 2010), http://www.wluml.org/node/6499, accessed August 25, 2011; Andrea K. Molnar, "Women's Agency in the Malay Muslim Communities of Southern Thailand with Comparative Observations on Women's Engagement in Timor Leste" (paper presented at the International Conference on International Relations, Development, and Human Rights, Thammasat University, Bangkok, 2011).

85 Interview with Rohanee Juenera, November 25, 2010. In one case, for instance, nineteen women were arrested for blocking the road to hinder security personnel from entering their village. Nine of them managed to receive support from the Muslim Attorney's Centre and had their charges dismissed at trial, yet the remaining ten were sentenced to three-and-a-half years' imprisonment and had to give up their land titles to receive bail. Field notes, January 27, 2011.

86 Interview with Aj. Pimolpan, Bangkok, February 9, 2011. On the terminology of *tom*, see Megan J. Sinnott, "The Language of Rights, Deviance, and Pleasure: Organizational Responses to Discourses of Same-Sex Sexuality and Transgenderism in Thailand," in *Queer Bangkok: Twenty-First-Century Markets, Media, and Rights*, ed. Peter Jackson (Hong Kong: Hong Kong University Press, 2011), 208.

87 Chaiwat Satha-Anand, *The Life of This World* (Singapore: Marshall Cavendish Academic, 2005), chap. 4.

88 Jon Fernquest, "Hijab Ban at Wat School," *Bangkok Post*, May 12, 2011, https://www.bangkokpost.com/learning/advanced/236707/hijab-ban-at-wat-school; "Pattani School Lifts Its Ban on Wearing Hijab," *Nation* (Thailand), May 21, 2018, https://www.nation-multimedia.com/detail/national/30345872.

89 Ruth Streicher, "Fashioning the Gentlemanly State: The Curious Charm of the Military Uniform in Southern Thailand," *International Feminist Journal of Politics* 14, no. 4 (2012): 471–89.

90 Group interview with female rangers, Ingkhayut Camp, Pattani, January 22, 2011 (group 2).

91 Group interview with female rangers, Ingkhayut Camp, Pattani, January 22, 2011 (group 1).

92 Group interview with female rangers, Ingkhayut Camp, Pattani, January 22, 2011 (group 1).

93 "Muslim Female Soldiers in the Deep South Want to Wear the Hijab," *Isra News*, January 30, 2016, http://www.isranews.org/south-news/english-article/item/44451-prime_44451.html. Modified from the original quote, which reads: "We hope the prime minister will understand our feeling and our obstacle if the people see us as their opposition side and look at us in an unfriendly manner simply because we do not have the head scarfs but they have—that we are different from them."

94 "Muslim Female Soldiers in the Deep South Want to Wear the Hijab"; "Police to End Female Admissions to Cadet School," *Bangkok Post*, September 2, 2018, https://www.bangkokpost.com/news/general/1532718/police-to-end-female-admissions-to-cadet-school.

95 Interview with Khaleeyoh, whose father was killed at Kru Ze, Pattani, January 14, 2011.

96   For a good overview on foreign aid to the southern provinces, see Adam Burke, "Peripheral Conflicts and Limits to Peacebuilding: Foreign Aid and the Far South of Thailand" (PhD diss., University of London, 2011), chap. 5.

97   Interview with Capt. Sukit, Pattani, January 17, 2011; interview with Capt. Pramuan, Yala, October 4, 2011; field notes, December 21, 2010. Pimonpan Ukroskit also writes about groups of housewives formed by the northeastern units stationed in Pattani Province: "Many groups of housewives were formed; one group sewed headscarves; another produced organic dishwashing liquid; another made fish sauce; and the last was involved in aromatherapy." Pimonpan, "Internal Culture of Military Units," 107.

98   Field notes, January 17, 2011.

99   Interviews with Capt. Sukit, Pattani, January 17, 2011; Capt. Wantana, Yala, December 20, 2010; Capt. Pramuan, Yala, October 4, 2011.

100 David Kilcullen, "Twenty-Eight Articles: Fundamentals of Company-Level Counterinsurgency," *Marine Corps Gazette* (Summer 2006): 33.

101 Barmé, *Woman, Man, Bangkok*, 5.

102 Vajiravudh, "Khrueangmai haeng khwamrungrueang khue saphap haeng satri" [The status of women: A symbol of civilization], in *Celebrating Queen Sirikit's 60th Birthday Anniversary* (in Thai) (Bangkok, 1992), 3, 6.

103 Carol Cohn and Cynthia Enloe, "A Conversation with Cynthia Enloe: Feminists Look at Masculinity and the Men Who Wage War," *Signs: Journal of Women in Culture and Society* 28, no. 4 (2000): 1201.

104 Interview with Lt. Col. Tanud, Yala, September 30, 2011.

105 Klaus Rosenberg, *Nation und Fortschritt: Der Publizist Thien Wan und die Modernisierung Thailands unter König Culalonkon (r. 1868–1910)* [Nation and progress: The political writer Thianwan and the modernization of Thailand under King Chulalongkorn (r. 1868–1910)] (Hamburg, Germany: Gesellschaft für Natur- und Völkerkunde Ostasiens e.V., 1980), 67.

CONCLUSION

1   John Sifton, "Thailand's Faux Democracy Shouldn't Be Treated Like a Real one," July 8, 2019, https://www.hrw.org/news/2019/07/08/thailands-faux-democracy-shouldnt-be-treated-real-one.

2   On the idea of colonies as "laboratories of modernity," see Frederick Cooper and Ann Laura Stoler, "Between Metropole and Colony: Rethinking a Research Agenda," in *Tensions of Empire: Colonial Cultures in a Bourgeois World*, ed. Frederick Cooper and Ann Laura Stoler (Berkeley: University of California Press, 1997), 5.

3   Ashby and Francis, "COIN in Thailand," 28, 32; Blaufarb, *Counterinsurgency Era*, 185; Kusuma Snitwongse, "Thai Government Responses to Armed Communist and Separatist Movements," in *Governments and Rebellions in Southeast Asia*, ed. Chandran Jeshurun (Singapore: ISEAS Publishing, 1985), 257.

4   Chambers, "In the Shadow of the Soldier's Boot." According to the ISOC's strategic plans of 2012 and 2017, possible threats to national security included "offences against the monarchy, ideological differences and conflict among Thai people, the southern border provinces, cyber threats, natural disasters, illegal workers and migrants, terrorism and transnational crimes, illicit drugs and natural resources and environmental problems." Cited in Pawakapan Puangthong, *The Central Role of Thailand's Internal Security Operations Command in the Post-Counter-Insurgency Period* (Singapore: ISEAS Publishing, 2017), 25.

5   "Thailand Unsettled #1: The Military (with Puangthong Pawakapan)," *New Mandala*, September 4, 2018, http://www.newmandala.org/thailand-unsettled-1-military-puangthong-pawakapan/; "ISOC's Political Role," Political Prisoners in Thailand website, June 18, 2019, https://thaipoliticalprisoners.wordpress.com/2019/06/18/isocs-political-role/.

6   Askew, "Fighting with Ghosts"; Tyrell Haberkorn and Thongchai Winichakul, "The Thai Junta's Doublespeak," *New Mandala*, June 8, 2015, http://asiapacific.anu.edu.au/newmandala/2015/06/08/the-thai-juntas-doublespeak.

7   On this interpretation of military reconciliation discourse, see also Duncan McCargo, "Thailand's Twin Fires," *Survival* 52, no. 4 (2010): 6.

8   An English translation of the song lyrics is available online. See Charlie Campbell, "The Thai Junta's 'Happiness' Song Is a Hit! (But Who'd Dare Say Otherwise?)," *Time*, June 10, 2014, http://time.com/2851467/thai-coup-junta-happiness-song/.

9 Stoler, "Affective States"; Herman, "Project Camelot and the Career of Cold War Psychology," 120; Laleh Khalili, "The Uses of Happiness in Counterinsurgencies," *Social Text* 32, no. 1 (2014): 23–43.

10 Benjamin Tausig, "A Division of Listening: Insurgent Sympathy and the Sonic Broadcasts of the Thai Military," *positions: asia critique* 24, no. 2 (2016): 403–33; Khalili, "Uses of Happiness in Counterinsurgencies," 37. For a contemporary advocate of such practices, see Montgomery McFate, "The Military Utility of Understanding Adversary Culture," *Joint Force Quarterly*, no. 38 (2005): 42–48.

11 Anand Panyarachun, "His Majesty's Role in the Making of Thai History" (speech delivered at the 14th Conference of the International Association of Historians of Asia, Bangkok, 1996), 2, http://www.anandp.in.th/en_speech/e010205.pdf1996.

12 On King Bhumipol's accession, see Urisara Kowitdamrong, "Truly the King of Hearts," *Nation* (Thailand), October 14, 2016, http://www.nationmultimedia.com/national/Truly-the-King-of-hearts-30297646.html.

13 Human Rights Watch, *Descent into Chaos: Thailand's 2010 Red Shirt Protests and the Government Crackdown* (Bangkok: Human Rights Watch, 2011), https://www.hrw.org/report/2011/05/03/descent-chaos/thailands-2010-red-shirt-protests-and-government-crackdown. For an elaboration on the historicity of ideas of crisis and apocalypse, see Mas, "On the Apocalyptic Tones of Islam."

14 Ishii, *Sangha, State, and Society*, 151.

15 Cited in Somboon, *Political Buddhism in Southeast Asia*, 94.

16 Yalannanbaru staff handbook, instructions for the third day.

17 Young, "Logic of Masculinist Protection."

18 See, for example, Thongchai Winichakul, "The Last Gasp of Royalist Democracy," *Cultural Anthropology*, September 23, 2014, https://culanth.org/fieldsights/the-last-gasp-of-royalist-democracy.

19 Andrew Harding and Peter Leyland, *The Constitutional System of Thailand: A Contextual Analysis* (Oxford: Hart, 2011), 12; Michael K. Connors, *Democracy and National Identity in Thailand* (Copenhagen: NIAS Press, 2003), 45.

20 Pravit Rojanaphruk, "Can We Talk about Thai-Style 'Democracy?,'" *Khaosod English*, January 20, 2018, http://www.Khaosodenglish.com/opinion/2018/01/20/can-talk-thai-style-democracy.

21 Inden, *Imagining India*.

22 Partha Chatterjee, *The Nation and Its Fragments* (Princeton, NJ: Princeton University Press, 1993), 22, 32.

23 Although Sarit died in 1963, his paternalistic government was continued by his close allies, Field Marshals Thanom Kittikachorn and Praphat Charusathien.

24 Quoted in Connors, *Democracy and National Identity in Thailand*, 9.

25 Thai Lawyers for Human Rights, *Collapsed Rule of Law: The Consequences of Four Years under the National Council for Peace and Order for Human Rights and Thai Society* (Bangkok, 2018); Sifton, "Thailand's Faux Democracy."

BIBLIOGRAPHY

Abadi, Jacob. *Israel's Quest for Recognition and Acceptance in Asia: Garrison State Diplomacy.* London: Routledge, 2004.

Abu-Lughod, Lila. "Do Muslim Women Really Need Saving? Anthropological Reflections on Cultural Relativism and Its Others." *American Anthropologist* 104, no. 3 (2002): 783–90.

Ahmed, Leila. *Women and Gender in Islam: Historical Roots of a Modern Debate.* New Haven, CT: Yale University Press, 1992.

Alatas, Syed Hussein. *The Myth of the Lazy Native.* London: Frank Cass, 1977.

Amnesty International. "Thailand: Torture in the Southern Counter-Insurgency." London: Amnesty International, 2009. http://www.amnesty.org/en/library/asset/ASA39/001/2009/en/45c1226f-dcd6-11dd-bacc-b7af5299964b/asa390012009eng.pdf, accessed April 2, 2010.

Amporn Marddent. "From Adek to Mo'ji: Identities of Southern Thai People and Social Realities." In *Knowledge and Conflict Resolution: The Crisis of the Border Region of Southern Thailand,* edited by Utai Dulyakasem, and Lertchai Sirichai, 269–338. Nakhon Si Thammarat, Thailand: Walailak University, 2005.

Amselle, Jean-Loup. *Affirmative Exclusion: Cultural Pluralism and the Rule of Custom in France.* Ithaca, NY: Cornell University Press, 2003.

Anand Panyarachun. "His Majesty's Role in the Making of Thai History." Speech delivered at the 14th Conference of the International Association of Historians of Asia, Bangkok, 1996. http://www.anandp.in.th/en_speech/e010205.pdf.

Andaya, Barbara Watson. "Localizing the Universal: Women, Motherhood, and the Appeal of Early Theravada Buddhism." *Journal of Southeast Asian Studies* 33, no. 1 (2002): 1–30.

Anderson, Benedict. "Studies of the Thai State: The State of Thai Studies." In *The Study of Thailand: Analyses of Knowledge, Approaches, and Prospects in Anthropology, Art History, Economics, History, and Political Science,* edited by Eliezer B. Ayal, 193–234. Athens: Ohio University Center for International Studies, 1978.

Anghie, Antony. *Imperialism, Sovereignty and the Making of International Law.* Vol. 37. Cambridge: Cambridge University Press, 2007.

Angkhana Neelapaijit. *Roles and Challenges for Muslim Women in the Restive Southern Border Provinces of Thailand.* Report, Working Group on Justice for Peace, Bangkok, 2010. http://www.wluml.org/node/6499, accessed August 25, 2011.

Anidjar, Gil. *Semites: Race, Religion, Literature.* Stanford, CA: Stanford University Press, 2008.

Asad, Talal. *Formations of the Secular: Christianity, Islam, Modernity.* Stanford, CA: Stanford University Press, 2003.

——. *Genealogies of Religion: Discipline and Reasons of Power in Christianity and Islam.* Baltimore: Johns Hopkins University Press, 1993.

Ashby, E. H., and D. G. Francis. "COIN in Thailand Jan 1967–Dec 1968." Contemporary Historical Evaluation of Combat Operations (CHECO), US Air Force, Washington, DC, 1969.

Askew, Marc. "Fighting with Ghosts: Querying Thailand's 'Southern Fire.'" *Contemporary Southeast Asia* 32, no. 2 (2010): 117–55.

——. "Sex and the Sacred: Sojourners and Vistors in the Making of the Southern Thai Borderland." In *Centering the Margin: Agency and Narrative in Southeast Asian Borderlands,* edited by Alexander Horstmann, and Reed L. Wadley, 177–206. Oxford: Berghahn, 2006.

——. "The Spectre of the South: Regional Instability as National Crisis." In *Legitimacy Crisis in Thailand,* edited by Marc Askew, 235–71. Chiang Mai, Thailand: Silkworm, 2010.

Askew, Marc, and Sascha Helbardt. "Becoming Patani Warriors: Individuals and the Insurgent Collective in Southern Thailand." *Studies in Conflict & Terrorism* 35 (2012): 779–809.

Aymonier, Étienne. *Le Cambodge*. Paris: Leroux, 1900.

Bachmann, Jan, Colleen Bell, and Caroline Holmqvist, eds. *War, Police, and Assemblages of Intervention*. London: Routledge, 2015.

Baker, Chris, trans. "The Antiquarian Society of Siam Speech of King Chulalongkorn." *Journal of the Siam Society* 89, nos. 1–2 (2001): 95–99.

Baker, Chris, and Pasuk Phongpaichit. *A History of Ayutthaya*. Cambridge: Cambridge University Press, 2017.

——. *A History of Thailand*. Cambridge: Cambridge University Press, 2005.

Bangkok Times. *Directory for Bangkok and Siam*. Bangkok: Bangkok Times Press, 1914.

Banivanua Mar, Tracey. "Stabilizing Violence in Colonial Rule: Settlement and the Indentured Labour Trade in Queensland in the 1870s." In *Writing Colonial Histories: Comparative Perspectives*, edited by Tracey Banivanua Mar and Julie Evans, 145–63. Melbourne, Australia: University of Melbourne Conference and Seminar Series, 2002.

Barmé, Scott. *Luang Wichit Wathakan and the Creation of Thai Identity*. Singapore: ISEAS Publishing, 1993.

——. *Woman, Man, Bangkok: Love, Sex, and Popular Culture in Thailand*. Chiang Mai, Thailand: Silkworm, 2002.

Barua, Pradeep. "Inventing Race: The British and India's Martial Races." *Historian* 58, no. 1 (1995): 107–16.

Battye, Noel Alfred. "The Military, Government, and Society in Siam, 1868–1910." PhD diss., Cornell University, 1974.

Bell, Colleen. "The Police Power in Counterinsurgencies: Discretion, Patrolling, and Evidence." In *War, Police, and Assemblages of Intervention*, edited by Jan Bachmann, Colleen Bell, and Caroline Holmqvist, 17–35. London: Routledge, 2015.

Bell, Peter F. "Thailand's Northeast: Regional Underdevelopment, 'Insurgency' and Official Response." *Pacific Affairs* 42, no. 1 (1969): 47–54.

——. "Western Conceptions of Thai Society: The Politics of American Scholarship." *Journal of Contemporary Asia* 12, no. 1 (1982): 61–74.

Berkwitz, Stephen C. "History and Gratitude in Theravāda Buddhism." *Journal of the American Academy of Religion* 71, no. 3 (2003): 579–604.

Blaufarb, Douglas. *The Counterinsurgency Era: US Doctrine and Performance 1950 to the Present*. New York: Free Press, 1977.

Bloembergen, Marieke, and Martijn Eickhoff. "Exchange and the Protection of Java's Antiquities: A Transnational Approach to the Problem of Heritage in Colonial Java." *Journal of Asian Studies* 72, no. 4 (2013): 1–24.

Bonura, Carlo. "Indeterminate Geographies of Political Violence in Southern Thailand." *Alternatives* 33, no. 4 (2008): 383–412.

Bowie, Katherine A. *Rituals of National Loyalty: An Anthropology of the State and the Village Scout Movement in Thailand*. New York: Columbia University Press, 1997.

Boycott, Divestment and Sanctions (BDS) Thailand. *Israel-Thailand Relations: Complicity of Thailand over Israel's Occupation, Colonialism, and Apartheid in Palestine*. Bangkok: Boycott, Divestment and Sanctions Thailand, 2014.

Bradley, Dan Beach. *Dictionary of the Siamese Language*. Bangkok, 1873.

Bradley, Francis R. *Forging Islamic Power and Place: The Legacy of Shaykh Dā'ūd bin 'Abd Allāh al-Faṭānī in Mecca and Southeast Asia*. Honolulu: University of Hawai'i Press, 2016.

Breazeale, Kennon. "A Transition in Historical Writing: The Works of Prince Damrong Rachanuphap." *Journal of the Siam Society* 59, no. 2 (1971): 25–49.

Brown, Wendy. "Finding the Man in the State," in *The Anthropology of the State: A Reader*, edited by Aradhane Sharma and Akhil Gupta, 187–210. Malden, MA: Blackwell, 2006.

Bunnag, Tej. *The Provincial Administration of Siam 1892–1915: The Ministry of Interior under Prince Damrong Rajanubhab*. Kuala Lumpur: Oxford University Press, 1977.

Burke, Adam. "Peripheral Conflicts and Limits to Peacebuilding: Foreign Aid and the Far South of Thailand." PhD diss., University of London, 2011.

Burton, Antoinette M. "The Feminist Quest for Identity: British Imperial Suffragism and 'Global Sisterhood' 1900–1915." *Journal of Women's History* 3, no. 2 (1991): 46–81.

Butler, Judith. *Bodies That Matter: On the Discursive Limits of "Sex."* London: Routledge, 1993.

——. "Endangered/Endangering." In *The Body: A Reader*, edited by Mariam Fraser and Monica Greco, 140–43. London: Routledge, 2005.

Campbell, J. G. D. *Siam in the Twentieth Century: Being the Experiences and Impressions of a British Official*. London: Edward Arnold, 1904.

Carter, A. Cecil. *The Kingdom of Siam*. New York: Knickerbocker, 1904.

Carter, John Ross. "Love and Compassion as Given." *Eastern Buddhist*, n.s., 22, no. 1 (1989): 37–53.

Chai-Anan Samudavanija. *The Thai Young Turks*. Singapore: ISEAS Publishing, 1982.

Chaiwat Satha-Anand. *The Life of This World*. Singapore: Marshall Cavendish Academic, 2005.

——. "The Silence of the Bullet Monument: Violence and "Truth" Management, Dusun-Nyor 1948, and Kru-Ze 2004." *Critical Asian Studies* 38, no. 1 (2006): 11–37.

Chakrabarty, Dipesh. *Provincializing Europe*. Princeton, NJ: Princeton University Press, 2000.

Chambers, Paul. "In the Shadow of the Soldier's Boot: Assessing Civil-Military Relations in Thailand." In *Legitimacy Crisis in Thailand*, edited by Marc Askew, 197–234. Chiang Mai, Thailand: Silkworm, 2010.

——. "US-Thai Relations after 9/11: A New Era of Cooperation?" *Contemporary Southeast Asia: A Journal of International and Strategic Affairs* 26, no. 3 (2004): 460–79.

Chao Phraya Thiphakorawong. *Nangsue sadaeng kitchanukit* [Elaboration on major and minor matters]. Bangkok, [1872] 1971.

Charnvit Kasetsiri. "Message." In *Through the Eyes of the King: The Travels of King Chulalongkorn to Malaya*, edited by Patricia Lim Pui Huen, x–xi. Singapore: ISEAS Publishing, 2009.

Chatterjee, Partha. *The Nation and Its Fragments*. Princeton, NJ: Princeton University Press, 1993.

Chladek, Michael. " 'They Will Be Like Diamonds': Novice Summer Camps, Being Riaproi, and Adjusting Selves." Unpublished paper presented at the Theravada Civilizations Workshop, Seattle, 2016.

——. "Making Monks, Making Men: The Role of Buddhist Monasticism in Shaping Northern Thai Identities." PhD diss., University of Chicago, 2016.

Christie, Clive J. *A Modern History of Southeast Asia: Decolonization, Nationalism, and Separatism*. New York: I. B. Tauris, 1996.

Chu, William. "Path." In *Encyclopedia of Buddhism*, edited by Robert E. Buswell, 635–40. New York: Macmillan Reference USA, 2004.

Clancy-Smith, Julia, and Frances Gouda. "Introduction." In *Domesticating the Empire: Race, Gender, and Family Life in French and Dutch Colonialism*, edited by Julia Clancy-Smith and Frances Gouda, 1–20. Charlottesville: University of Virginia Press, 1998.

Cohn, Bernard S. *Colonialism and Its Forms of Knowledge: The British in India*. Princeton, NJ: Princeton University Press, 1996.

Cohn, Carol, and Cynthia Enloe. "A Conversation with Cynthia Enloe: Feminists Look at Masculinity and the Men Who Wage War." *Signs: Journal of Women in Culture and Society* 28, no. 4 (2000): 1187–1207.

Connell, R. W., and James W. Messerschmidt. "Hegemonic Masculinity: Rethinking the Concept." *Gender & Society* 19, no. 6 (2005): 829–59.

Connors, Michael K. *Democracy and National Identity in Thailand*. Copenhagen: NIAS Press, 2003.

Cook, Joanna. *Meditation in Modern Buddhism: Renunciation and Change in Thai Monastic Life*. Cambridge: Cambridge University Press, 2010.

Cooke, Miriam. "Saving Brown Women." *Signs: Journal of Women in Culture and Society* 28, no. 1 (2002): 468–70.

Cooper, Frederick, and Ann Laura Stoler. "Between Metropole and Colony: Rethinking a Research Agenda." In *Tensions of Empire: Colonial Cultures in a Bourgeois World*, edited by Frederick Cooper and Ann Laura Stoler, 1–58. Berkeley: University of California Press, 1997.

Coronil, Fernando. "After Empire: Reflections on Imperialism from the Americas." In *Imperial Formations*, edited by Ann Laura Stoler, 241–71. Santa Fe, NM: James Currey, 2007.

Crosby, Kate. *Theravada Buddhism: Continuity, Diversity, and Identity*. Malden, MA: Wiley-Blackwell, 2014.

Damrong Rajanubhab. *Chao Phraya Yomarat*. Bangkok: Samnakphim Praphat Ton, 1948.

——. "Laksana kanpokkhrong prathet sayam tae boran" [The nature of government in Siam since antiquity]. In *Prawatisat lae kanmuang: nangsu an prakop wicha phunthan arayatham thai* [History and politics: Reading book for a course on Thai civilization], 1–30. Bangkok: Thammasat University Press, [1927] 1975.

Das, Veena. "Violence, Gender, and Subjectivity." *Annual Review of Anthropology*, no. 37 (2008): 283–99.

Davidson, Naomi. *Only Muslim: Embodying Islam in Twentieth-Century France*. Ithaca, NY: Cornell University Press, 2012.

Davisakd Puaksom. "Of a Lesser Brilliance: Patani Historiography in Contention." In *Thai South and Malay North: Ethnic Interactions on a Plural Peninsula*, edited by Michael J. Montesano and Patrick Jory, 71–88. Singapore: NUS Press, 2008.

Day, Tony. *Fluid Iron: State Formation in Southeast Asia*. Honolulu: University of Hawai'i Press, 2002.

Decha Tangseefa. "Reading 'Bureaucrat Manuals,' Writing Cultural Space: The Thai State's Cultural Discourses and the Thai-Malay in-between Spaces." In *Imagined Land? The State and Southern Violence in Thailand*, edited by Chaiwat Satha-Anand, 121–44. Tokyo: Research Institute for Languages and Cultures of Asia and Africa, 2009.

Denny, Frederick M. "Tawba." In *Encyclopaedia of Islam*, edited by P. Bearman, Th. Bianquis, C. E. Bosworth, E. van Donzel, and W. P. Heinrichs. 2nd ed. Leiden, The Netherlands: Brill, 2012.

Diller, Anthony V. N. "Islam and Southern Thai Ethnic Reference." In *Politics of the Malay-Speaking South*. Vol. 1, *Historical and Cultural Studies*, edited by Andrew D. W. Forbes, 153–67. Gaya, India: Centre for South East Asian Studies, 1989.

——. "What Makes Central Thai a National Language?" In *National Identity and Its Defenders: Thailand, 1939–1989*, edited by Craig J. Reynolds, 71–107. Clayton, Australia: Centre of Southeast Asian Studies Monash University, 1991.

Dirks, Nicholas B. "The Policing of Tradition: Colonialism and Anthropology in Southern India." *Society for Comparative Study of Society and History* 39, no. 1 (1997): 182–212.

Dodd, William Clifton. *The Tai Race: Elder Brother of the Chinese*. Cedar Rapids, IA: Torch, 1923.

Dorairajoo, Saroja. "All My Men Are Dead: Women, the Real Victims of Violence in Southern Thailand." Paper presented at International Symposium: Gender and Islam in Southeast Asia, University of Passau, Germany, 2005. http://www.susanne-schroeter.de/pdf/all_my_men_are_dead.pdf, accessed June 3, 2010.

——. "Peaceful Thai, Violent Malay (Muslim): A Case Study of the 'Problematic' Muslim Citizens of Southern Thailand." *Copenhagen Journal of Asian Studies* 27, no. 2 (2009): 61–83.

Doyle, Michael W. *Empires*. Ithaca, NY: Cornell University Press, 1986.

Dyvik, Synne Laastad. "Women as 'Practitioners' and 'Targets': Gender and Counterinsurgency in Afghanistan." *International Feminist Journal of Politics* 16, no. 3 (2013): 1–20.

Edwards, Penny. *Cambodge: The Cultivation of a Nation*. Honolulu: University of Hawai'i Press, 2007.

Elshtain, Jean Bethke. "Moral Woman and Immoral Man: A Consideration of the Public-Private Split and Its Political Ramifications." *Politics & Society* 4, no. 4 (1974): 453–73.

Enloe, Cynthia. *Bananas, Beaches, and Bases: Making Feminist Sense of International Politics*. Berkeley: University of California Press, 2014.

"Ethnographische Karte: Verbreitung der Menschenrassen" [Ethnographic map: Distribution of human races], in *Meyers Konversationslexikon: Eine Encyklopädie des allgemeinen Wissens* [Meyers encyclopedia of general knowledge], 4th edition. Leipzig: Meyers und Verlag des Bibliographischen Institut Autorenkollektiv, 1885–1892. https://commons.wikimedia.org/wiki/File:Meyers_b11_s0476a.jpg.

Fabian, Johannes. *Time and the Other: How Anthropology Makes Its Objects*. New York: Columbia University Press, 1983.

Fanon, Frantz. *A Dying Colonialism*. New York: Grove, 1965.

Farrelly, Nicholas, Craig J. Reynolds, and Andrew Walker. "Practical and Auspicious: Thai Handbook Knowledge for Agriculture and the Environment." *Asian Studies Review* 35, no. 2 (2011): 235–51.

Feierman, Steven "Africa in History: The End of Universal Narratives." In *After Colonialism: Imperial Histories and Postcolonial Displacements*, edited by Gyan Prakash, 40–65. Princeton, NJ: Princeton University Press, 1995.

Fishel, Thamora V. "Romances of the Sixth Reign: Gender, Sexuality, and Siamese Nationalism." In *Genders & Sexualities in Modern Thailand*, edited by Peter A. Jackson and Nerida M. Cook, 154–67. Chiang Mai, Thailand: Silkworm, 1999.

Ford, Eugene. *Cold War Monks: Buddhism and America's Secret Strategy in Southeast Asia*. New Haven, CT: Yale University Press, 2017.

Forte, Maximilian C. "The Human Terrain System and Anthropology: A Review of Ongoing Public Debates." *American Anthropologist* 113, no. 1 (2011): 149–53.

Foucault, Michel. *Discipline and Punish: The Birth of the Prison.* New York: Vintage, [1975] 1995.

——. "Nietzsche, Genealogy, History." In *Language, Counter-Memory, Practice: Selected Essays and Interviews,* edited by Donald Bouchard, 139–64. Ithaca, NY: Cornell University Press, 1977.

——. *Security, Territory, Population: Lectures at the Collège de France, 1977–78.* Edited by Michel Senellart. Translated by Graham Burchell. London: Palgrave Macmillan, 2007.

——. *"Society Must Be Defended": Lectures at the Collège De France, 1975–1976.* Edited by Mauro Bertani, Alessandro Fontana, François Ewald, and David Macey. Vol. 1. New York: Picador, [1976] 2003.

Freeman, John H. *An Oriental Land of the Free.* Philadelphia: Westminster, 1910.

Frevert, Ute. "Das Militär als Schule der Männlichkeiten" [The military as a school of masculinities]. In *Männlichkeiten und Moderne: Geschlecht in den Wissenskulturen um 1900* [Masculinities and modernity: Gender in cultures of knowledge around 1900], edited by Ulrike Brunotte and Rainer Herrn. Bielefeld, Germany: Transcript Verlag, 2008.

Friis, Karsten. "Peacekeeping and Counter-Insurgency—Two of a Kind?" *International Peacekeeping* 17, no. 1 (2010): 49–66.

Fuhrmann, Arnika. *Ghostly Desires: Queer Sexuality and Vernacular Buddhism in Contemporary Thai Cinema.* Durham, NC: Duke University Press, 2016.

Gallagher, John, and Ronald Robinson. "The Imperialism of Free Trade." *Economic History Review* 6, no. 1 (1953): 1–15.

Galula, David. *Counterinsurgency Warfare: Theory and Practice.* New York: Greenwood, 1964.

Gesick, Lorraine M. *In the Land of Lady White Blood: Southern Thailand and the Meaning of History.* Ithaca, NY: Cornell University Press, 1995.

Gong, Gerrit W. *The Standard of "Civilization" in International Society.* Oxford: Clarendon, 1984.

González, Roberto. "Indirect Rule and Embedded Anthropology: Practical, Theoretical, and Ethical Concerns." In *Anthropology and Global Counterinsurgency,* edited by John D. Kelly, Beatrice Jauregui, Sean T. Mitchell, and Jeremy Walton, 231–44. Chicago: University of Chicago Press, 2010.

——. "Towards Mercenary Anthropology? The New UU Army Counterinsurgency Manual FM 3–24 and the Military-Anthropology Complex." *Anthropology Today* 23, no. 3 (2007): 14–19.

Gouda, Frances. "The Gendered Rhetoric of Colonialism and Anti-Colonialism in Twentieth-Century Indonesia." *Indonesia* 55 (1993): 1–22.

Grabowsky, Volker. "The Thai Census of 1904: Translation and Analysis." *Journal of the Siam Society* 84, no. 1 (1996): 49–85.

Gray, Christine E. "Hegemonic Images: Language and Silence in the Royal Thai Polity." *Man,* n.s., 26, no. 1 (1991): 43–65.

Gregory, Derek. "The Biopolitics of Baghdad: Counterinsurgency and the Counter-City." *Human Geography* 1, no. 1 (2008): 6–27.

——. "'The Rush to the Intimate': Counterinsurgency and the Cultural Turn." *Radical Philosophy,* no. 150 (2008): 8–23.

Haberkorn, Tyrell, and Thongchai Winichakul. "The Thai Junta's Doublespeak." *New Mandala,* June 8, 2015. http://asiapacific.anu.edu.au/newmandala/2015/06/08/the-thai-juntas-doublespeak.

Hacking, Ian. *Historical Ontology.* Cambridge, MA: Harvard University Press, 2002.

Hall, Stuart. "Conclusion: The Multi-Cultural Question." In *Un/Settled Multiculturalisms: Diasporas, Entanglements, 'Transruptions,'* edited by Barnor Hesse, 209–41. London: Zed, 2000.

Halley, Janet, and Kerry Rittich. "Critical Directions in Comparative Family Law: Genealogies and Contemporary Studies of Family Law Exceptionalism." *American Journal of Comparative Law* 58 (2010): 753–76.

Handley, Paul M. *The King Never Smiles: A Biography of Thailand's Bhumibol Adulyadej.* New Haven, CT: Yale University Press, 2006.

Hanstaad, Eric J. "Constructing Order through Chaos: A State Ethnography of the Thai Police." PhD. diss., University of Wisconsin–Madison, 2008.

Haraway, Donna. "Situated Knowledges: The Science Question in Feminism and the Privilege of Partial Perspective." *Feminist Studies* 14, no. 3 (1988): 575–99.

Harding, Andrew, and Peter Leyland. *The Constitutional System of Thailand: A Contextual Analysis.* Oxford: Hart, 2011.

Haschemi Yekani, Elahe. "'Enlightened Imperialism'—Der englische Gentleman-Hero als Erlös(t)er" ["Enlightened Imperialism"—the English gentleman-hero as savior]. In *Erlöser: Figurationen männlicher Hegemonie* [Saviors: Figurations of male hegemony], edited by Sven Glawion, Elahe Haschemi Yekani, and Jana Husmann-Kastein, 97–109. Bielefeld, Germany: Transcript Verlag, 2007.

Helbardt, Sascha. "Deciphering Southern Thailand's Violence: Organisation and Insurgent Practices of BRN-Coordinate." PhD diss., University of Passau, 2011.

Herman, Ellen. "Project Camelot and the Career of Cold War Psychology." In *Universities and Empire: Money and Politics in the Social Sciences during the Cold War,* edited by Christopher Simpson, 97–133. New York: New Press, 1998.

Herzfeld, Michael. "The Conceptual Allure of the West: Dilemmas and Ambiguities of Crypto-Colonialism in Thailand." In *The Ambiguous Allure of the West: Traces of the Colonial in Thailand,* edited by Rachel V. Harrison and Peter A. Jackson, 173–86. Hong Kong: Hong Kong University Press, 2010.

Heymann, Hans. *Seminar on Development and Security in Thailand—Part II: Development-Security Interactions.* Santa Monica, CA: RAND Corporation, 1969.

Higate, Paul. "Martial Races and Enforcement Masculinities of the Global South: Weaponising Fijian, Chilean, and Salvadoran Postcoloniality in the Mercenary Sector." *Globalizations* 9, no. 1 (2012): 35–52.

——. "Peacekeepers, Masculinities, and Sexual Exploitation." *Men and Masculinities* 10, no. 1 (2007): 99–119.

Hochberg, Gil Z. "'Check Me Out': Queer Encounters in Sharif Waked's *Chic Point: Fashion for Israeli Checkpoints.*" *GLQ* 16, no. 4 (2010): 577–97.

Hooker, M. B. "The 'Europeanization' of Siam's Law 1855–1908." In *Laws of South-East Asia.* Vol. 2, *European Laws in South-East Asia,* edited by M. B. Hooker, 531–77. Singapore: Butterworth, 1988.

——. "Introduction: European Laws in South-East Asia." In *Laws of South-East Asia.* Vol. 2, *European Laws in South-East Asia,* edited by M. B. Hooker, 1–26. Singapore: Butterworth, 1988.

Horstmann, Alexander. "Ethnohistorical Perspectives on Buddhist-Muslim Relations and Coexistence in Southern Thailand." *SOJOURN: Journal of Social Issues in Southeast Asia* 19, no. 1 (2004): 76–92.

——. "The Inculturation of a Transnational Islamic Missionary Movement: Tablighi Jamaat Al-Dawa and Muslim Society in Southern Thailand." *SOJOURN: Journal of Social Issues in Southeast Asia* 22, no. 1 (2007): 107–30.

Human Rights Watch. "'It Was Like Suddenly My Son No Longer Existed': Enforced Disappearances in Thailand's Southern Border Provinces." *Human Rights Watch Report* 19, no. 5 (2007).

——. "No One Is Safe: Insurgent Attacks on Civilians in Thailand's Southern Border Provinces" *Human Rights Watch Report* 19, no. 13 (2007).

——. *Descent into Chaos: Thailand's 2010 Red Shirt Protests and the Government Crackdown.* Bangkok: 2011. https://www.hrw.org/report/2011/05/03/descent-chaos/thailands-2010-red-shirt-protests-and-government-crackdown.

Hyun, Sinae. "Building a Human Border: The Thai Border Patrol Police School Project in the Post–Cold War Era." *SOJOURN: Journal of Social Issues in Southeast Asia* 29, no. 2 (2014): 332–63.

International Commission of Jurists. *Thailand's Internal Security Act: Risking the Rule of Law?* Report by the International Commission of Jurists, Bangkok, 2010.

International Crisis Group. *Recruiting Militants in Southern Thailand.* Asia Report no. 170. Bangkok/Brussels, 2009.

——. *Southern Thailand: Dialogue in Doubt.* Asia Report no. 270. Bangkok/Brussels, 2015.

——. *Southern Thailand: The Impact of the Coup.* Asia Report no. 129. Bangkok/Brussels, 2007.

——. *Southern Thailand: Insurgency, Not Jihad.* Asia Report no. 98. Bangkok/Brussels, 2005.

——. *Southern Thailand: The Problem with Paramilitaries.* Asia Report no. 140. Bangkok/Brussels, 2007.

——. *Southern Thailand's Peace Dialogue: No Traction.* Asia Briefing no. 148. Bangkok/Brussels, 2016.

Inden, Ronald. *Imagining India.* Oxford: Basil Blackwell, 1990.

Internal Security Operations Command (ISOC) 5th Operational Cooperation Centre. "Khumue chut ong khwamru prakopkan damnoenkan khong chao nathi phu patibat ngan nai phuen thi changwat chaidaen phak tai" [Handbook of operational knowledge for officers working in the southern border provinces]. Bangkok, 2010.

Ishii, Yoneo. *Sangha, State, and Society: Thai Buddhism in History.* Honolulu: University of Hawai'i, 1986.

——. "Thai Muslims and the Royal Patronage of Religion." *Law & Society Review* 28, no. 3 (1994): 453–60.

Ivarsson, Soren. "Making Laos 'Our' Space: Thai Discourses on History and Race, 1900–1941." In *Contesting Visions of the Lao Past: Lao Historiography at the Crossroads,* edited by Soren Ivarsson and Christopher E. Goscha, 239–64. Copenhagen: NIAS Press, 2003.

Ivarsson, Soren, and Lotte Isager. "Strengthening the Moral Fibre of the Nation: The King's Sufficiency Economy as Etho-Politics." In *Saying the Unsayable: Monarchy and Democracy in Thailand,* edited by Soren Ivarsson and Lotte Isager, 223–40. Copenhagen: NIAS Press, 2010.

Jackson, Peter A. "The Ambiguitites of Semicolonial Power in Thailand." In *The Ambiguous Allure of the West: Traces of the Colonial in Thailand,* edited by Rachel V. Harrison and Peter A. Jackson, 37–56. Hong Kong: Hong Kong University Press, 2010.

Janjira Sombutpoonsiri. "Policing Protest in Ethnic Minority Conflict: A Case of Thai State Agents' Policing of the 2007 Pattani Protest." Master's thesis, University of Queensland, 2008.

Jeganathan, Pradeep. "Checkpoint: Anthropology, Identity, and the State." In *Anthropology in the Margins of the State,* edited by Veena Das and Deborah Poole, 67–81. Santa Fe, NM: School for Advanced Research Press, 2004.

Jerryson, Michael. "Appropriating a Space for Violence: State Buddhism in Southern Thailand." *Journal of Southeast Asian Studies* 40, no. 1 (2009): 33–57.

——. *Buddhist Fury: Religion and Violence in Southern Thailand.* Oxford: Oxford University Press, 2011.

Joll, Christopher M. *Muslim Merit-Making in Thailand's Far-South.* Heidelberg, Germany: Springer, 2012.

——. "Thailand's Muslim Kaleidoscope between Central Plains and Far-South: Fresh Perspectives from the Sufi Margins." In *Ethnic and Religious Identities and Integration in Southeast Asia,* edited by Volker Grabowsky and Oi Keat Jin, 319–58. Chiang Mai, Thailand: Silkworm, 2016.

——. "Why Monolingual Mind-Sets, Linguistic Justice, and Language Policy Are All Central to a Peaceful, Political Resolution to Thailand's Southern Impasse." Paper presented at the International Conference on Political Transition, Non-Violence and Communication in Conflict Transformation, Pattani, January 24–27, 2017.

Jory, Patrick. "Books and the Nation: The Making of Thailand's National Library." *Journal of Southeast Asian Studies* 31, no. 2 (2000): 351–73.

——. "Thai and Western Buddhist Scholarship in the Age of Colonialism: King Chulalongkorn Redefines the Jatakas." *Journal of Asian Studies* 61, no. 3 (2002): 891–918.

——. "Thailand's Politics of Politeness: Qualities of a Gentleman and the Making of 'Thai Manners.'" *South East Asia Research* 23, no. 3 (2015): 357–75.

Kalir, Barak. "The Field of Work and the Work of the Field: Conceptualising an Anthropological Research Engagement." *Social Anthropology* 14, no. 2 (2006): 235–46.

Kanok Wongtrangan. "Change and Persistence in Thai Counter-Insurgency Policy." ISIS Occasional Paper no. 1, Institute of Security and International Studies, Chulalongkorn University, Bangkok, 1983.

Kaplan, Amy. "Manifest Domesticity." *American Literature* 70, no. 3 (1998): 581–606.

Kasian Tejapira. *Commodifying Marxism: The Formation of Modern Thai Radical Culture, 1927–1958.* Kyoto: Kyoto University Press, 2001.

Keyes, Charles F. "Buddhism and National Integration in Thailand," *Journal of Asian Studies* 30, no. 3 (1971): 551–67.

——. "Mother or Mistress but Never a Monk: Buddhist Notions of Female Gender in Rural Thailand." *American Ethnologist* 11, no. 2 (1984): 223–41.

——. "Muslim 'Others' in Buddhist Thailand." *Thammasat Review* 13, no. 1 (2009): 19–42.

———. "Political Crisis and Militant Buddhism in Contemporary Thailand." In *Religion and Legitimation of Power in Thailand, Laos, and Burma*, edited by Bardwell L. Smith, 147–64. Chambersburg, PA: ANIMA, 1978.

Khalili, Laleh. "Gendered Practices of Counterinsurgency." *Review of International Studies* 37 (2011): 1471–91.

———. "The Location of Palestine in Global Counterinsurgencies." *International Journal of Middle East Studies* 42, no. 3 (2010): 413–33.

———. *Time in the Shadows: Confinement in Counterinsurgencies*. Stanford, CA: Stanford University Press, 2013.

———. "The Uses of Happiness in Counterinsurgencies." *Social Text* 32, no. 1 (2014): 23–43.

Kienscherf, Markus. "Plugging Cultural Knowledge into the U.S. Military Machine: The Neo-Orientalist Logic of Counterinsurgency." *Topia: Canadian Journal of Cultural Studies* 23–24 (2010): 121–43.

———. "A Programme of Global Pacification: US Counterinsurgency Doctrine and the Biopolitics of Human (In)Security." *Security Dialogue* 42, no. 6 (2011): 517–35.

Kilcullen, David. "Twenty-Eight Articles: Fundamentals of Company-Level Counterinsurgency." *Marine Corps Gazette* (Summer 2006): 29–35.

Knemeyer, Franz-Ludwig. "Polizei." *Economy and Society* 9, no. 2 (1980): 172–96.

Knodel, John, Chanpen Saengtienchai, Mark Vanlandingham, and Rachel Lucas. "Sexuality, Sexual Experience, and the Good Spouse: Views of Married Thai Men and Women." In *Genders & Sexualities in Modern Thailand*, edited by Peter A. Jackson and Nerida M. Cook, 93–113. Chiang Mai, Thailand: Silkworm, 1999.

Kotef, Hagar, and Merav Amir. "(En)Gendering Checkpoints: Checkpoint Watch and the Repercussions of Intervention." *Signs: Journal of Women in Culture and Society* 32, no. 4 (2007): 973–96.

Kusuma Snitwongse. "Thai Government Responses to Armed Communist and Separatist Movements." In *Governments and Rebellions in Southeast Asia*, edited by Chandran Jeshurun, 251–66. Singapore: ISEAS Publishing, 1985.

Lacouperie, Terrien de. *The Languages of China before the Chinese*. London: David Nutt, 1887.

Lak than prasa nayobai samrap monthon Patani [Policy principles for the monthon Patani], B.E. 2466 [1923], reprinted in *Naeo thang patibat ratchakan: Samrap kha ratchakan nai phuen thi changwat chai daen pak tai* [Methods for the performance of officers: For officers in the area of the southern border provinces], 5–9. Bangkok, Thailand: Ministry of the Interior, 2004.

Lemire, Charles. *La France et le Siam*. Paris: A. Challamel, 1903.

Lennon, Kathleen. "Feminist Perspectives on the Body." *The Stanford Encyclopedia of Philosophy*, Fall 2010 edition. https://plato.stanford.edu/entries/feminist-body/.

Leow, Rachel. *Taming Babel: Language in the Making of Malaysia*. Cambridge: Cambridge University Press, 2016.

Lieberman, Victor B. "Ethnic Politics in Eighteenth-Century Burma." *Modern Asian Studies* 12, no. 3 (1978): 455–82.

Liow, Joseph Chinyong. *Islam, Education, and Reform in Southern Thailand: Tradition and Transformation*. Singapore: ISEAS Publishing, 2009.

Loos, Tamara. "Competitive Colonialisms: Siam and the Malay Muslim South." In *The Ambiguous Allure of the West: Traces of the Colonial in Thailand*, edited by Rachel V. Harrison and Peter A. Jackson, 75–92. Hong Kong: Hong Kong University Press, 2010.

———. "Gender Adjudicated: Translating Modern Legal Subjects in Siam." PhD diss., University of Michigan, 1999.

———. "Sex in the Inner City: The Fidelity between Sex and Politics in Siam." *Journal of Asian Studies* 64, no. 4 (2005): 881–909.

———. *Subject Siam: Family, Law, and Colonial Modernity in Thailand*. Ithaca, NY: Cornell University Press, 2002.

Lowe, Lisa. *The Intimacies of Four Continents*. Durham, NC: Duke University Press, 2015.

Lysa, Hong. "Palace Women at the Margins of Social Change: An Aspect of the Politics of Social History in the Reign of King Chulalongkorn." *Journal of Southeast Asian Studies* 30, no. 2 (1999): 310–24.

———. "'Stranger within the Gates': Knowing Semi-Colonial Siam as Extraterritorials." *Modern Asian Studies* 38, no. 2 (2004): 327–54.

Lyttleton, Chris. "Magic Lipstick and Verbal Caress: Doubling Standards in Isan Villages." In *Coming of Age in South and Southeast Asia: Youth, Courtship, and Sexuality*, edited by Lenore Manderson and Pranee Liamputtong, 165–87. Richmond, UK: Psychology Press, 2002.

Mahmood, Saba. *Politics of Piety: The Islamic Revival and the Feminist Subject*. Princeton, NJ: Princeton University Press, 2005.

——. *Religious Difference in a Secular Age: A Minority Report*. Princeton, NJ: Princeton University Press, 2015.

——. "Religious Reason and Secular Affect: An Incommensurable Divide?" *Critical Inquiry* 35, no. 4 (2009): 836–62.

Marks, Thomas A. "The Thai Approach to Peacemaking since World War II." *Journal of East and West Studies: Perspectives on East Asian Economies and Industries* 7, no. 1 (1978): 133–55.

Marquis, Jefferson P. "The Other Warriors: American Social Science and Nation Building in Vietnam." *Diplomatic History* 24, no. 1 (2000): 79–105.

Mas, Ruth. "On the Apocalyptic Tones of Islam in Secular Time." In *Secularism and Religion-Making*, edited by Markus Dressler and Arvind-Pal S. Mandair, 87–103. Oxford: Oxford University Press, 2011.

——. "Secular Couplings: An Intergenerational Affair with Islam." In *New Dangerous Liaisons: Discourses on Europe and Love in the Twentieth Century*, edited by Luisa Passerini, Liliana Ellena, and Alexander Greppert, 269–88. Oxford: Berghahn, 2010.

Masuzawa, Tomoko. *The Invention of World Religions: Or, How European Universalism Was Preserved in the Language of Pluralism*. Chicago: University of Chicago Press, 2005.

McBride, Keally, and Annick T. R. Wibben. "The Gendering of Counterinsurgency in Afghanistan." *Humanity: An International Journal of Human Rights, Humanitarianism, and Development* 3, no. 2 (2012): 199–215.

McCargo, Duncan. "Co-Optation and Resistance in Thailand's Muslim South: The Changing Role of Islamic Council Elections." *Government and Opposition* 45, no. 1 (2010): 93–113.

——. "The Coup and the South." *NIAS nytt—Asia Insights* 3 (2007): 12–14.

——. "Patani Militant Leaflets and the Uses of History." In *Ghosts of the Past in Southern Thailand*, edited by Patrick Jory. 277–97. Singapore: NUS Press, 2013.

——. "The Politics of Buddhist Identity in Thailand's Deep South: The Demise of Civil Religion?" *Journal of Southeast Asian Studies* 40, no. 1 (2009): 11–32.

——. "Security, Development, and Political Participation in Thailand: Alternative Currencies of Legitimacy." *Contemporary Southeast Asia* 24, no. 1 (2002): 50–67.

——. *Tearing Apart the Land: Islam and Legitimacy in Southern Thailand*. Ithaca, NY: Cornell University Press, 2008.

——. "Thai Buddhism, Thai Buddhists, and the Southern Conflict." *Journal of Southeast Asian Studies* 40, no. 1 (2009): 1–10.

——. "Thailand's Twin Fires." *Survival* 52, no. 4 (2010): 5–12.

——. "Thaksin and the Resurgence of Violence in the Thai South: Network Monarchy Strikes Back?" *Critical Asian Studies* 38, no. 1 (2006): 39–71.

McClintock, Anne. *Imperial Leather: Race, Gender, and Sexuality in the Colonial Contest*. London: Routledge, 1995.

McFate, Montgomery. "Anthropology and Counterinsurgency: The Strange Story of Their Curious Relationship." *Military Review* 85, no. 2 (2005): 24–38.

——. "The Military Utility of Understanding Adversary Culture." *Joint Force Quarterly*, no. 38 (2005): 42–48.

McMahan, David L. "Buddhist Modernism." In *Buddhism in the Modern World*, edited by David L. McMahan, 160–76. London: Routledge, 2012.

Military Research and Development Center, "Rai ngan khrongkan wichai khang san nai changwat chaidaen phak tai (khumue si changwat chaidaen phak tai" [Report on the research project concerning the southern border provinces (handbook for the four southern border provinces)]. Bangkok, 1974.

Milner, Anthony. *The Invention of Politics in Colonial Malaya*. Cambridge: Cambridge University Press, 1994.

——. *The Malays*. Malden, MA: Wiley, 2008.

Mohamad, Muhammad Arafat Bin. "Be-Longing: Fatanis in Makkah and Jawi." PhD diss., Harvard University, 2013.

Mohanty, Chandra Talpade. "Under Western Eyes: Feminist Scholarship and Colonial Dis-
    courses." *Feminist Review*, no. 30 (1988): 61–88.
Molnar, Andrea K. "Women's Agency in the Malay Muslim Communities of Southern Thai-
    land with Comparative Observations on Women's Engagement in Timor Leste." Paper
    presented at the International Conference on International Relations, Development, and
    Human Rights, Thammasat University, Bangkok, 2011.
Montesano, Michael J., and Patrick Jory. "Introduction." In *Thai South and Malay North: Ethnic
    Interactions on a Plural Peninsula*, edited by Michael J. Montesano and Patrick Jory, 1–24.
    Singapore: NUS Press, 2008.
Müller, Friedrich Max. *Letter to Chevalier Bunsen on the Classification of the Turanian Languages:*.
    London: A. and P. A. Spottiswoode, 1854.
Murashima, Eiji. "The Origin of Modern Official State Ideology in Thailand." *Journal of South-
    east Asian Studies* 19, no. 1 (1988): 80–96.
Nagl, John A. *Counterinsurgency Lessons from Malaya and Vietnam: Learning to Eat Soup with a Knife.*
    Westport, CT: Praeger, 2002.
Nantawan Haemindra. "The Problem of the Thai-Muslims in the Four Southern Provinces of
    Thailand (Part Two)." *Journal of Southeast Asian Studies* 8, no. 1 (1977): 85–105.
Naphang Kongsetthagul, and Pimonpan Ukoskit. *The Study of Female Ranger Operation in 3
    Southern Border Provinces through the Thought of Technology of the Self.* [In Thai with an English
    abstract.] Bangkok: Chulachomklao Royal Military Academy, 2007.
National Reconciliation Commission. "Overcoming Violence through the Power of Reconcili-
    ation." Report of the National Reconciliation Commission. Bangkok, 2006.
Neelawat Ngoensongsee and Nootarat Saengsooree. "The Military Operations of Task Force
    23 at the Checkpoint of Yan Pana, Pattani Province." Master's thesis, Prince of Songkhla
    University, 2010.
Neocleous, Mark. "Theoretical Foundations of the 'New Police Science.'" In *The New Police Sci-
    ence: The Police Power in Domestic and International Governance*, edited by Mariana Valverde and
    Markus D. Dubber, 17–41. Stanford, CA: Stanford University Press, 2006.
——. *War Power, Police Power*. Edinburgh: Edinburgh University Press, 2014.
Ochs, Juliana. *Security and Suspicion: An Ethnography of Everyday Life in Israel*. Philadelphia: Uni-
    versity of Pennsylvania Press, 2011.
Ockey, James. "Thailand: The Struggle to Redefine Civil-Military Relations." In *Coercion and
    Governance: The Declining Political Role of the Military in Asia*, edited by Muthiah Alagappa,
    187–208. Stanford, CA: Stanford University Press, 2001.
——. "Thailand in 2006: Retreat to Military Rule." *Asian Survey* 47, no. 1 (2007): 133–40.
Olender, Maurice. *The Languages of Paradise: Race, Religion, and Philology in the Nineteenth Century*.
    Cambridge, MA: Harvard University Press, 2008.
Pallegoix, Jean-Baptiste. *Déscription du Royaume de Siam*. Bangkok: DK Book House,
    [1854] 1976.
——. *Siamese, French, English Dictionary*. Bangkok: Imprimerie de la Mission Catholique, 1896.
Pathan, Don, and Joseph Liow. *Confronting Ghosts: Thailand's Shapeless Southern Insurgency*. Syd-
    ney: Lowy Institute for International Policy, 2010.
Pattana Kitiarsa. "An Ambiguous Intimacy: Farang as Siamese Occidentalism." In *The Am-
    biguous Allure of the West: Traces of the Colonial in Thailand*, edited by Rachel V. Harrison
    and Peter A. Jackson, 57–74. Hong Kong: Hong Kong University Press, 2010.
Pavin Chachavalpongpun. "Thaksin, the Military, and Thailand's Protracted Political Crisis."
    In *The Political Resurgence of the Military in Southeast Asia: Conflict and Leadership*, edited by
    Marcus Mietzner, 45–62. London: Routledge, 2011.
Pawakapan Puangthong. *The Central Role of Thailand's Internal Security Operations Command in the
    Post-Counter-Insurgency Period*. Singapore: ISEAS Publishing, 2017.
Peleggi, Maurizio. "From Buddhist Icons to National Antiquities: Cultural Nationalism and
    Colonial Knowledge in the Making of Thailand's History of Art." *Modern Asian Studies* 47,
    no. 5 (2013): 1520–48.
——. *Lords of Things: The Fashioning of the Siamese Monarchy's Modern Image*. Honolulu: University
    of Hawai'i Press, 2002.
——. "Refashioning Civilization: Dress and Bodily Practice in Thai Nation-Building." In *The
    Politics of Dress in Asia and the Americas*, edited by Mina Roces and Louise Edwards, 65–80.
    Brighton, UK: Sussex University Press, 2008.

Peletz, Michael G. *Islamic Modern: Religious Courts and Cultural Politics in Malaysia.* Princeton, NJ: Princeton University Press, 2002.

Peterson, V. Spike. "Gendered Identities, Ideologies, and Practices in the Context of War and Militarism." In *Gender, War, and Militarism: Feminist Perspectives*, edited by Laura Sjoberg and Sandra Via, 17–29. Santa Barbara, CA: Praeger, 2010.

Pimonpan Ukoskit. "The Internal Culture of Military Units and Its Impact on the Conflict Resolution in Thailand's Far South." In *Imagined Land? The State and Southern Violence in Thailand*, edited by Chaiwat Satha-Anand, 93–120. Tokyo: Research Institute for Languages and Cultures of Asia and Africa, 2009.

Piyada Chonlaworn. "Contesting Law and Order: Legal and Judicial Reform in Southern Thailand in the Late Nineteenth to Early Twentieth Century." *Southeast Asian Studies* 3, no. 3 (2014): 527–46.

Pletsch, Carl E. "The Three Worlds, or the Division of Social Scientific Labor, circa 1950–1975." *Comparative Studies in Society and History* 23, no. 4 (1981): 565–90.

Porter, Patrick. *Military Orientalism: Eastern War through Western Eyes.* London: Oxford University Press, 2009.

Powers, John. *A Bull of a Man: Images of Masculinity, Sex, and the Body in Indian Buddhism.* Cambridge, MA: Harvard University Press, 2009.

Preecha Juntanamalaga. "Thai or Siam?" *Names: Journal of the American Name Society* 36, nos. 1–2 (1988): 69–84.

Price, David. "Faking Scholarship." In *The Counter-Counterinsurgency Manual: Or, Notes on Demilitarizing American Society*, edited by the Network of Concerned Anthropologists, 59–76. Chicago: Prickly Paradigm, 2009.

Puar, Jasbir K., and Amit S. Rai. "Monster, Terrorist, Fag: The War on Terrorism and the Production of Docile Patriots." *Social Text* 20, no. 3 (2002): 117–48.

Pupavac, Vanessa. "War on the Couch: The Emotionology of the New International Security Paradigm." *European Journal of Social Theory* 7, no. 2 (2004): 149–70.

Razack, Sherene. "A Hole in the Wall; a Rose at a Checkpoint: The Spatiality of Colonial Encounters in Occupied Palestine." *Journal of Critical Race Inquiry* 1, no. 1 (2010): 90–108.

"Report of the Seminar on Village Defence and Development, Bangkok, March 15–21, 1970." Thailand Information Center, Bangkok, SVDD/70/REP.

Reynolds, Craig J. "Buddhist Cosmography in Thai History, with Special Reference to Nineteenth-Century Culture Change." *Journal of Asian Studies* 35, no. 2 (1976): 203–20.

——. "Chumchon/Community." In *Words in Motion: Toward a Global Lexicon*, edited by Carol Gluck and Anna Lowenhaupt Tsing, 286–305. Durham, NC: Duke University Press, 2009.

——. "Introduction: National Identity and Its Defenders." In *National Identity and Its Defenders: Thailand, 1939–1989*, edited by Craig J. Reynolds, 1–41. Clayton, Australia: Centre of Southeast Asian Studies, Monash University, 1991.

——. "Power." In *Critical Terms for the Study of Buddhism*, edited by Donald S. Lopez, 211–28. Chicago: University of Chicago Press, 2005.

——. *Seditious Histories: Contesting Thai and Southeast Asian Pasts.* Seattle: University of Washington Press, 2006.

Reynolds, Craig J., and Hong Lysa. "Marxism in Thai Historical Studies." *Journal of Asian Studies* 43, no. 1 (1983): 77–104.

Rid, Thomas. "The Nineteenth Century Origins of Counterinsurgency Doctrine." *Journal of Strategic Studies* 33, no. 5 (2010): 727–58.

Rosenberg, Klaus. *Nation und Fortschritt: Der Publizist Thien Wan und die Modernisierung Thailands unter König Culalonkon (R. 1868–1910)* [Nation and progress: The political writer Thianwan and the modernization of Thailand under King Chulalongkorn (r. 1868–1910)]. Hamburg, Germany: Gesellschaft für Natur- und Völkerkunde Ostasiens e.V., 1980.

Royal Thai Embassy. *The Eagle and the Elephant: Thai-American Relations since 1833; Part 3: Current Cooperation.* Washington DC: Royal Thai Embassy, 2009.

Rubin, Gayle. "The Traffic in Women: Notes on the Political Economy of Sex." In *The Second Wave: A Reader in Feminist Theory*, edited by Linda Nicholson, 27–62. London: Routledge, [1975] 1997.

Rungrawee Chaloemsripinyorat. "The Security Forces and Human Rights Violations in Thailand's Insurgency-Wrecked South." In *Imagined Land? The State and Southern Violence in Thailand*, edited by Chaiwat Satha-Anand, 73–92. Tokyo: Research Institute for Languages and Cultures of Asia and Africa, 2009.

Ruth, Richard A. *In Buddha's Company: Thai Soldiers in the Vietnam War.* Honolulu: University of Hawai'i Press, 2011.

Saichol Sattayanurak. "The Construction of Mainstream Thought on 'Thainess' and the 'Truth' Constructed by 'Thainess.'" Translated by Sarinee Achavanuntakul. Paper presented at Conference on Thai Humanities II, 2005, Chiang Mai University. https://pdfs.semanticscholar.org/9a10/5c84daaca1b2d41b93aaa5885acd18de 7b28.pdf.

Sarosi, Diana, and Janjira Sombutpoonsiri. "Arming Civilians for Self-Defense: The Impact of Firearms Proliferation on the Conflict Dynamics in Southern Thailand." *Global Change, Peace & Security* 23, no. 3 (2011): 387–403.

Schaper, Ulrike. "Universalizing the Province Europe in Early German Legal Anthropology." *TRAFO—Blog for Transregional Research*, 2016. https://trafo.hypotheses.org/3982.

Schatz, Edward. "Introduction: Ethnographic Immersion and the Study of Politics." In *Political Ethnography. What Immersion Contributes to the Study of Power*, edited by Edward Schatz, 1–22. London: University of Chicago Press, 2009.

Scupin, Raymond. "Islam in Thailand before the Bangkok Period." *Journal of the Siam Society* 68, no. 1 (1980): 55–71.

Sears, Laurie J. "Intellectuals, Theosophy, and Failed Narratives of the Nation in Late Colonial Java." In *A Companion to Postcolonial Studies*, edited by Henry Schwarz and Sangeeta Ray, 333–59. Malden, MA: Blackwell, 2000.

Sedgwick, Eve Kosofsky. *Between Men: English Literature and Male Homosocial Desire.* New York: Columbia University Press, 2015.

Simpson, Christopher. "Universities, Empire, and the Production of Knowledge: An Introduction." In *Universitites and Empire. Money and Politics in the Social Sciences During the Cold War*, edited by Christopher Simpson, xi–xxxiv. New York: New Press, 1998.

Sinha, Mrinalini. "Colonial and Imperial Masculinities." In *International Encyclopedia of Men and Masculinities*, edited by Michael Flood, Judith Kegan Gardiner, Bob Pease, and Keith Pringle, 73–76. London: Routledge, 2007.

——. *Colonial Masculinity: The "Manly Englishman" and the "Effeminate Bengali" in the Late Nineteenth Century.* Manchester, UK: Manchester University Press, 1994.

——. "Mapping the Imperial Social Formation: A Modest Proposal for Feminist History." *Signs: Journal of Women in Culture and Society* 25, no. 4 (2000): 1077–82.

Sinnott, Megan J. "The Language of Rights, Deviance, and Pleasure: Organizational Responses to Discourses of Same-Sex Sexuality and Transgenderism in Thailand." In *Queer Bangkok: Twenty-First-Century Markets, Media, and Rights*, edited by Peter Jackson, 205–28. Hong Kong: Hong Kong University Press, 2011.

Sjoberg, Laura. "Women Fighters and the 'Beautiful Soul' Narrative." *International Review of the Red Cross* 92, no. 877 (2010): 53–68.

Sjoberg, Laura, and Jessica Peet. "A(nother) Dark Side of the Protection Racket." *International Feminist Journal of Politics* 13, no. 2 (2011): 163–82.

Skinnider, Eileen, Ruth Montgomery, and Stephanie Garrett. *The Trial of Rape: Understanding the Criminal Justice System Response to Sexual Violence in Thailand and Viet Nam.* Bangkok: United Nations Women, United Nations Development Program, United Nations Office of Drugs and Crime, 2017.

Somboon Suksamran. *Political Buddhism in Southeast Asia: The Role of the Sangha in the Modernization of Thailand.* London: Hurst, 1977.

Spivak, Gayatri Chakravorti. "Can the Subaltern Speak?" In *The Post-Colonial Studies Reader*, edited by Bill Ashcroft, Gareth Griffiths, and Helen Tiffin, 28–37. London: Routledge, 1996.

Srisompob Jitpiromsri. "The New Challenge of Thailand's Security Forces in the Southern Frontiers." In *Knights of the Realm: Thailand's Military and Police, Then and Now*, edited by Paul Chambers, 541–82. Bangkok: White Lotus, 2013.

Srisompob Jitpiromsri, and Duncan McCargo. "The Southern Thai Conflict Six Years On: Insurgency, Not Just Crime." *Contemporary Southeast Asia* 32, no. 2 (2010): 156–83.

Steinmetz, George. "The Sociology of Empires, Colonies, and Postcolonialism." *Annual Review of Sociology* 40 (2014): 70–103.

Stoler, Ann Laura. "Affective States." In *A Companion to the Anthropology of Politics*, edited by David Nugent, 4–20. Oxford: Wiley-Blackwell, 2004.

——. *Carnal Knowledge and Imperial Power.* Berkeley: University of California Press, 2002.

——. "Intimidations of Empire: Predicaments of the Tactile and Unseen." In *Haunted by Empire: Geographies of Intimacy in North American History*, edited by Ann Laura Stoler, 1–23. Durham, NC: Duke University Press, 2006.

——. "On Degrees of Imperial Sovereignty." *Public Culture* 18, no. 1 (2006): 125–46.

——. *Race and the Education of Desire: Foucault's History of Sexuality and the Colonial Order of Things.* Durham, NC: Duke University Press, 1995.

——. "Rethinking Colonial Categories: European Communities and the Boundaries of Rule." *Society for Comparative Study of Society and History* 31, no. 1 (1989): 134–61.

——. "'The Rot Remains': From Ruins to Ruination." In *Imperial Debris: On Ruins and Ruination*, edited by Ann Laura Stoler, 1–58. Durham, NC: Duke University Press, 2013.

Stoler, Ann Laura, Carole McGranahn, and Peter C. Perdue, eds. *Imperial Formations.* Santa Fe, NM: School for Advanced Research Press, 2007.

Strate, Shane. *The Lost Territories: Thailand's History of National Humiliation.* Honolulu: University of Hawai'i Press, 2015.

Streckfuss, David. "The Mixed Colonial Legacy in Siam: Origins of Thai Racialist Thought, 1890–1910." In *Autonomous Histories, Particular Truths: Essays in Honor of John R. W. Smail*, edited by Laurie J. Sears, 123–53. Madison: University of Wisconsin Center for Southeast Asian Studies, 1993.

Streicher, Ruth. "Fashioning the Gentlemanly State: The Curious Charm of the Military Uniform in Southern Thailand." *International Feminist Journal of Politics* 14, no. 4 (2012): 471–89.

——. "Imperialism, Buddhism, and the Secular in 19th-Century Siam—Notes on Provincializing Secularism." *TRAFO—Blog for Transregional Research*, 2016. https://trafo.hypotheses.org/3941.

——. "Die Macht des Feldes: Für Selbstreflexivität als Methodologische Strategie Feministischer Feldforschung in Konfliktgebieten" [The power of the field: Self-reflexivity as a methodological strategy of feminist research in areas of conflict]. In *Geschlechterverhältnisse, Frieden und Konflikt: Feministische Denkanstöße für die Friedens- und Konfliktforschung* [Gender relations, peace and conflict: Feminist food for thought for peace and conflict studies], edited by Bettina Engels and Corinna Gayer, 65–77. Baden-Baden, Germany: Nomos, 2011.

Streicher, Ruth, and Schirin Amir-Moazami. "Reflections on Hegemonies of Knowledge Production and the Politics of Disciplinary Divisions." *TRAFO—Blog for Transregional Research*, August 4, 2016. https://trafo.hypotheses.org/3439.

Suchit Bunbongkarn. *The Military in Thai Politics.* Singapore: ISEAS Publishing, 1987.

Sudarat Musikawong. "Art for October: Thai Cold War State Violence in Trauma Art." *Positions: East Asia Cultures Critique* 18, no. 1 (2010): 19–50.

Sukunya Bumroongsook. "Chulachomklao Royal Military Academy: The Modernization of Military Education in Thailand, 1887–1948." PhD diss., Northern Illinois University, 1991.

Sunait Chutintaranond. "The Image of the Burmese Enemy in Thai Perceptions and Historical Writing." *Journal of the Siam Society* 80, no. 1 (1992): 89–98.

Supik, Linda. *Statistik und Rassismus: Das Dilemma der Erfassung von Ethnizität* [Statistics and racism: The dilemma of recording ethnicity]. Frankfurt, Germany: Campus, 2014.

Surin Pitsuwan. "Islam and Malay Nationalism: A Case Study of the Malay-Muslims of Southern Thailand." PhD diss., Harvard University, 1982.

Suwadee Tanaprasitpatana. "Thai Society's Expectations of Women, 1851–1935." PhD diss., Sydney University, 1989.

Szanton, David, ed. *The Politics of Knowledge: Area Studies and the Disciplines.* Berkeley: University of California Press, 2003.

Tambiah, Stanley. "The Galactic Polity: The Structure of Traditional Kingdoms in Southeast Asia." *Annals of the New York Academy of Science* (1976): 69–97.

Tanguay, Pascal. "Kratom in Thailand: Decriminalisation and Community Control?" Series on Legislative Reform of Drug Policies, no. 13, Transnational Institute, April 2011. https://www.tni.org/en/page/introduction.

Tausig, Benjamin. "A Division of Listening: Insurgent Sympathy and the Sonic Broadcasts of the Thai Military." *Positions: East Asia Cultures Critique* 24, no. 2 (2016): 403–33.

Terwiel, B. J. *The Ram Kamhaeng Inscription: The Fake That Did Not Come True.* Gossenberg, Germany: Ostasien Verlag, 2010.

Thai Lawyers for Human Rights. *Collapsed Rule of Law: The Consequences of Four Years under the National Council for Peace and Order for Human Rights and Thai Society.* Bangkok, 2018.

Thak Chaloemtiarana. *Thai Politics: Extracts and Documents, 1932–1957.* Bangkok: Thammasat University Printing Office, 1978.

———. *Thailand: The Politics of Despotic Paternalism.* Chiang Mai, Thailand: Silkworm, 2007.

Thanet Aphornsuvan. "History and Politics of the Muslims in Thailand." Working paper, Thammasat University, 2003.

———. "Slavery and Modernity: Freedom in the Making of Modern Siam." In *Asian Freedoms: The Idea of Freedom in East and Southeast Asia,* edited by David Kelly and Anthony Reid, 161–86. Cambridge: Cambridge University Press, 1998.

———. "The West and Siam's Quest for Modernity: Siamese Responses to Nineteenth Century American Missionaries." *South East Asia Research* 17, no. 3 (2009): 401–31.

Thongchai Winichakul. "Buddhist Apologetics and a Genealogy of Comparative Religion in Siam." *Numen* 62, no. 1 (2015): 76–99.

———. "The Last Gasp of Royalist Democracy." *Cultural Anthropology,* September 23, 2014. https://culanth.org/fieldsights/the-last-gasp-of-royalist-democracy.

———. "The Others Within: Travel and Ethno-Spatial Differentiation of Siamese Subjects 1885–1910." In *Civility and Savagery: Social Identity in Tai States,* edited by Andrew Turton, 38–62. Richmond, UK: Psychology Press, 2000.

———. "The Quest for 'Siwilai': A Geographical Discourse of Civilizational Thinking in the Late Nineteenth and Early Twentieth-Century Siam." *Journal of Asian Studies* 59, no. 3 (August 2000): 528–49.

———. *Siam Mapped: A History of the Geo-Body of a Nation.* Honolulu: University of Hawai'i Press, 1994.

———. "Siam's Colonial Conditions and the Birth of Thai History." In *Southeast Asian Historiography: Unraveling the Myths,* edited by Volker Grabowsky, 21–43. Bangkok: River Books, 2011.

Turner, Alicia. *Saving Buddhism: The Impermanence of Religion in Colonial Burma.* Honolulu: University of Hawai'i Press, 2014.

Ukrist Pathmanand. "Thaksin's Achilles' Heel: The Failure of Hawkish Approaches in the Thai South." *Critical Asian Studies* 38, no. 1 (2006): 73–93.

United Nations Office for the Coordination of Humanitarian Affairs. "The Monthly Humanitarian Bulletin." East Jerusalem: United Nations Office for the Coordination of Humanitarian Affairs, September 2018. https://www.ochaopt.org/content/monthly-humanitarian-bulletin-september-2018.

US Army. *Counterinsurgency (Field Manual, FM 3–24).* Washington DC: US Army, 2006.

US Marine Corps. *Small Wars Manual (NAVMC 2890).* Washington DC: US Marine Corps, 1940.

Vajiravudh. "Khrueangmai haeng khwamrungrueang khue saphap haeng satri" [The status of women: A symbol of civilization]. In *Celebrating Queen Sirikit's 60th Birthday Anniversary.* [In Thai.] 1–8. Bangkok, 1992.

———. *Lectures on Religious Topics.* 1914. https://archive.org/details/cu31924022930204/page/n18.

Vajiravudh [Asvabahu, pseud.]. *The Jews of the Orient.* Bangkok: Siam Observer Press, 1914.

Van Esterik, Penny. *Materializing Thailand.* New York: Berg, 2000.

Vella, Walter F. *Chaiyo! King Vajiravudh and the Development of Thai Nationalism.* Honolulu: University of Hawai'i, 1978.

Vichitr Vadakarn. *Thailand: Thai-Khmer Racial Relations.* Bangkok: Department of Publicity, 1940.

———. *Thailand's Case.* Bangkok: Thai Commercial Press, 1941.

Wakin, Eric. *Anthropology Goes to War: Professional Ethics and Counterinsurgency in Thailand.* Madison: University of Wisconsin Press, 1992.

Weber, Max. *Wirtschaft und Gesellschaft: Die Wirtschaft und die Gesellschaftlichen Ordnungen und Mächte* [Economy and society: The economy and the arena of normative and de facto powers]. Tübingen, Germany: Mohr Siebeck, [1922] 2005.

Wedeen, Lisa. "Scientific Knowledge, Liberalism, and Empire: American Political Science in the Modern Middle East." In *Middle East Studies for the New Millennium: Infrastructures of*

Knowledge, edited by Seteney Shami and Cynthia Miller-Idriss, 31–81. New York: Social Science Research Council and New York University Press, 2016.

Weisman, Jan Robyn. "Tropes and Traces: Hybridity, Race, Sex and Responses to Modernity in Thailand." PhD diss., University of Washington, 2000.

Wheeler, Matt. "People's Patron or Patronizing the People? The Southern Border Provinces Administrative Centre in Perspective." *Contemporary Southeast Asia* 32, no. 2 (2010): 208–33.

White, Erick. "Fraudulent and Dangerous Popular Religiosity in the Public Sphere: Moral Campaigns to Prohibit, Reform, and Demystify Thai Spirit Mediums." In *Spirited Politics: Religion and Public Life in Contemporary Southeast Asia*, edited by Andrew C. Wilford and Kenneth M. George, 69–91. Ithaca, NY: Southeast Asia Program Publications, Cornell University, 2005.

Whittaker, Andrea. *Abortion, Sin, and the State in Thailand*. New York: Routledge, 2004.

Wildenthal, Lora. *German Women for Empire, 1884–1945*. Durham, NC: Duke University Press, 2001.

Winai Pongsripian. "Traditional Thai Historiography and Its Nineteenth-Century Decline." PhD diss., University of Bristol, 1983.

Wiphusana Klaimanee. "The Need to Improve Population and Resource Control in Thailand's Counterinsurgency." Master's thesis, Naval Postgraduate School, 2008.

Wood, W. A. R. *A History of Siam*. London: T. Fisher Unwin, 1926.

Woodhouse, Leslie Ann. "A 'Foreign' Princess in the Siamese Court: Princess Dara Rasami, the Politics of Gender, and Ethnic Difference in Nineteenth-Century Siam." PhD diss., University of California, 2009.

Wyatt, David K. *The Politics of Reform in Thailand: Education in the Reign of King Chulalongkorn*. New Haven, CT: Yale University Press, 1969.

Young, Iris Marion. "The Logic of Masculinist Protection: Reflections on the Current Security State." *Signs: Journal of Women in Culture and Society* 29, no. 1 (2003): 1–25.

Yusuf, Imtiyaz. "Islam and Democracy in Thailand: Reforming the Office of *Chularajamontri/ Shaikh Al-Islam*." *Journal of Islamic Studies* 9, no. 2 (1998): 277–98.

INDEX

Figures are indicated by page numbers in *italics*.

CPSIA information can be obtained
at www.ICGtesting.com
Printed in the USA
LVHW060845250322
714380LV00008B/485